P9-CDL-922

THE SPORTS 100

The 100 Greatest Athletes of the 20th Century And Their Greatest Career Moments

AP
THE ASSOCIATED PRESS

SUSAN M. MCKINNEY, Director of Production

MICHAEL G. PEARSON, Coordinating Editor

TERRY N. HAYDEN, Book and Cover Design

TERRENCE C. MILTNER, Photo Editor

SCOT MUNCASTER, Photo Production Editor

JEFFREY J. D'ALESSIO, Research Editor

DAVID HAMBURG, Proofreader

CRYSTAL L. GUMMERE, Production Assistant

Copyright © 1999 The Associated Press. All Rights Reserved.
The reprinted articles and photographs were originally published through The Associated Press. No part of this work covered by the copyright hereon may be reproduced or used in any form or by any means graphic, electronic, or mechanical, including photographing, recording, taping or in information storage and retrieval systems without the written permission of the publisher. In some instances, articles appearing in this book have been edited to accommodate certain space limitations. However, whenever possible, we have included articles in their entirety. We have made every effort to ascertain the ownership of all copyrighted photographs, reproduced herein and to secure permission from copyright holders. In the event of any inadvertent omission of credit, we will be pleased to make the necessary corrections in the future printing.

ISBN: 1-58261-206-4
Library of Congress Catalog Card Number: 99-67716

Published by Sports Publishing Inc.
www.SportsPublishingInc.com

Printed in the United States

THE SPORTS 100

The 100 Greatest Athletes of the 20th Century
And Their Greatest Career Moments

From the archives of

AP

THE ASSOCIATED PRESS

Published by Sports Publishing Inc.
www.Sports PublishingInc.com

CONTENTS

HANK AARON HOLDS THE BALL HE HIT FOR HIS 715TH CAREER HOME RUN ON APRIL 8, 1974 AT ATLANTA STADIUM TO BREAK BABE RUTH'S LONG-STANDING RECORD OF 714. (AP/WIDE WORLD PHOTOS)

HANK AARON

THE ALL-TIME HOME RUN KING

On the crisp evening of April 8, 1974, before the largest crowd ever to jam into Atlanta Stadium and millions watching on television, Henry Louis Aaron caught a fastball thrown by Al Downing of the Los Angeles Dodgers on the fat part of his bat and sent it soaring over the left-field fence, triggering a wild celebration and at the same time a touch of remorse at the passing of one of baseball's cherished records.

Hail the new home run king, Hammerin' Hank, sultan of the game's premier thrill—the massive one-shot blow out of the park, now with 715 homers. But no goodbyes for the great Babe Ruth, savior of the game, whose place in baseball can never pale.

Aaron's erasing of a mark that most people felt would never be broken was a stark testament to changing times and an irony in the contrast of personality and lifestyles.

The Babe emerged in the wild, swinging era of the Golden Twenties and partook of the period to its fullest. He was big, lovable and outgoing, with a massive appetite for food, women and song, and basked in the limelight of the biggest city and most glamorous team, the New York Yankees.

Aaron was a product of the Jim Crow South, born at the height of the Great Depression. He had to struggle through early want and racial indignities and spend most of his career in virtual obscurity with a team in the so-called hinterlands.

Most baseball followers felt that if Ruth's record was to be challenged, Mickey Mantle and Willie Mays would be the ones to do it. So, while these two charismatic figures on popular teams pursued the goal, Aaron methodically kept smashing 25, 30, or 40 home runs a year with the shifting Braves, who moved from Boston to Milwaukee to Atlanta.

A strong body, powerful wrists, and perseverance proved the determining factors, as Aaron's career spanned 23 years. During that time, he played for 12 managers and not only broke Ruth's record, but extended his home run total to 755. He also set other baseball records that have become a lasting tribute to his conditioning, consistency and durability.

He played in the most games (3,298), had the most plate appearances (13,940), the most official times at bat (12,364) and the most runs batted in (2,297), 93 more than Ruth. He set 11 major league and 18 National League records.

A notorious bad-ball hitter, Aaron developed into a record breaker through hard work and intelligence. Many attributed his power to strong wrists—eight inches around—and an ability to wait until the last fraction of a second to snap his bat into action.

Aaron's advice to young hitters always was succinct: "Just be quick with your hands." He prided himself on his ability to assess pitchers. "I never forget a pitcher," he said.

HANK AARON AT EBBETS FIELD IN BROOKLYN BEFORE THE 1961 SEASON. (AP/WIDE WORLD PHOTOS)

HANK AARON TAKES BATTING PRACTICE AS HE CLOSES IN ON HIS 3,000TH HIT IN
1971. (AP/WIDE WORLD PHOTOS)

HANK AARON EYES THE FLIGHT OF THE BALL AFTER HITTING HIS 715TH CAREER HOMER, APRIL 8, 1974, AGAINST THE LOS ANGELES DODGERS. THE BLAST ECLIPSED THE 714 MARK HELD FOR YEARS BY BABE RUTH. (AP/WIDE WORLD PHOTOS)

Aaron was born February 5, 1934, in Mobile, Alabama, the third child of Herbert and Estella Aaron. His father was an unskilled shipyards worker; his mother tended a vegetable garden to help feed the family in a $9-a-month shack in a black district known as Texas Hill.

When Aaron was 6, the family moved to a larger house, with no electricity and primitive plumbing, but with a backyard big enough for the kids in the neighborhood to hit tin cans and rag balls in one-eyed-cat games.

At 11, he was the shortstop on a kids' team managed by his father, and at 16 he was playing semipro ball with the Mobile Bears, collecting $10 a week. He was good enough in high school to be offered a college scholarship, but his mind was made up, over the objections of his mother, to play pro baseball.

He was 18 when, with two pairs of pants, $2 in his pockets and lunch in a paper bag, he caught a train to Indianapolis to join the Indianapolis Clowns, a black professional team whose manager had been impressed by the teenage shortstop in an exhibition game against the Bears in Mobile. Aaron was paid $200 a month.

By this time, with Jackie Robinson the pioneer, blacks were being integrated into major league baseball, and young Aaron was too fine a talent to be confined to the Negro League. In May 1952, the Braves outbid the New York Giants and signed the 18-year-old for $350. Aaron was assigned to the Braves' Class C farm club at Eau Claire, Wisconsin.

Aaron batted .336 and was named Rookie of the Year in the Northern League. From Eau Claire, he went to Jacksonville, Florida, in the South Atlantic League, where he became the most valuable player despite insults and abuses from the biased fans in the South.

He couldn't stay in the hotel with his teammates but had to be hauled to a boarding house in the black end of town. He couldn't eat with them at restaurants. Despite his production, he was jeered on and off the field. Tragically, similar resentment surfaced two decades later, when he began threatening the precious record of the immortal Ruth.

A loner by nature, Aaron took the indignities hard. Even on the field and in the clubhouse, he failed to join in the camaraderie. He never argued with an umpire. He stayed to himself and avoided confrontations.

He joined the Braves in spring training in March 1954, but was limited to pinch-hitting duties until outfielder Bobby Thomson suffered a broken leg in an exhibition game. Suddenly, Aaron was thrust into the lineup—a job he wasn't to relinquish until 23 years later. Ten days after the season opened, playing in St. Louis, he hit a Vic Raschi fastball over the left-field fence for the first of his 755 home runs.

Aaron now serves as Senior Vice President of the Atlanta Braves. In April 1999, Baseball Commissioner Bud Selig announced the creation of a hitting award in his honor. The Hank Aaron Award will be presented annually to the best hitter in each league.

KAREEM ABDUL-JABBAR
DISPLAYS HIS FAMOUS
SKYHOOK AGAINST THE
BOSTON CELTICS' ROBERT
PARISH DURING THE 1987
REGULAR SEASON.
(AP/WIDE WORLD PHOTOS)

KAREEM ABDUL-JABBAR

THE SKY HOOK WAS HIS CALLING CARD

The towering figure with the bald spot on the back of his head and industrial goggles that made him look like a masked man from outer space took a stutter step, spun, rose in the air like a graceful dove in flight and, with a flick of one of his long arms, dropped the basketball—almost gently—through the iron hoop. Defenders could only gape.

Such was Kareem Abdul-Jabbar's renowned "sky hook," the virtually unstoppable and unmatchable maneuver that shall forever mark the legacy of one of the most overwhelming, magnetic and complex personalities ever to play the game.

The 7-foot-2, 230-pound Jabbar dominated his sport from the moment he first picked up a basketball as a tyke in a Harlem playground in New York until retiring as the NBA's all-time leading scorer in 1989.

No other man had endured so many years in the tough, run-and-shoot pro game. No one had ever run up and down as many thousand hardwood floors, scored as many points, grabbed as many rebounds or achieved as much success on every rung of his career ladder—high school, college and the big time. The sky hook was his calling card. And nobody could copy it.

"It's a matter of triangulation," he told *Sports Illustrated* after being named that magazine's Sportsman of the Year in 1985, sounding like a college professor lecturing a science class.

"A normal shot is easier to triangulate. The three corners of the triangle are your eyes, the ball and the rim, and most players shoot from near their eyes. But on the sky hook the ball is way up there and that . . . keeps most players from getting the coordination of it."

The sky hook and a unique training regimen—swimming, jumping a heavy rope and especially yoga, hours of meditation at the Yoga College in Los Angeles—provided the somber, enigmatic giant a durability and longevity that defied the imagination of his peers. The normal career life of a pro basketball player is less than four years.

Jabbar, as a converted Muslim, didn't drink or eat red meats. He shunned social functions and informal parties. While he never shirked heavy practice, he learned to pace himself in a game and not exert unnecessary energy. His younger teammates treated him reverentially and went to extra lengths in the later years to shield him from pressure by rolling up big leads so he wouldn't be forced to play more than 40 minutes a game.

Jabbar set NBA records for most seasons played, most games played and most minutes played. In 1985, he surpassed Wilt Chamberlain's NBA career record of 31,419 points, finishing with a record 38,387. And on

LEW ALCINDOR, LATER KNOWN AS KAREEM ABDUL-JABBAR, BRINGS DOWN A REBOUND FOR UCLA. (AP/WIDE WORLD PHOTOS)

ALCINDOR, AS A FRESHMAN AT UCLA, LED HIS TEAM TO A WIN OVER THE UCLA VARSITY TEAM. (AP/WIDE WORLD PHOTOS)

ABDUL-JABBAR, SHOWN HERE WITH THE MILWAUKEE BUCKS, CONTESTS A LAYUP BY THE CHICAGO BULLS' JERRY SLOAN. (AP/WIDE WORLD PHOTOS)

February 20, 1987, he became the first to reach 36,000 points. He held records also for most field goals and most blocked shots.

Six times he was voted the league's MVP, 15 times selected for the NBA All-Star game, 10 as a starter.

His legs, the first thing usually to go under basketball's constant pounding, stood up like stanchions of steel. He never suffered a serious injury, although twice he broke a hand in an altercation with an opposing player—a reaction to the elbow liberties he felt referees gave to the smaller men.

Jabbar, who abandoned his Christian name while in college, appeared destined for a king-sized role in life—physically as well as athletically—from the moment he arrived. Ferdinand Lewis Alcindor was born in New York April 16, 1947, the only child of middle-class parents. Lew was a big baby—22 1/2 inches long and 12 pounds at birth.

Entering kindergarten, he was head and shoulders taller than his classmates. By the time he reached the seventh grade he was 6-3 and upon entering high school 6-11. His size turned him into a shy, retiring kid who felt uncomfortable with others, and he stayed largely to himself. For company, he turned to books and the be-bop and swing music of his times. His home life didn't help bring him out of his shell. His mother, Cora, was very possessive, and his father, Big Al, a transit cop and trombone player, was uncommunicative.

Because of his size and natural talent, young Lew could find some pride in his basketball ability. At Power Memorial High School, he led his team to a 95-6 record, a winning streak of 71 games, and three New York City championships.

Perhaps no high school player in history was more widely recruited. Lew chose UCLA, and as a three-time All-American, proceeded to lead the Bruins to three consecutive NCAA titles, losing only two of 90 games.

In 1969 he signed a $1.4 million contract with the Milwaukee Bucks of the NBA, who six years later sent him to the Lakers in a five-player trade. His salary rose from $500,000 to $2 million a year.

It was while a junior at UCLA that Jabbar adopted the Muslim faith, as Muhammad Ali had done earlier, although it was not until 1971 that he made it public. It was a time of racial turmoil, and Jabbar, studious and sensitive to the social injustices, became even more sullen and reclusive.

He criticized the people of Los Angeles as "phonies" and "hate-filled." He expressed resentment that he was accepted only as a jock and not a human being. He cold-shouldered the press and avoided people. He boycotted the 1968 Olympics. He distanced himself from his family. He broke up with his wife, mother of three of his children, taking another mate.

It was not until his Bel Air mansion and many of his prized possessions burned in a January 1983 fire that he seemed to mellow—touched by public response to his tragedy—and to rejoin the human race.

Since retiring, he has worked in the entertainment business, served as a "basketball ambassador" and helped to fight hunger and illiteracy.

In 1998, the Hall of Famer gave coaching a whirl, signing a $1 contract to lead the boys' basketball team at Arizona's Alchesay High School on the Fort Apache Indian Reservation.

CASSIUS CLAY, SOON TO BE KNOWN AS MUHAMMAD ALI, STANDS OVER SONNY LISTON AFTER DEFENDING HIS HEAVYWEIGHT TITLE IN 1965. (AP/WIDE WORLD PHOTOS)

MUHAMMAD ALI

"FLOAT LIKE A BUTTERFLY, STING LIKE A BEE"

"ALI, ALI, ALI!"

It was a cry that started as a chant in the early 1960s and grew in volume over the next two decades, reverberating around the world from London to New York, Manila to Zaire to the accompaniment of flailing leather gloves.

Muhammad Ali won the heavyweight boxing championship an unprecedented three times. He fought monsters and pushovers, once compiling a winning streak of 31 straight fights, yet his greatest victory was scored outside the ring.

He beat Uncle Sam. He reversed public opinion. Down but not out, he struggled back to become one of the most popular and celebrated athletes of his time.

Refusing to take the step for military service when drafted in 1967, during the Vietnam War, he was stripped of his title, indicted by the government and, while never jailed, was forced into professional exile for three years.

Although he became a symbol of resistance for fellow blacks and the oppressed people of the world, much of the American public slapped him with the label "slacker"—one of the most reprehensible of terms. After three years, he was vindicated by the Supreme Court.

He returned to reclaim his crown dramatically, lose it, regain it a second time and then a third.

After winning the heavyweight crown, the puckish son of a Kentucky sign painter adopted the Muslim faith, changing his name from Cassius Marcellus Clay—as he was christened—to Muhammad Ali. It was uncomfortable for the public to accept at first.

"I am 90 percent preacher and 10 percent fighter," he contended in Houston when he rejected the military draft on the grounds—upheld later by the highest court—that he was a conscientious objector.

The taint of the experience faded, and Ali's popularity soared. He was a superb fighter, a sleek punching machine with quick hands, dancing feet and blows that carried the sting of a sabre thrust. More than that, he was a personality—brash and brassy at times, "The Mouth That Roared," they said, cocky almost to the point of arrogance, but rarely offensive.

He intrigued the masses and charmed potentates and kings, who courted his favors. There was no more recognizable personality in the world.

He gave the world some of its greatest ring battles—two

SPRAY FLIES FROM THE HEAD OF CHALLENGER JOE FRAZIER (LEFT) AS HEAVYWEIGHT CHAMPION MUHAMMAD ALI CONNECTS WITH A RIGHT IN THE FAMED "THRILLA IN MANILA" FIGHT OF 1975. (AP/WIDE WORLD PHOTOS)

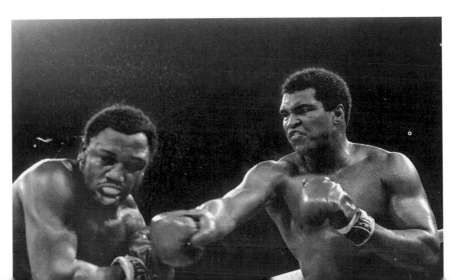

MUHAMMAD ALI

CHAMPION GEORGE FOREMAN COVERS UP AS MUHAMMAD ALI UNLEASHES A FLURRY OF PUNCHES DURING THEIR HEAVYWEIGHT TITLE FIGHT IN KINSHASA, ZAIRE, AFRICA IN 1974. ALI REGAINED HIS BOXING CROWN WITH AN EIGHTH-ROUND KNOCKOUT. (AP/WIDE WORLD PHOTOS)

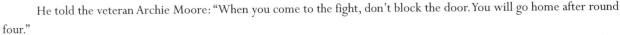

MUHAMMAD ALI LIT THE
TORCH TO OPEN THE
1996 SUMMER OLYMPIC
GAMES IN ATLANTA.
(AP/WIDE WORLD
PHOTOS)

knockouts of the fearsome Sonny Liston, his "Rope a Dope" tactics against George Foreman in Zaire and three great slugfests with Smokin' Joe Frazier.

He was always on stage—boasting, chiding, philosophizing, spouting kindergarten poetry.

"They all must fall, in the round I call."

He told the veteran Archie Moore: "When you come to the fight, don't block the door. You will go home after round four."

He was indeed a tremendous specimen—6 feet, 3 inches tall and 210 pounds at top fighting trim—with a blacksmith's shoulders and arms, but lean legs that moved like fleeting light.

"Float like a butterfly, sting like a bee" became his clarion call as he danced about the ring, challenging his foes to land a damaging blow and then moving in with a left jab punctuated by a bone-rattling right.

Son of a house painter, the boy known as Cassius dropped out of school early, haunted the playgrounds and boxed in the local gym. He piled up 108 victories as an amateur and battled his way onto the U.S. Olympic team at age 18, winning the light heavyweight gold medal in Rome in 1960.

The Louisville youngster won 19 fights before he was considered ready for a shot at the heavyweight crown, held by an awesome bear of a man named Sonny Liston, who had twice battered Floyd Patterson into insensibility in the first round.

The fight was set for Miami, February 25, 1964. Everybody considered Cassius a sacrificial lamb. When the challenger staged a wild tantrum at the weigh-in, doctors attributed it to fear and considered calling off the fight.

But the fight went on. A calm, methodical challenger danced and stabbed and made a monkey of the fearsome titleholder, who failed to come out for the seventh round. It was after this fight that Cassius announced his conversion to the Muslim faith and a new name: Muhammad Ali. In his first defense in May of the following year, Ali knocked out Liston with a historic "phantom punch" in the first round at Lewiston, Maine.

Then followed a series of victories, the draft tribulations, the three-year banishment from the game and finally vindication.

Wild excitement greeted his comeback October 26, 1970—a bout in a 5,000-seat Atlanta gym against brawling Jerry Quarry, who lasted only three rounds. But 300 million—live and on TV—reportedly witnessed the "Battle of the Century" in New York's Madison Square Garden against Smokin' Joe Frazier, the reigning champion, March 8, 1971.

It was a brutal fight, slugger against scientific boxer, won by the slugger Frazier, but a battle that left both gladiators so battered that they needed medical attention. It was Ali's first defeat after 31 straight victories.

Ali later scored a close decision over Frazier in a non-title bout, regained his title by stopping big George Foreman in Kinshasa, Zaire, in October 1974. He kept the crown three years, winning a "rubber" battle over old rival Frazier in the bloody and brutal so-called "Thrilla in Manila," before losing lackadaisically to outsider Leon Spinks in 1978.

The great Ali defeated Spinks later in the year to become the only man ever to win the heavyweight title three times, but age and ring punishment had taken their toll. He announced his retirement in 1981 after losses to Larry Holmes and Trevor Berbick.

"I am still the greatest," he bellowed in a tired, almost inaudible voice. The world echoed agreement.

MARIO ANDRETTI CELEBRATES WITH HIS TROPHY AFTER WINNING A RACE IN BUENOS AIRES IN 1978. (AP/WIDE WORLD PHOTOS)

MARIO ANDRETTI

KING OF THE ROAD

Mario Andretti never asked for any special favors. The competitive dynamo who won races in each of four decades always gave no quarter and asked none, even when racing against his own sons.

"Sure, I knew they were out there," Andretti said. "But when we were on the track, they were just another car I had to beat. And it was a thrill if I beat them."

Andretti, at age 54, completed his season-long "Arrivederci, Mario" Tour in the 1994 Bank of America 300 at Laguna Seca Raceway, his 407th and last Indy-car event.

Andretti grew up in Italy, where his family sold grapes to local wineries. From 1948 to 1955, the Andretti family lived in a refugee camp in Tuscany after their hometown of Montona became part of Yugoslavia.

When Andretti was 15, his family was granted visas to the United States, and they settled in Pennsylvania.

Andretti made his way into the sport on the dirt tracks of the Northeast and Midwest with an obvious flair for speed and excitement. He quickly graduated to the big leagues.

He was a winner in his first love, Formula One, earning 12 victories and the 1978 World Championship while splitting his time between Europe and America.

On the Indy-car circuit, the masterful driver won four championships and 52 races—second only to A.J. Foyt's 67. Those wins include the 1969 Indianapolis 500.

Perhaps the most versatile driver of all time, Andretti also won the 1967 Daytona 500 and a number of sport-car endurance events and has been named Driver of the Year in three different decades. He was the first Driver of the Year, in 1967.

Andretti won at Phoenix early in 1993, ending a five-year winless streak, but he wasn't fooled.

"I think I could probably be effective for another year or so, but I don't want to get to the point where I'm not quick enough to justify being involved," he said. "So, I knew it was time."

Most of his family were on hand for his last Indy-car race, including eldest son Michael, who's now starring on the Championship Auto Racing Team's circuit.

After retiring from racing, Andretti bought his own winery in Napa, California. He now serves as an advisor to CART.

MARIO ANDRETTI, IN THE FOREGROUND, LEADS TEAMMATE RONNIE PETERSON TO ONE OF ANDRETTI'S MANY CAREER VICTORIES. (AP/WIDE WORLD PHOTOS)

CITATION, CENTER, WITH EDDIE ARCARO ABOARD, COMES UP ON COALTOWN ON THE WAY TO WINNING THE 1948 KENTUCKY DERBY. CITATION AND ARCARO TOOK THE PREAKNESS AND BELMONT AS WELL TO WIN THE TRIPLE CROWN IN 1948. (AP/WIDE WORLD PHOTOS)

EDDIE ARCARO

RACING'S GRAND SLAM KING

"Eddie Arcaro," said Willie Shoemaker, "was the greatest rider I ever saw. He could do everything. I know he beat me more times than I beat him."

No greater tribute could befall a man than that delivered by a respected rival, particularly one of Shoemaker's stature, who over four decades won more races and more prize money than any jockey who ever lived.

"He could do everything," Shoemaker added. "He was a good gate boy, had the intelligence to make the right moves and was in a good position when he needed it. And there was nobody like him for finishing on a horse."

If Shoemaker was thoroughbred racing's all-time winningest rider, as records attest, then Eddie Arcaro must be judged the best ever in the big-time events. Arcaro, who died in 1997 at the age of 81, was once proclaimed the "King of the Stakes Riders." He accumulated 554 stakes, a mark broken by Shoemaker. Arcaro was racing's Grand Slam King, however. In a career spanning 31 years between 1931 and 1961, Arcaro rode an unchallenged 17 winners in the three Triple Crown events—five Kentucky Derbys, six Preaknesses and six Belmont Stakes—holding or sharing records in all. He was the only rider to score a double in the Triple Crown races—aboard Whirlaway in 1941 and Citation in 1948.

He rode 4,779 winners and finished in the money on more than half of the 24,092 horses he rode and earned $30,039,543, a sum exceeded only by his friend and golfing companion, Shoemaker.

Although he had a hard time breaking in, Arcaro developed an artistry in his craft that earned him the nickname "The Master" from his contemporaries, while railbirds affectionately called him "Banana Nose," because of his elongated beak.

"A strong pair of hands and a sense of rhythm," was Eddie's own assessment of the requisites of a good jockey. "That and a good horse," he said. "You've got to make the horse think you are part of him."

There was a confidence bordering on arrogance in the way Eddie sat on a horse, and he often drew boos from the fans.

"They never expect you to lose," Arcaro was once told.

"Oh, well," he said, "it's their money."

Eddie had to conquer a once-violent temper and a wild abandon to attain stardom. It was costly.

He drew a six-month suspension at Pimlico in 1936 for deliberately colliding with nearby horses and was set down in 1941 for blocking.

Arcaro was suspended for a year in September 1942, when after being bumped by jockey Vincent Nodarse coming out of the gate, Arcaro tried to push him into the infield.

Snapped Arcaro: "I'd have killed that SOB if I could."

EDDIE ARCARO, SHOWN HERE IN A 1951 PHOTO, WON 4,779 RACES IN HIS CAREER. (AP/WIDE WORLD PHOTOS)

HENRY ARMSTRONG IN
A 1937 PUBLICITY PHO-
TOGRAPH. (AP/WIDE
WORLD PHOTOS)

HENRY ARMSTRONG

THE HUMAN BUZZSAW

In winning the lightweight championship, one of an unprecedented three world titles he held simultaneously, Henry Armstrong epitomized the sum and substance of his boxing career.

This was on August 17, 1938, against Lou Ambers in Madison Square Garden, and although Armstrong was ahead on points late in the fight, he had been taking a severe beating from his rugged opponent.

In the 11th round, referee Arthur Donovan wanted to stop the fight because Armstrong had been bleeding profusely.

"I told him I was ahead on points and why stop it?" Armstrong later remembered. "He said, 'Look at the ring, it's covered with blood—your blood.' I told him I'd stop bleeding, then, so I swallowed the blood."

Literally bloody but unbowed, Armstrong went on to a 15-round decision over Ambers, climaxing a spectacular flurry that gained him his third world title within the short space of 10 months. In October 1937 he had knocked out Petey Sarron for the featherweight championship, and in May 1938 had taken the welterweight title from Barney Ross.

Although he had to eventually relinquish the featherweight championship because of weight-making difficulties and later lost the lightweight title back to Ambers, Armstrong's place in ring history was secure. His achievement of three simultaneous major championships was a euphoric peak never scaled by other boxers.

By the time he retired in 1945, Armstrong had participated in 175 professional fights in 15 years, winning 97 by knockouts and 47 by decisions. He had eight draws, one no-decision, and only 22 losses, most of them early in his career when he hadn't yet developed the princely skills that would take him to the top of the boxing world.

Remarkably, he narrowly missed winning a fourth championship, falling short when he battled middleweight titleholder Ceferino Garcia to a 10-round draw and the title was retained by the champion.

One of 15 children in a poverty-ravaged St. Louis family, Armstrong had to fight for everything growing up, and observers believe this was the motivational force of his career.

Armstrong, who died in 1988, is widely considered one of the best pound-for-pound fighters of all time. Jack Dempsey once described the Hall of Famer's fights as "a million punches thrown as fast and hard as he could let them go."

HIS HAND RAISED IN VICTORY, HENRY ARMSTRONG ADDS THE LIGHTWEIGHT TITLE TO THE WELTERWEIGHT AND FEATHERWEIGHT TITLES HE WON IN 1938. (AP/WIDE WORLD PHOTOS)

SAMMY BAUGH IN ACTION BEFORE THE 1938 ALL-STAR GAME IN CHICAGO. (AP/WIDE WORLD PHOTOS)

SAMMY BAUGH

THE FIRST GREAT PASSER

The first forward pass in football reportedly was thrown around 1913, its perpetrator still a source of debate among historians. But it flowered as an offensive weapon with the wild "aerial circus" maneuvers of the Southwest Conference in the 1930s and found its greatest exponent in a skinny, slingshot-armed Texan named Sammy Baugh.

For decades, football had been a dull, head-butting, body-slamming exercise fought on the ground with little or no scoring. It remained for a few imaginative coaches in the cowboy country to introduce a new "razzle dazzle" attack, fill the sky with spirals and prove that—in football, as in traveling—one can get there more quickly through the air.

Baugh, a kicker as well as a passer, became the symbol of this revolution in the sport. A gifted all-around athlete courted by baseball's major leagues, Slingin' Sammy, as he was called, became a ball-tossing Houdini, first at Texas Christian University and later with the Washington Redskins, where he played for 16 seasons.

He spanned two generations and two eras of the sport. When he hung up his No. 33 jersey in 1952, he left a long string of collegiate and pro records. He was elected to the College Football Hall of Fame in 1951 and as a charter member of the Pro Football Hall of Fame in 1963.

Baugh could throw the ball like a bullet and with the ease of a man flipping a baseball. He could nail a running target half the length of the field away.

He was a college All-American in 1935 and 1936, completing 109 passes for 1,371 yards the latter year, upsetting undefeated Santa Clara in the season's final game, then leading TCU to a Cotton Bowl victory.

With the Redskins, he led the NFL in passing six times and set records that were to last for years—such as most seasons played, 16; most passes thrown, 3,016; most passes completed, 1,709; and most yards gained, 22,085.

He still holds a share of the NFL record for most seasons leading the league in passing, which he and Steve Young both did six times.

Said Sid Luckman, Baugh's rival back then with the Bears: "I like to just sit and watch him."

"In his worst games," wrote historian Roger Treat, "Baugh is as good as most quarterbacks in their best days."

Another, Kevin Roberts said, "He is to passing what Lindbergh was to the airplane."

SAMMY BAUGH LEAVES THE FIELD IN WASHINGTON D.C. FOR THE LAST TIME IN HIS FINAL GAME IN 1952. (AP/WIDE WORLD PHOTOS)

ELGIN BAYLOR IN ACTION IN 1958 WITH THE MINNE-APOLIS LAKERS. (AP/WIDE WORLD PHOTOS)

ELGIN BAYLOR

THE FRANCHISE SAVER

The term "franchise player" is loosely applied to an individual who can singularly take a team to a higher plane, usually transforming a loser into a winner. In the case of charismatic Elgin Baylor, it was more literal than most.

The Minneapolis Lakers were down on their luck when Baylor signed with them out of Seattle University in 1958. "All I know is that he saved my franchise when it appeared that I was going to die," said Robert Short, owner of the Lakers then. "If I had moved to Los Angeles, nobody would have come out to see us play. He was the salvation of us all."

Baylor became an instant star in Minneapolis, in his first season establishing himself as one of the league's premier forwards. He averaged 24.9 points, 15 rebounds and 4.1 assists and was named to the all-National Basketball Association first team for the first of seven consecutive seasons. More important, the Lakers improved dramatically as a team. The previous season, they made it to the NBA Finals, losing there to mighty Boston.

Baylor's presence alone made the Lakers a more valuable commodity, and Short, who bought the team for $200,000, eventually sold it for $5.1 million to Jack Kent Cooke, who moved it to Los Angeles.

"If Baylor had turned me down," Short recalled, "I'd have gone out of business. The club would have gone bankrupt."

Named one of the NBA's 50 Greatest Players of All Time in 1996, Baylor ranks with the top scorers in league history.

His 71 points against the Knicks in 1960 set a league record at the time. His 61 against the Celtics in 1961 is still a record for an NBA finals game. His 27.4 career scoring average is third all time—behind only Michael Jordan and Wilt Chamberlain.

He's stayed in basketball, and Los Angeles, where he's now in his 14th season as vice president of Basketball Operations for the Clippers.

ELGIN BAYLOR, SHOWN HERE DRIVING AGAINST MCCOY MCLEMORE OF THE GOLDEN STATE WARRIORS, TURNED AROUND THE LAKERS FRANCHISE. (AP/WIDE WORLD PHOTOS)

Matt Biondi celebrates winning the gold medal in the 50-meter freestyle at the 1988 Summer Olympics in Seoul. (AP/Wide World Photos)

MATT BIONDI

SWIMMING'S MEDAL DETECTOR

Matt Biondi, a long-armed, 6-foot-7 swimming machine from Moraga, California, is one of three U.S. Olympians to capture 11 medals.

He won seven swimming medals at the 1988 Games, matching the seven-medal achievement of Mark Spitz in 1972. Biondi's catch wasn't all gold, like Spitz's, but five golds, a silver and a bronze were hardly a disappointment.

He also set a world record in the 50-meter freestyle and participated in world records in three relay events in the Seoul Games.

In 1992, the two-time USOC SportsMan of the Year award winner, found himself in the uncommon role of spectator. Yet he wound up in the role of Olympic medalist.

Biondi, one of America's greatest freestyle swimmers, earned his record-tying 11th medal—and his eighth gold— while watching the race from the stands.

In his last Olympic race, Biondi anchored the U.S. 400-meter medley relay team to the top time in the qualifying heats. But he sat out the final, where swimmers were chosen based on their finishes in the 100-meter individual races. The top U.S. finisher in that event, Jon Olsen swam the anchor instead.

Biondi was merely a cheerleader as Jeff Rouse, Nelson Diebel, Pablo Morales and Olsen won the race in 3:36.93, matching the world record.

The gold medals went not only to the four men who swam the final, but also to the four who competed in the preliminary. That allowed Biondi to tie swimmer Mark Spitz and shooter Carl Osburn for the most medals won by a U.S. Olympian.

"It feels a litle anticlimactic now just because I didn't swim at night," Biondi said at the time. "But I think when the years go by the fact that I have put my name on 11 Olympic medals will stand as my greatest achievement in swimming."

The 26-year-old Biondi, of Castro Valley, California, expressed mixed feelings about the way he won the medal.

"I certainly didn't want to piggyback," he said. "Will I take it? Definitely."

During the final, Biondi stood with the rest of the American team and joined in chants of "USA, USA."

He wanted to soak it all in. It would be his last Olympics.

"I've got no voice left," he said afterward.

MATT BIONDI WON A TOTAL OF 11 OLYMPIC MEDALS, INCLUDING THE SILVER MEDAL IN THE 100-METER BUTTERFLY, BELOW, IN THE 1988 SUMMER OLYMPICS IN SEOUL. (AP/WIDE WORLD PHOTOS)

BIRD HELPED THE BOSTON CELTICS WIN THREE NBA CHAMPIONSHIPS AND WAS TWICE THE NBA FINALS MVP. (AP/WIDE WORLD PHOTOS)

LARRY BIRD

"HE'D CUT YOUR HEART OUT TO WIN"

In 1986, after Larry Bird had played only seven years with the Boston Celtics, a *Dallas Morning News* poll of 60 leading professional basketball authorities selected him as the greatest forward ever to play the game. The hand-picked panel chose Bird over Elgin Baylor, Julius Erving, Rick Barry and the old St. Louis Hawks' floor wizard Bob Pettit.

There have been others ready to acclaim—without the further proof that comes with aging—the cotton-haired, ballhandling Houdini from French Lick, Indiana, to be the most complete player in the sport's history.

While admittedly debatable, it was a remarkable tribute at this early stage of the gifted Hoosier's career and ironic since it became a story-book saga that almost didn't happen.

At Springs Valley High School, Bird, thin and gawky, played the first two years in the shadow of a more highly regarded teammate, Steve Land, and, although later a state all-star, he failed to impress college scouts.

Bird wanted to play at the University of Kentucky, but Coach Joe B. Hall, after looking him over, said he was too slow to fit into the Wildcats' fast-break, fire-engine style of basketball.

Larry became so discouraged that he was prepared to give up a college education altogether. "Larry really didn't want to go to college anywhere," his widowed mother said. "He feels he should get a job, so I won't have to work so hard."

Larry's father had died in 1961 after separating from his mother and going to Tucson, Arizona, in hopes that a drier climate would help his emphysema. Larry's mother sold the family farm and took her flock—three boys and one girl—to live with her own widowed mother. Times were hard.

Larry finally was persuaded to enter Indiana University, but left after six weeks because he was used so sparingly in basketball practice. Coming from a small town and small school, he felt smothered by the size of the university.

He enrolled in a 200-student junior college, Northwood in West Baden, Indiana, but dropped out when he learned that he would have to stay two years before applying to a four-year college. His cage career appeared doomed.

He drove a garbage truck and played AAU basketball on the side with a construction company,

NO. 33 WAS INDIANA STATE'S GREATEST PLAYER EVER. (AP/WIDE WORLD PHOTOS)

Larry Bird was selected as an All-Star in 12 of his 13 NBA Seasons. (AP/Wide World Photos)

THE LEGENDARY CONFRONTATIONS BETWEEN LARRY BIRD AND MAGIC JOHNSON BEGAN WITH THE 1979 CHAMPIONSHIP GAME. (AP/WIDE WORLD PHOTOS)

getting occasional headlines in state tournaments. He had an unsuccessful six-month marriage. His life appeared to be drifting until, out of the blue, he was recruited by Indiana State University.

Red-shirted for a year at the rather obscure Terre Haute institution, he played three seasons, climaxing in 1978-79 when he gained All-America recognition for the second year, led his team to the NCAA Championship finals against Magic Johnson's Michigan State powerhouse and won the NCAA Player of the Year award. He was the first-round draft choice of the Boston Celtics.

Bird's professional career was meteoric. He was the National Basketball Association's Rookie of the Year in 1980 and a member of the league's All-Rookie team. He proceeded to win a place on the All-NBA team and qualify for the mid-season All-Star Game 12 times, as well as being named the playoff MVP in 1984 and 1986. He joined Wilt Chamberlain and Bill Russell as the only players in league history to win MVP honors for three consecutive seasons. He did it in 1984, 1985 and 1986.

One of the game's most durable athletes in his first several years, a chronic back ailment sidelined him in his latter seasons. Inducted into the Basketball Hall of Fame in 1998, Bird wound up his Celtic career with 21,791 points, 8,974 rebounds and 5,695 assists in 897 regular-season games. He registered an amazing 69 triple-doubles, with individual game bests of 60 points, 21 rebounds and 17 assists.

Although having filled out his once bony, 6-foot-9 frame with 220 solid pounds, Bird was not the biggest nor the strongest player in the league. He lacked the speed of some of his contemporaries and couldn't jump as high as many, yet he managed to dominate the floor with his intense competitiveness and instinctive skills.

He compensated for his lack of jumping ability by perfecting the three-point field goal, setting an NBA record for that specialty with 649 during his career. Five times he won the NBA's All-Star Three-Point Shootout.

The three-point goal is a climactic art that pulled out many close games for the Celtics, and Bird insisted that it was not a gift but the product of hard work. He built a special court at his home to practice hours at a time.

"If you go to the gym with the other guys, you may get 100 shots," he said. "By yourself you get 1,000."

"Larry's just a player who continued to grow," Celtics' assistant coach Jimmy Rodgers said. "When you think you've seen everything, he came up with another gimmick, another approach."

Added Pete Newell, Golden State's director of player personnel: "He rebounds, scores, passes, picks up the tough guy on defense, can play inside or outside and is as good as any guard handling the break and hitting the open man. He's as skilled a forward as I've ever seen."

Matt Guokas, coach of the Philadelphia 76ers, said, "Bird's approach to the game is unparalleled. He will cut your heart out to win."

"I maintain the championship was won when Larry Bird was born," commented teammate Bill Walton after a Celtics' title in 1985-86.

Larry was born December 7, 1956, and he never forgot his roots, maintaining always that he was "just the hick from French Lick," a resort town of about 1,800 where he'd go back to see old buddies and even mow the lawn. He showed up for black-tie dinners in a sport shirt and blue jeans, admitting: "I eat, drink and sleep basketball 24 hours a day."

On May 8, 1997, Bird accepted the Indiana Pacers' head coaching position. One year later, he was honored as the NBA's Coach of the Year. Just prior to the 1999-2000 season, Bird announced that this would be his last, citing a heart problem as part of his decision.

BONNIE BLAIR SHOWS OFF ONE OF HER FIVE GOLD MEDALS, THIS ONE FROM THE 500-METER EVENT AT THE 1994 WINTER OLYMPICS IN HAMAR. (AP/WIDE WORLD PHOTOS)

BONNIE BLAIR

A FANTASTIC FINISH

They sang "My Bonnie" one last time for American speedskater Bonnie Blair as she took a final shot at her world record in the 500 meters and capped off a career for the record books on March 18, 1995 in Calgary.

The five-time Olympic gold medalist finished well ahead of the pack at 38.87 seconds, just shy of her 38.69 record set earlier that year.

But Blair achieved her goal going into her speedskating finale. As always.

She shaved her old U.S. record of 1 minute, 18.31 seconds down to 1:18.05 in what was her final race. She left on top of the world.

Blair is the only U.S. Winter Olympian to win a gold medal in the same event in three separate Olympic Games and the only woman to win consecutive gold medals in the 500 meters.

After making Olympic history in Lillehamer, Norway, she's raked in numerous awards, including the 1994 Sportswoman of the Year from *Sports Illustrated* magazine and the 1994 Female Athlete of the Year from The Associated Press.

About 25 family members and friends made the trek from Champaign, Illinois, to Calgary's Olympic Oval for her last hurrah. They sang "Happy Birthday" and "My Bonnie," as the world champion—who turned 31—warmed up for the last two races of her career.

"I'm sad to be leaving the sport, but I also know I'm ready," Blair told a boisterous crowd at a brief ceremony honoring her after the races. Her voice cracked as she recalled her career, which includes five Olympic gold medals, world championships and records.

Event officials read a letter from President Bill Clinton congratulating her, and she was presented with a Calgary-trademark white Stetson.

Blair helped make sprint speedskating a glamor event in North America—unlike in Europe where distance skaters tend to get the glory.

She has amazed those in her sport with consistent drive and determination, even when she didn't have a competitor on her heels.

"I think it's because she has done it for fun and she discovered that a lot of her fun was in competition," said her mother, Eleanor Blair, who attended skating practices and competitions since her daughter first wobbled onto the ice when she was 2. "She lives a pretty well-organized life. Organization and determination, I think, are a great part of her success."

After hanging up her skates, Blair took to the motivational speaking circuit and worked with young speedskaters in Milwaukee.

BONNIE BLAIR RACES TO HER FOURTH CAREER GOLD MEDAL IN THE 1994 WINTER GAMES, WINNING THE 500-METER EVENT. (AP/WIDE WORLD PHOTOS)

Bjorn Borg moments after he won the final point of his fifth consecutive Wimbledon singles title in 1980. (AP/Wide World Photos)

BJORN BORG

SWEDEN'S GOLDEN BOY OF TENNIS

Bjorn Borg burst upon the tennis scene at age 15, a golden-haired "Wonder Child" with a suspect fighting heart, and retired at the age of 26 with a great sigh of relief, as if he had just been freed from some dreadful dungeon.

In those intervening years, from 1971 through 1982, this somber, steely Swede with his devastating topspin shots and thundering serve, provided audiences with the most gripping drama ever unfolded within those white rectangles that make up the arena of the sport.

His principal stage was the ancient turf of historic Wimbledon, although he kept so-called "teeny-boppers" squealing with delight from Paris' Roland Garros to Melbourne's Kooyong and New York's Madison Square Garden throughout his self-shortened career.

Wimbledon is the oldest and most prestigious of the world's tennis tournaments, and it is on Wimbledon's archaic but storied Center Court turf that tennis heroes are forged, and none stood taller than the Scandinavian golden child.

Starting in 1976, at the age of 20, he stormed to five consecutive singles championships, an unbelievable feat that escaped such greats as Big Bill Tilden, Fred Perry, Don Budge, Jack Kramer and Rod Laver. It was Bjorn's one great badge of grandeur, although he also won an unprecedented six French Opens, the Italian twice, the Masters in New York and World Championship of Tennis in Dallas. Strangely, his Achilles' heel was the U.S. Open, which repeatedly escaped his grasp.

Borg never won the U.S. Open, although he was runner-up four times, twice to Jimmy Connors and twice to John McEnroe, his chief rivals for world supremacy. A moody, private person, the young Swede never seemed comfortable in the teeming, fast-paced atmosphere he found in America, and thus his performances suffered as a result. Five times he qualified for the WCT Finals in Dallas, winning only in 1976.

His battles with Connors and McEnroe, both left-handers, became classics—duels matching markedly contrasting personalities and game styles. Connors was a feisty, alley fighter, a constant attacker who played every point as if it might be his last. McEnroe was a sulking, spoiled racket genius with tremendous natural talent and instincts.

Connors and McEnroe were given to court tantrums, constant bickering with umpires and linesmen and frequent antagonism toward fans and the press.

Both became natural villains in the scenarios that featured Borg as the good guy. A

BJORN BORG REACHES FOR A SHOT IN A TOURNAMENT IN 1976. (AP/WIDE WORLD PHOTOS)

BJORN BORG WITH HIS MEN'S SINGLES TROPHY AFTER HIS FOURTH TITLE AT WIMBLEDON IN 1979. (AP/WIDE WORLD PHOTOS)

BJORN BORG SHAKES HANDS WITH JOHN MCENROE AFTER LOSING THE U.S. OPEN FINAL IN 1981. FOLLOWING THIS LOSS, BORG LEFT THE COURT AND ANNOUNCED HIS RETIREMENT FROM TENNIS. (AP/WIDE WORLD PHOTOS)

handsome athlete, close to six feet tall and slender at 160 pounds, Borg was a sphinx on the court. His strong, Viking features never showed any emotion. He never argued a point. He typified controlled strength as he literally pounded his adversaries into submission from the backcourt with his rocket-like, two-fisted backhand and accentuated topspin forehand. Although a foreigner facing Americans, he was the idol of American fans.

Borg was born June 6, 1956, in the small community of Sodertlage, just outside Stockholm. He took up tennis at an early age, playing on slow clay courts, and while still in elementary school caught the eye of Lennart Bergelin, a former member of the Swedish Davis Cup team. In a land of snow and ice, where skiing and hockey vie with soccer for the attention of youths, tennis was largely an orphan sport.

Bjorn was a court prodigy. Even before he got into his teens, he could beat top men in his community. At 14, he was an internationalist, traveling to Miami to win the first of his two junior titles in the Orange Bowl. At 15, he captured the junior crown at Wimbledon and made the Swedish Davis Cup team, the youngest ever to compete for the famous trophy.

In 1974, a scrawny kid of 17, he won the Italian National and captured the first of his six French crowns, beating Manuel Orantes after dropping the first two sets. A year later, he led Sweden to its first Davis Cup victory.

By this time Borg was the toast of the tennis world, although the huge Swedish press corps that followed him around the globe was creating negative vibes because of his continued frustrations in the United States, particularly in the Open and WCT Finals in Dallas.

The knock: "No heart. Can't win the big one."

They began asking: "Is Sweden's Golden Boy just a mechanical robot? Is what we took for tremendous calm merely a lack of fire and spirit?"

The doubts were soon shattered on the taut tension strings of Borg's familiar wooden racket.

Bjorn, twice beaten in the quarterfinals as a teenager, won his first Wimbledon in 1976 after just turning 20. He crushed flashy Ilie Nastase in the final, 6-4, 6-2, 9-7, causing the Romanian to wonder if the kid was human.

"He's a robot from outer space," said Ilie, not questioning his rival's courage. "A Martian."

In 1978, the young Swede became the first man since Rod Laver in 1962 to win the Italian, French and Wimbledon titles in the same year. He didn't lose a match over a seven-month period, finally bowing to Connors in the U.S. Open.

Borg saved his greatest Wimbledon effort for his last in 1980—a knock-down, drag-out slugfest against McEnroe in the final. After dropping a heartbreaking tie-breaker 18-16 in the fourth set, he allowed McEnroe only three points against his service in the decisive set, winning it 8-6. That was the year also that Borg was married to his longtime fiance, Mariana Simionescu, whom he divorced 2 1/2 years later, and began contemplating retirement. A wealthy man who had earned $8 million a year in prize money and endorsements with vast business interests, Borg retired to the life of a jet-setter on the French Riviera. He's still active, playing Conners, McEnroe and other old rivals these days on the ATP's senior circuit.

JIM BROWN TEARS THROUGH THE PHILADELPHIA EAGLES LINE FOR HIS 106TH CAREER TOUCHDOWN BREAKING DON HUTSON'S RECORD ON SEPTEMBER 20, 1965. (AP/WIDE WORLD PHOTOS)

JIM BROWN

SHEER POWER AND DESIRE

Jim Brown was considered a villain on and off the football field—a Tarzan-like and complex black man who shredded tacklers, allegedly beat up women, carried on a running feud with the law, starred in more than a dozen movies, yet spent much of his later life trying to provide jobs, milk and bread for the less fortunate members of his race.

He never denied that he was tough, sometimes downright mean, and basically a brooding loner, but he strongly resented the figure he often was publicly portrayed as.

"There is the image and the man," he said. "The image is what the public thinks he is. The man is what he is—I am no angel. If I was a goody-goody, I'd be a psychological wreck—in a straitjacket."

Succeeding generations will remember him as neither devil nor angel but as one of the greatest athletes of all time, potentially another Jim Thorpe, who excelled in many athletic activities but chose football.

In high school, he won 13 letters in five sports—baseball, football, basketball, track and lacrosse. Recruited by Syracuse University for lacrosse, he turned to football and proceeded to run for 2,091 yards and 25 touchdowns as a slashing, almost unstoppable halfback and fullback.

His exploits made him the first-round draft choice of the Cleveland Browns, with whom over nine seasons he stormed over would-be tacklers like a tornado, leaving shattered records in his wake.

He led the National Football League in rushing in eight of the nine seasons he played from 1957 through 1965 which is still an NFL record. With 12,312 career yards, he held the league's all-time rushing record until former Chicago Bears great Walter Payton broke it in 1984.

Magnificently built, 6 feet, 2 inches and 230 pounds, with broad shoulders, a 32-inch waist and narrow hips, he ran close to the ground, spinning and dodging and brutally stampeding over frustrated would-be tacklers.

"He was most dangerous when you thought you had him," said Sam Huff, the New York Giants' great linebacker. "He'd gather himself up and you'd find yourself empty-handed."

"Superhuman," acknowledged the Philadelphia Eagles' Chuck Bednarik. "He had finesse, ability, power—sheer power and desire."

Defensive back Henry Carr said, "He ran like he had a halo over his head saying you can't touch."

JIM BROWN SPEAKS TO A CROWD OF CLEVELAND BROWNS FANS AT A RALLY IN 1998, ONE YEAR BEFORE THE NEW CLEVELAND BROWNS TAKE THE FIELD AGAIN. (AP/WIDE WORLD PHOTOS)

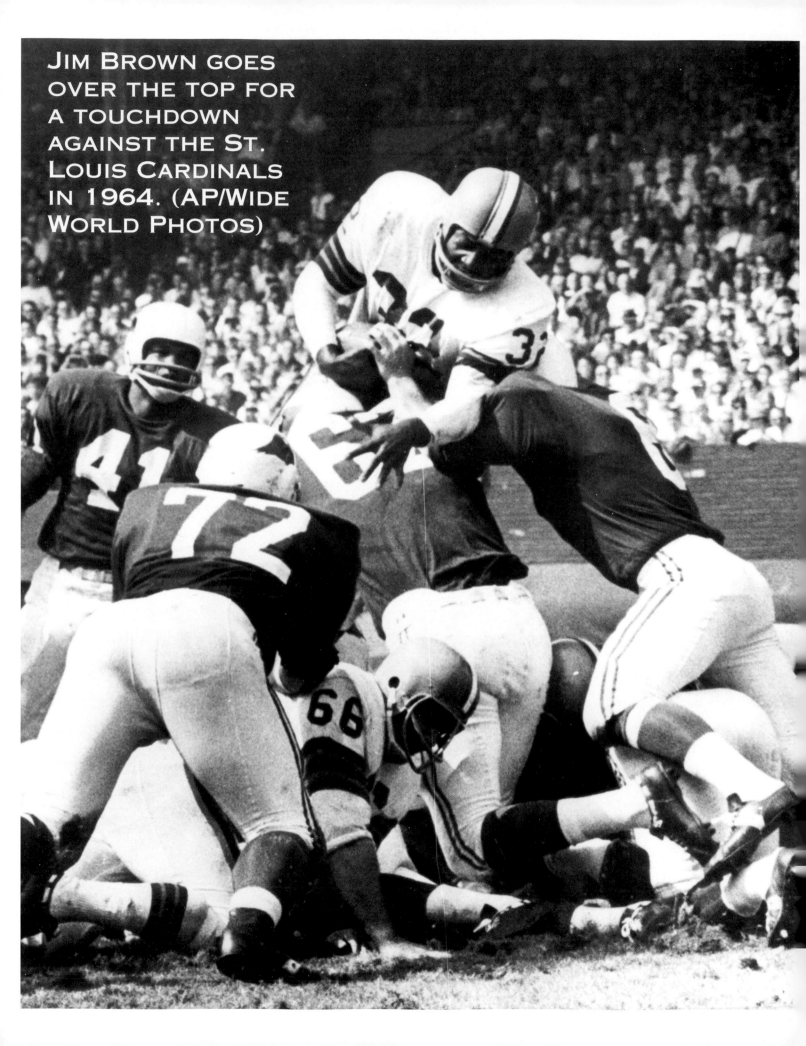

JIM BROWN GOES OVER THE TOP FOR A TOUCHDOWN AGAINST THE ST. LOUIS CARDINALS IN 1964. (AP/WIDE WORLD PHOTOS)

JIM BROWN AT THE UNVEILING OF A BUST HONORING HIM AT A SYRACUSE UNIVERSITY FOOTBALL GAME IN 1996. (AP/WIDE WORLD PHOTOS)

Brown disdained the suggestion that he had some extraordinary power. "There were a lot of running backs as good as me," he said. "The real difference was that I could focus. I never laid back and relied on natural ability."

Born in 1936, James Nathaniel Brown spent the first nine years of his life in the care of a great-grandmother on a small island off the coast of southern Georgia after being deserted by a philandering father and a mother who moved north.

When Brown was nine, he joined his mother, a housemaid, and took up residence in the home of his mother's employer, in the affluent community of Manhasset, Long Island. The homeowner saw that the boy had the best clothes and went to the best schools.

At Manhasset High School, Brown became an outstanding all-around athlete, particularly gifted in football and lacrosse. In his senior year, he averaged 14.9 yards a carry in football, 38 points a game in basketball and was a standout high jumper. Recruited by close to 50 colleges, Brown chose Syracuse, where at first the coaches sought to make him into a tackle. Later he found his proper position, running back, and won All-America honors his senior year.

Signed by Cleveland at the end of the 1956 season, he immediately turned around the Browns' fortunes. Having finished with a 5-7 record in 1956, the Browns won the Eastern Conference title with a 9-2-1 record in 1957, with Brown rushing for 942 yards.

Brown led a players' revolt in 1962 that resulted in the removal of Paul Brown as coach and followed that with his finest season in 1963, when he ran for 1,863 yards and 12 touchdowns. The Browns won the NFL crown in 1964 and another Eastern title in 1965, with Brown rushing for 1,544 yards.

He had been voted the NFL's Most Valuable Player when he retired July 14, 1966, at the age of 30. He estimated he had six top-flight seasons remaining. Brown's decision to quit football came while he was in London making his second movie, *The Dirty Dozen*, with Lee Marvin. The picture grossed $63 million, the most successful of the 17 films he was to make over the next 15 years.

Although football's highest-paid star at $75,000 a year, he had decided it was time to strike out on a new course.

"The money was more than I ever dreamed of," he said about his shift in careers. "I was still young. The movies gave me dignity and a chance to do something for my race."

Brown had earlier married a childhood sweetheart, the former Sue Jones, "a country girl out of Columbus, Georgia," with whom he had three children before she finally found it impossible to adjust to the great football star's lifestyle.

Over a period of years, Brown was hit with paternity suits, charges of tossing a model from a second-floor balcony, assaulting a cop and leaving the scene of an accident after a collision on a Los Angeles thruway.

"Harassment," Brown charged. "They couldn't make any of the charges stick. They have made me a target."

Brown did some broadcasting, became a strident black activist and founded the Black Economic Union, designed to set up blacks in business. Few of his enterprises succeeded.

In 1971, his first year of eligibility, he was elected to the Pro Football Hall of Fame. He took his trophy to his retreat in the Hollywood Hills. "I am a loner," he said.

SERGEI BUBKA BECAME THE FIRST MAN TO CLEAR 20 FEET OUTDOORS IN THE POLE VAULT WITH THIS ATTEMPT AT A MEET IN MALMO, SWEDEN IN 1991. (AP/WIDE WORLD PHOTOS)

SERGEI BUBKA

NOBODY DOES IT BETTER

Six for six. The amazing Sergei Bubka had won gold in the pole vault at all six World Championships, an unprecedented streak that dates back to 1983.

His sixth title, which came on the final night of the 1997 championships, may have been the most dramatic of all.

The Ukrainian star, written off by many people after a career-threatening injury kept him out of the 1996 Atlanta Olympics, produced a magical performance in a compelling duel with Russian rival Maksim Tarasov and U.S. upstart Dean Starkey.

"It's not my best victory at the championships," said Bubka, 33 when he did it. "But I can say it is maybe the most difficult. After Atlanta, many said, 'He's finished, he's dead.' Maybe for that reason I tried to find motivation and come back."

Bubka, who underwent surgery on his torn right Achilles tendon in December 1997, had competed only twice that year, and failed to go higher than 18 feet, 4 3/4 inches.

But he clinched victory by clearing 19-8 1/2, a championship record and one of the many highlights in a career that includes 35 world records (18 indoors, 17 outdoors) and has spanned two decades.

"It's quite amazing to see someone winning six titles in a row," Tarasov said afterward.

"He's unbelievable," Starkey added. "He never ceases to amaze me. No one will ever been able to duplicate what he's done."

The closest is Lars Riedel of Germany, who won his fourth consecutive world title in the men's discus with a throw of 224-10.

The secret for Bubka's longevity?

"I love the sport because of the competition and the atmosphere," said Bubka, who missed the 1999 championships due to injury. "I want to be the best."

Bubka was named the top athlete of 1997 by *L'Equipe*, the French daily.

It might have been his last hurrah. Bubka's career has been on the decline since the Ukraine turned in a disappointing showing at the 1998 Goodwill Games.

The world record holder remains the only vaulter to clear 20 feet.

SERGEI BUBKA WON HIS THIRD MEET IN TWO WEEKS AT THE RUSSIAN WINTER TRACK MEET BY VAULTING 19.5 FEET ON HIS FIRST ATTEMPT IN 1996. (AP/WIDE WORLD PHOTOS)

SERGEI BUBKA

DON BUDGE IN ACTION AT THE 1937 WIMBLEDON, WHICH HE WON. (AP/WIDE WORLD PHOTOS)

DON BUDGE

THE COMPLETE TENNIS PLAYER

"Playing tennis against Don Budge was like playing against a concrete wall—there was nothing to attack," said former Wimbledon champion Sidney Wood, a contemporary.

"Budge had to be the greatest player of all time, the records prove it," insisted Walter Pate, a player of the Bill Tilden era and for 11 years captain of the U.S. Davis Cup team.

Neither got an argument from the late Bobby Riggs, the feisty court hustler, himself a one-time champion, whose career touched six decades from Tilden to Jack Kramer to Billie Jean King and who faced Budge as both an amateur and a pro.

"Tilden toyed with opponents—he teased them by letting them get close," said Riggs. "Ellsworth Vines was inconsistent. Kramer was troubled with a bad back. Budge wasn't just steady. He was explosive. He blew you off the court."

Budge, who played in the shadow of a developing World War II, had a comparatively brief career and thus from a public-appreciation standpoint, found himself sandwiched between the euphoria of Tilden's "Golden Twenties" and the emergence of a postwar breed of tough, young professionals who hit the ball at 120 miles an hour and competed for purses that soared into millions of dollars.

Yet none of the widely acclaimed international stars who preceded him, nor the hard-hitting champions who followed managed to cram as much success and dominance into such a small package.

In 1937, Budge won both the Wimbledon and the U.S. men's singles championships. In 1938 he repeated those two triumphs and added the Australian and French crowns to score the first Grand Slam sweep of the sport's major titles. He didn't lose a single match during that two-year span.

A complete player and a powerful server with a steady, effective forehand, Don's greatest weapon was a whiplash backhand, a carryover from his baseball-playing days as a kid. It was deadly.

He made his mark in tennis, but his first love as a kid was baseball. After becoming famous, Budge had a chance to meet one of his baseball heroes, Joe DiMaggio at a New York restaurant.

"You know, Don," DiMaggio told him, "I always envied you. As a kid I dreamed of becoming a tennis champion."

"That's funny," Budge replied. "I always wanted to be a baseball player.

DON BUDGE DURING A TOURNAMENT IN 1937. (AP/WIDE WORLD PHOTOS)

DICK BUTKUS CLOSES IN
FOR A TACKLE AGAINST
THE ST. LOUIS CARDINALS
IN 1969. (AP/WIDE WORLD
PHOTOS)

DICK BUTKUS

THE BRUISING, BATTERING BEAR

In the memory of the oldest living naturalist, no grizzly bear has ever been spotted prowling the streets of Chicago.

Except one: Dick Butkus, who was 245 pounds of snarling, seething muscle at a middle linebacker post for the Chicago Bears from 1965 to 1973. He was Rambo without automatic weapons, using only his hands, shoulders, legs, feet and—it was charged—his teeth.

"The Animal" was the nickname fastened to Dick by the teams he terrorized. Butkus didn't seem to appreciate that handle, but neither did he overly resent it. "I guess people think the Bears keep me in a cage and only let me out on Sundays to play football," he growled. "Nobody thinks I can talk, much less write my own name."

Butkus roamed a football field sideline to sideline. There were no sophisticated defenses in his day that gave him areas to guard. No offensive keys to read. He went where the ball went, and when he found it, he tried to knock the helmet off the guy who had it into the 20th row.

"Dick rattles your brains when he tackles you," former Green Bay quarterback Bart Starr said.

"Butkus is so physical, he puts the fear of God into you," Detroit's Greg Landry said.

About that business of using his teeth: Accused a couple of times of biting another player in the heat of battle, Butkus drew himself to his full height of 6-3 and replied reproachfully: "I'm a football player, not a gourmet."

Dick was an All-Pro seven times in his nine NFL seasons but never realized a pro football player's dream of taking the field in a Super Bowl game or even a league title game. In most of his seasons with the Bears, they had a losing record. There were times when he seemed to be a lone defender.

He won every football award there is, earning a spot on the NFL's 75th Anniversary All-Time Team and a plaque in the Pro Football Hall of Fame. The former University of Illinois standout even had an award named after him—the Butkus Award, which goes each year to college football's top linebacker.

But one of the finest tributes Butkus ever received was unofficial. In a 1970 poll of NFL coaches, Butkus was named by nine of them as the first player they'd pick if they were starting a team from scratch.

His nine votes were three more than any other star, including Jets sensation Joe Namath, who was in his prime at the time.

DICK BUTKUS (51) HELPS JOE TAYLOR TACKLE THE GREEN BAY PACKERS' JOHN BROKINGTON IN THIS 1972 GAME. (AP/WIDE WORLD PHOTOS)

DICK BUTTON IN FRONT OF ST. BASIL'S CATHEDRAL IN MOSCOW WHILE ON TOUR WITH THE HOLIDAY ON ICE SHOW. (AP/WIDE WORLD PHOTOS)

DICK BUTTON

A FIGURE GREAT

Dick Button was the most dominant male figure skater over a six-year period and later became the most visible and one of the most influential voices in the sport.

Button started receiving instruction in 1942 and a year later, he entered his first competition at age 14.

From 1946 to 1952, he dominated the world of figure skating. Button captured the first of seven consecutive U.S. men's titles in 1946 and a year later he became the first American in 23 years to to win the North American championship. He won that championship again in 1949 and 1951.

In 1948 and 1949, while attending Harvard, he became the first person to hold five figure skating titles at the same time: the U.S., North American, European, world and Olympic.

Button took the European title in 1948, the last time Americans were allowed to compete in the event.

That year he also took the Olympic gold medal at St. Moritz, Switzerland. He defended his title four years later in Oslo, Norway. He was the first to complete a first triple jump with a triple loop at those 1952 Olympics opening a new era of athleticism in the sport.

In addition to his two Olympic gold medals, he won five straight world titles from 1948 through 1952.

In 1953 he turned professional, signing a contract to appear with the Ice Capades.

Button has been analyzing and explaining the finer points of figure skating for television audiences since 1960. He has become the most visible and one of the most influential voices in the sport, winning an Emmy Award for his work in 1981.

Thanks greatly to Button, figure skating's popularity on this continent has soared. As women such as Peggy Fleming and Dorothy Hamill, men like John Curry, Robin Cousins and Scott Hamilton, and all the Soviet pairs dominated the ice, Button was there to interpret their moves, query them about technique, emotion and the judging.

DICK BUTTON WAS THE FIRST AMERICAN TO CAPTURE FIGURE SKATING GOLD IN THE OLYMPICS. (AP/WIDE WORLD PHOTOS)

WILT CHAMBERLAIN COVERS THE FACE OF THE NEW YORK KNICKS' BILL BRADLEY DURING THE 1970 NBA FINALS. (AP/WIDE WORLD PHOTOS)

WILT CHAMBERLAIN

CENTER OF ATTENTION

If George Mikan was the first of the big men in basketball, then Wilt Chamberlain was the first of the agile giants, triggering the "Seven-Foot Revolution" for muscular beanstalks who could move with the grace of ballerinas, fake, pass, shoot and slam dunk.

At 7 feet, 1 inch and 275 pounds, Wilt the Stilt emerged as the Goliath by whom all future titans—and they proliferated—had to be measured. He wrote the book. He copyrighted the slam dunk, broke the dam that unleashed capitalistic six-figure salaries and set records in such abundance that it took two pages of five-point type to record them all in the *National Basketball Association Register*.

It was Chamberlain who erased the words "klutz" and "ox" from the basketball dictionary and relegated to oblivion the notion that all big men had to be dumb, awkward stumblebums. Chamberlain was an athlete of superb potential who might have been a champion in any athletic field he chose.

One of his early ambitions was to be a decathlon competitor in the Olympic Games. As a schoolboy, he was a good runner and high jumper and, because of his unusual strength, was outstanding in such field events as the javelin, shot put and discus. "One of my regrets," he said later, "was that I never pursued this dream."

He raced boats and learned to water ski. He took up volleyball and even tried his hand at polo, although he never found a big enough pony.

Reflective of the range of his talents, he both played tennis and boxed. After retirement, he once seriously considered challenging Muhammad Ali for the heavyweight championship, but later abandoned the idea, for which Ali was most thankful. "Only one man in this whole world might beat me," Ali said, "and that's that big, tough dude, the Stilt. It scares me just to think about getting in the ring with him."

So Wilt the Stilt—a label he abhorred—confined himself to busting basketball records instead of beaks, and no one in the game did it on such an overwhelming scale.

In his 14 years as a professional, from 1959 through 1973, he twice scored more than 3,000 points in a season and once went over the 4,000 mark—plateaus no other player ever reached. Playing with Philadelphia's Warriors and 76ers, the San Francisco Warriors and Los Angeles Lakers, he accumulated a career total of 31,419 points, a record that lasted until Kareem Abdul-Jabbar, playing in his 16th season, broke it in 1985.

WILT CHAMBERLAIN HOLDS A SIGN FOR THE 100 POINTS HE SCORED AGAINST THE KNICKERBOCKERS IN 1962. (AP/WIDE WORLD PHOTOS)

WILT CHAMBERLAIN ROLLS IN TWO POINTS FOR THE PHILADELPHIA
WARRIORS AGAINST THE DETROIT PISTONS DURING THE 1959
SEASON. (AP/WIDE WORLD PHOTOS)

CHAMBERLAIN TRIES TO
SHOOT OVER BILL
RUSSELL OF THE
BOSTON CELTICS IN THE
1969 NBA FINALS.
(AP/WIDE WORLD
PHOTOS)

He led the league in rebounding in 11 of his 14 years and in field-goal percentage in nine. Seven times he was the NBA's leading scorer. His one crowning season was 1961-62, when he scored a total of 4,029 points and averaged 50.4 points a game. It was climaxed when he rammed in 100 points— seemingly an untouchable mark—against the New York Knicks in Hershey, Pennsylvania, on March 2, 1962.

His records ranged from career rebounds, totaling 2,075, to consecutive field goals, minutes played and other statistics. He was four times the league's Most Valuable Player and seven times a starter in the All-Star Game. He entered basketball's Hall of Fame in 1978.

Wilt was born in Philadelphia on August 21, 1936, the son of a handyman and one of nine children. Growing up, he was always taller than his schoolmates, a condition that made him self-conscious and unsocial. Young friends dubbed him "The Dipper," "Dippy" and "Dip."

By the time he reached Overbrook High School, Wilt was 6 feet, 11 inches tall, a torso on pipestem legs. Yet he had good coordination and became the star of the team, sometimes scoring 70 to 90 points a game. Courted by more than 200 colleges, he chose the University of Kansas, where he led the Jayhawks to the NCAA finals in 1957, losing a four-overtime thriller to North Carolina in Kansas City.

He quit college after his junior year to join the Harlem Globetrotters for a salary of $65,000. On May 30, 1959, Owner Eddie Gottlieb of the Philadelphia Warriors signed the prize prospect for $30,000 plus fringe benefits. An immediate sensation, Wilt scored 43 points and grabbed 28 rebounds in his debut against the Knicks. Gottlieb began dreaming of a championship.

Unfortunately, Wilt was unable to deliver titles as easily as he could stuff basketballs through the hoop.

In his 14 years in the NBA, Chamberlain had the satisfaction of playing on only two championship teams— Philadelphia in 1967 and Los Angeles in 1972. This gave rise to comparisons with Bill Russell, the 6-foot-10 ballhandling wizard of the Boston Celtics, who beat his teams twice in the NBA championship series and five times in conference finals. In all, the Celtics won 11 titles behind Russell, nine in the 10 years the two giant stars clashed—a source of pain for Wilt.

"I scored more points against the Celtics than anybody else," Chamberlain argued. "I outscored Russell in head-to-head meetings 440 to 212—two to one."

After retiring, Chamberlain wrote four books, played professional volleyball, owned racehorses and made a mint in the restaurant business. He lived in a mansion in Bel Air, California, which he helped design. Of his retirement, Chamberlain said, "I'm busier now than I was 30 years ago," he said. "I own a few businesses. I develop land in countries all over the world. I play the stock market. I sponsor youth track and volleyball teams. So I've got a full schedule."

Chamberlain, who died October 12, 1999 of apparent heart failure at his home in Bel Air, California, took that marvelous ability and tremendous size—7-foot-1, 290 pounds—and made the most of it. He was 63 years old.

Ty Cobb waits for a pitch during his early days with the Detroit Tigers in this 1905 photo. (AP/Wide World Photos)

TY COBB

THE FIERY GEORGIA PEACH

In 1951, when The Associated Press released the results of a sportswriters' poll naming the greatest athletes by sport of the first half-century, the telephone rang on the desk of Joe Reichler, the AP's baseball editor. The call came from Atlanta, and there was a raspy, agitated voice at the other end.

The caller was Ty Cobb. He was livid, having read in the *Atlanta Journal* that Babe Ruth had been chosen over him as the greatest baseball player of the past 50 years. In angry, no uncertain terms, Cobb made it known that the poll was a farce. Baseball's greatest player, Ty Cobb insisted, was Ty Cobb.

Such was the nature of the man—fiery, arrogant, egotistical, combative, outspoken. Yet there were many of his contemporaries who conceded that, love him or hate him (and most were in the latter category), the crusty old "Georgia Peach" may have been correct. He may well have been the greatest all-around ballplayer, if not the most popular, of all time. There were statistics to support the theory.

Playing 22 years with the Detroit Tigers and two with the Philadelphia Athletics, the rock-hard redneck from red clay country compiled records that endured for generations. In the 1936 voting for original inductees into baseball's Hall of Fame, Cobb led them all, including the great Ruth, with 222 of 226 votes.

He had a lifetime batting average of .367, the game's highest, with three seasons of better than .400. He won 12 batting titles, nine in a row, and never fell below .368 from 1909 through 1919. He was the first to get more than 4,000 hits. He scored 2,245 runs and stole 892 bases. It was not until more than half a century later that Pete Rose surpassed his mark of 4,191 hits and Lou Brock bettered his career stolen base record.

Cobb was not a slugger, in the sense of a Ruth, Hank Aaron, or a Mark McGwire, who thrilled crowds later. He was a slashing left-handed hitter whose line drives rocketed over the heads of infielders. Once on base, he was a scheming strategist who drove defenders to nervous distraction with his speed and daring.

The "Georgia Peach" played in the "dead ball era," when runs were scarce and had to be milked around the bases. He had the tools for the times. He was leather tough, lightning quick and meaner than a bed of rattlesnakes. He treasured his reputation as a diamond villain—generally heckled by fans, resented by teammates, detested and feared by opponents.

Stories that he filed the spikes of his shoes in the locker room are probably untrue, but there is nothing fictional about his aggressiveness and tenacity on the base paths. He shunned the head-on slide and preferred to go into a base full tilt, spikes flying, unmindful of the opposing player.

To Cobb, baseball wasn't a game, it was a war. And his animosity wasn't confined to the playing field. Contemporaries attributed it to an early tragedy in his life.

Cobb was born December 18, 1886, in the small north Georgia village of Narrows. His father

TY COBB SLIDES INTO A BASE IN THIS 1925 PHOTO. (AP/WIDE WORLD PHOTOS)

Ty Cobb warming up before a game in 1922. He would compile a .401 average that year. (AP/Wide World Photos)

TY COBB SLIDES UNDER THE TAG IN THIS UNDATED
PHOTO. (AP/WIDE WORLD PHOTOS)

was a man of local esteem—a teacher, farmer, weekly newspaper publisher, later mayor and state senator. Tyrus was the first child, named for the ancient city of Tyre. The elder Cobb wanted his son to go to college and be a lawyer or a doctor. Athletically inclined and very competitive, Ty demurred.

At 17, he was a star of the local team in Royston, Georgia, played briefly with Augusta in the South Atlantic League and some semipro ball in Anniston, Alabama, before getting a chance with the Detroit Tigers in 1905. He was a scrawny, gristly kid of 18, 5 feet, 11 inches and 155 pounds.

This break coincided with news that his father had been killed—shot by his mother upon returning home late at night from a business trip. The mother claimed she had mistaken him for a burglar, but there were reports of a secret lover.

Cobb became bitter, and his rage continued to manifest itself as he sought to gain a spot with the team. He was five years younger than any of the other Tigers' regulars and the only Southerner—a firebrand generally disliked by teammates because of his temper and aggressiveness.

"He was still fighting the Civil War," said Sam Crawford, a contemporary. "We were all damn Yankees."

Cobb's first years with the Tigers were turbulent. Because of his cockiness, he was ostracized and hazed by his fellow players. His bats were sawed in half. He got into fights with teammates. Catcher Charlie Smith broke his nose. He knocked down and kicked a pitcher named Ed Siever. He had to be separated from a fellow outfielder, Matty McIntyre.

As Cobb got older, he got bigger (6-1, 175 pounds), more audacious and meaner. He taunted pitchers and kept rival infielders in a tizzy by getting caught between bases and dodging back and forth to force a mistake.

In 1912, he leaped into the stands in New York and punched and kicked a fan who was badgering him. There was a celebrated hotel brawl with Buck Herzog of the Giants in 1917. In 1921, he challenged umpire Billy Evans under the stands. He was constantly having scrapes with blacks off the field—a street worker, an elevator operator, a watchman.

At age 34, he became playing manager of the Tigers and had six years of moderate success. He played his final two years, 1927 and 1928, with the Philadelphia Athletics.

Even after retiring, Cobb became involved in many public scrapes. A friend sued him for $50,000. He was barred from some golf courses in California. Nevertheless, he was a shrewd businessman, investing in firms such as General Motors and Coca-Cola. Twice married and twice divorced, he died July 17, 1961, a multimillionaire, angry at the world.

Nadia Comeneci after she earned the first perfect score of 10 in Olympic history. She repeated the perfect score two more times during the 1976 Summer Olympics in Montreal. (AP/Wide World Photos)

NADIA COMENECI

PRINCESS OF THE BARS AND BEAMS

She was just a sprite of a child, a brooding, dark-eyed girl of 14, a little more than 4 feet tall and less than 80 pounds—seemingly a windup toy on a stick, spinning, leaping, somersaulting with a cold, mechanical precision while millions, watching in the flesh and on television, cheered.

Her name was Nadia Comaneci. The icicle princess of the bars and beams in the 1976 Olympics became the first gymnast in history to score a perfect "10"—she did it seven times and turned her once neglected and cult discipline into an exact science.

The world fell in love with her, but the little girl from behind Romania's Communist curtain refused to respond with even a smile. Her aloof reserve remained impenetrable.

"In 1976," said Gordon Maddux, a gymnastics authority who did TV commentary on the Olympics' gymnastic competition, "Nadia was the best athlete in the world, all sports included."

Nadia and her cordon of teammates, all looking like cub Girl Scouts as they marched in unison through Montreal's Olympic Village, came to the Games in the shadow of the Soviets' celebrated Olga Korbut, the cute, outgoing heroine of the 1972 Games in Munich, Germany.

It was actually Olga, 84 pounds of personality and flying pigtails, who made the world conscious of her sport, a dizzying routine of swinging on bars, staging daring loops on narrow beams and doing barefoot exercises to music much in the fashion of figure skaters on ice.

A TV reporter had noticed Korbut doing a difficult back somersault on the uneven bars and persuaded ABC to alter its program and include a segment of Korbut's routine in its broadcast. The network was hooked. Before it had finished, its cameras were giving special attention to the 17-year-old Russian girl and, before long, it had its viewers joining the live chorus of "Olga! Olga! Olga!"

Olga won the balance beam and free exercises—only two gold medals—but television made her a world personality and she relished the role. A natural "ham," she was the star of the Russian team that toured the United States in 1976.

The ever-smiling, effervescent Olga, although then a maturing 21, was still the main attraction on the stage when the gymnastics competition

COMENECI PERFORMS DURING THE 1976 OLYMPIC GAMES. COMENECI TOOK HOME THE GOLD IN THE 1976 GAMES. (AP/WIDE WORLD PHOTOS)

Nadia Comaneci dismounts from the uneven parallel bars during one of her perfect "10" performances at the 1976 Summer Olympics in Montreal. (AP/Wide World Photos)

NADIA COMENECI STOLE THE SPOTLIGHT FROM RIVAL OLGA
KORBUT WITH HER PERFORMANCE AT THE 1976 OLYMPICS.
(AP/WIDE WORLD PHOTOS)

began in Montreal in 1971. Few paid much attention to Comaneci until the Romanian schoolgirl began whizzing through her routines, her supple body performing like a metronome on the platforms, bars and beams.

Nadia was not a complete unknown. She was one of an underaged brood, look-alike miniatures in their white leotards with a bold stripe down the side ostensibly being groomed by Romanian coach Bela Karolyi for some future Games. A year earlier Nadia had scored an upset over the Soviet Union's veteran European champion Ludmilla Turischeva.

But interest was quickened when Nadia scored her first "10"—an unheard-of achievement in 80 years of the sport—and soon fans began flocking to the big hall and fighting for tickets to get a look at the newest sports phenomenon.

Flawlessly, Comaneci swept to gold medals in the balance beam and uneven parallel bars and captured all-around individual honors while Korbut, a forlorn and distraught figure, slipped from the limelight, finally winning the free exercises to the delight of her faithful followers.

While Nadia inspired admiration and wonderment among specialists and ordinary spectators alike, she never was able to engender the warmth and personal attachment that had marked the reign of her Russian rival.

"Nadia was extremely stoic, a robot," said the coach of the American team, Don Peters. "But she was in a class by herself—head and shoulders above the rest."

Whereas Olga had been bouncy and ebullient, Nadia was as cold as the blade of a rapier. She never showed emotion—not even to the crowd that was constantly bursting into wild applause. She swept through her routines as if pushed by some unseen button, then, having finished, she sought quick refuge in the privacy of the Village.

Some of her aloofness was accountable. The daughter of an auto mechanic, she was discovered by Karolyi when she was 6 years old doing flip-flops in a schoolyard. Karolyi immediately enrolled her in a training class. She never had a childhood as such. All she knew were rings, bars and beams.

At 14, she was unprepared for the public and media attention which poured down on her at Montreal. She was timid and half-scared. But under that schoolgirl facade was a competitive drive as cold and sharp as steel.

Her and Olga's impact on their sport was dramatic. Gymnastics interest mushroomed throughout the world. In the United States alone, the gymnastics pool grew from 15,000 in 1972 to 150,000.

Nadia had a nervous breakdown, tried to commit suicide but righted her life and showed up at the 1984 Olympics in Los Angeles—a bright, mature young woman no longer scared of the public. Karolyi, distressed over the Romanian government's attempt to exploit his prize pupil, moved to America and began turning out a new class of champions, including Mary Lou Retton, Dominique Moceanu and Kerri Strug.

In 1996, Comaneci married American gymnastics great Bart Conner in Bucharest, Romania. "Sometimes the story just seems a little too cute," Conner said. "Joe Midwest and the mysterious beauty from Transylvania."

BJORN DAHLIE COLLAPSES AT THE FINISH LINE OF THE 50 KM FREESTYLE CROSS-COUNTRY EVENT AT THE 1998 WINTER OLYMPICS IN NAGANO. (AP/WIDE WORLD PHOTOS)

BJORN DAHLIE IN ACTION IN THE 10KM CLASSICAL CROSS-COUNTRY EVENT IN NAGANO. (AP/WIDE WORLD PHOTOS)

BJORN DAHLIE

IS EIGHT ENOUGH?

It was the hardest race of his career, perhaps his greatest victory—and maybe his last in Olympic competition.

After seeing Bjorn Dahlie collapse in a heap as he won the gold medal in the 50K freestyle cross-country race, it was easy to understand why he may want to quit after the 1998 Winter Olympics. What else was there for the great Norwegian to prove?

With his victory in Nagano, Japan, Dahlie had eight Winter Olympic gold medals, more than anyone else before him.

Dahlie had beaten the old record of six golds even before the 50K, the blue-ribbon event of the sport, the marathon of cross-country, the toughest race there is.

And still he kept pushing, not wanting to lose that gold even as his tired legs were giving way late in the race. In the end, he beat Niklas Jonsson of Sweden by 8.1 seconds, finishing in two hours, 5 minutes, 8.2 seconds.

He fell flat on his face and lay in snow on the Snow Harp course even as Christian Hoffmann of Austria came in 53.6 seconds later to clinch the bronze and Russia's Alexei Prokurorov finished fourth, 1:33.3 behind.

Then Norwegian trainers picked him up and supported him as he struggled to regain his breath.

"I think it's my hardest race ever," Dahlie said after winning his third gold medal of the Nagano Games.

"On the morning of the race I didn't believe in a medal at all. Mentally, I was finished with these Olympics. I was quite tired. Right now I feel I have finished my skiing career. I have no motivation left."

A year after announcing he was probably finished, Dahlie was back on the slopes—and back dominating—winning his sixth Nordic Cup world title at age 31 in Lahti, Finland.

Sportswriters used the word "semi-retired" to describe his status.

So will he be back in 2002, the year of the next Winter Olympics?

Maybe. While his place in Olympic history is secure—12 medals are more than any Winter Games athlete ever—in Salt Lake City, Utah, site of the 2002 Games, has a special place in Dahlie's heart. It's where he won his first race at age 20.

And Dahlie's surely aware that one more gold medal would give him a share of the all-time Olympic record of nine, now jointly held by Carl Lewis, Paavo Nurmi, Laryssa Latynina and Mark Spitz.

Two more victories would put Dahlie ahead of them all.

He's been a success off the slopes, too. Dahlie is co-host of a popular TV show, has his own line of sportswear and makes about $1.5 million a year, the highest individual earner in Norwegian sports after soccer players.

BJORN DAHLIE ACCEPTS HIS EIGHTH OLYMPIC GOLD MEDAL AFTER WINNING THE 50-KILOMETER CROSS COUNTRY RACE AT THE 1988 WINTER GAMES IN NAGANO. (AP/WIDE WORLD PHOTOS)

JACK DEMPSEY IN
A 1925 PUBLICITY
PHOTO. (AP/WIDE
WORLD PHOTOS)

JACK DEMPSEY

THE DEVASTATING MANASSA MAULER

Of all a nation's sports heroes, traditionally, none is more revered than the heavyweight boxing champion of the world. He stimulates a pride and near idolatry that traces back to the gladiators of ancient Rome and the knights of the Middle Ages—a passion fed by the symbol of great strength and survival in raw, primitive, man-to-man combat.

Of America's unending parade of fighting greats, dating back a century or more, none has so captivated the people's fancy as the pug-faced, beetle-browed, one-time hobo out of Montana's mine country whom they called "The Manassa Mauler."

One can visualize gray-haired fathers and grandfathers decades in the future, discussing some current champion with their offspring, saying, "Well, son, let me tell you about a man named Jack Dempsey."

Jack Dempsey, a tough, fierce, devastating ring brawler, emerging just after World War I when the strife-weary nation was thirsting for some emotional relief, became the measuring rod by which all future champions would be judged.

He held the title for seven years. He eschewed the classic style. A crouching, weaving, bold aggressor with the kick of a mule in each hand, he battered opponents into pulps. He popularized the knockout punch and became the sport's first "Ring Killer."

When he fought, commerce stopped. Families gathered around their radios for details. Thousands stood in town squares to see the round-by-round flashed on giant screens.

He introduced the "Million Dollar Gate." In 1950 a nationwide poll of sportswriters and sportscasters by The Associated Press named him the greatest fighter of the first half of the 20th century.

Ironically, Dempsey's greatest popularity came not while he was battering opponents into unconsciousness but after he had lost his title to a handsome ex-Marine, Gene Tunney, and failed to regain it in two of boxing's most historic fights.

During his career, the Manassa Mauler had been the object of much negative publicity. Some sportswriters referred to him as "an animal hypnotized by his own ferocity." He was labelled a "slacker," because he failed to don a uniform while America's young men were sailing off to war in Europe. He was even accused of sneaking plaster of paris

JACK DEMPSEY WAITS IN THE CORNER AS THE REFEREE COUNTS OVER DOWNED CHAMPION GENE TUNNEY IN THIS 1927 TITLE BOUT. (AP/WIDE WORLD PHOTOS)

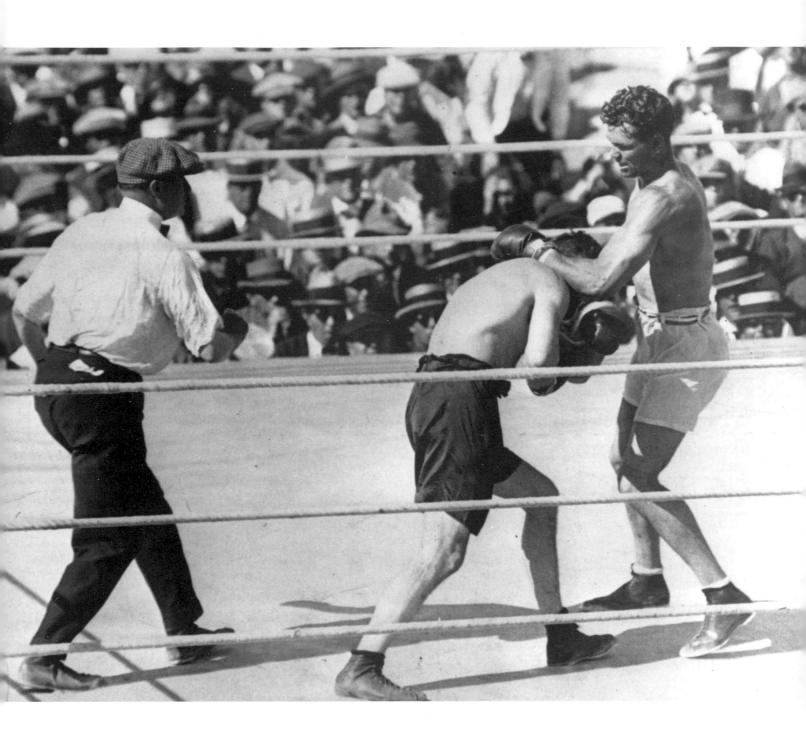

JACK DEMPSEY, RIGHT, DURING HIS HEAVYWEIGHT TITLE BOUT WITH TOMMY GIBBONS IN 1923. (AP/WIDE WORLD PHOTOS)

JACK DEMPSEY, LEFT,
SHAKES HANDS WITH HIS
MANAGER JACK KEARNS IN
THIS 1923 PHOTO.
(AP/WIDE WORLD PHOTOS)

into his gloves, giving him a rock-hard substance for his punishing knockouts.

He not only weathered these barbs but saw his popularity mushroom in his final years and upon retirement when he became a prominent restaurateur on New York's Broadway, always sitting in a corner ready to sign autographs and to converse with tourists.

He remained forever "The Champ." The public never forgave Tunney, who wrested the title from him in 1926 and repeated the victory in 1927 in the famous "long count" battle that will be a source of debate as long as men pull on padded gloves. Dempsey praised Tunney and never complained.

The legend that grew around this dark-visaged, head-bashing warrior stemmed from the rags-to-riches nature of his early life. He was born in the small mining town of Manassa, Montana, June 24, 1895, the ninth of 11 children, and was given the presidential name of William Harrison Dempsey.

The family, seeking to scrub out an existence, moved from place to place—Denver, Provo, Salt Lake City and finally a farm near Utah Lake. Dempsey shined shoes, grudgingly fanned and finally began fighting in a chicken coop gym along with an older brother, Jack, whose name he adopted while substituting on a local fight card.

Jack left home at 16 and took up the life of a hobo, riding in freight cars and fighting in saloons until he fell under the influence of a wily manager named Jack Kearns.

Kearns brought his protégé along judiciously and finally got him a shot at the heavyweight title against Jess Willard on a sizzling afternoon, July 4, 1919, in Toledo, Ohio. Willard was an awesome hulk of a man, 6 feet, 6 1/2 inches tall and 230 pounds, who had wrested the crown from Jack Johnson. Dempsey looked overmatched at 6-1 and 187 pounds.

However, Dempsey, lightning fast and attacking like an enraged panther, hammered the gigantic champion into submission in three rounds, knocking out six teeth, breaking Willard's jaw and leaving him a helpless, bleeding mass.

Dempsey's reputation was made. "A killer," wrote Grantland Rice. "A superhuman wild man."

The Manassa Mauler's reputation as a brutal ring assassin was enhanced by two of his most famous title defenses, and boxing, with the aid of promoter Tex Rickard, was thrust into the era of its first million-dollar gates.

Fans paid $1,789,238 to witness Dempsey's title defense against classy Georges Carpentier, the idol of France, in 1921. The Frenchman was demolished in three rounds. In September of 1923, Dempsey flattened Luis Firpo, "the Wild Bull of the Pampas," in 68 seconds of the second after having been sent reeling out of the ropes by the Argentine brawler in the opening round. It, too, grossed more than $1 million.

Now a national hero and with no worthy challengers, Dempsey drifted into the free-swinging high life of society and Hollywood. Both his brine-hardened fists and competitive fire had become soft when Gene Tunney burst on the scene as a contender three years after the Firpo fight.

Fighting in the rain in Philadelphia on September 23, 1926, the former Marine, dancing and jabbing, outboxed Dempsey for 10 rounds to take the title. A year later, Dempsey, seeking revenge before 100,000 in Chicago's Soldier Field, smashed Tunney to the canvas in the seventh round but failed to go to a neutral corner. Tunney, with the benefit of a 17-second "long count," recovered to win the controversial bout.

Dempsey ultimately retired to his Broadway restaurant, took his fourth wife, Deanna Piattelli, and lived to the ripe old age of 87—a growing legend. He died on May 31, 1983.

BABE DIDRICKSON WITH
HER JAVELIN AT THE 1932
SUMMER OLYMPICS IN LOS
ANGELES WHERE SHE WON
THE GOLD MEDAL.
(AP/WIDE WORLD PHOTOS)

BABE DIDRICKSON ZAHARIAS

THE PHENOMENAL WONDER WOMAN

During the 1970s and 1980s, tykes and grown people alike were enthralled by the mighty deeds of a fictional character called "Wonder Woman," who could leap over the tallest skyscraper in a bound, choke a lion to death with her bare hands and destroy an evil enemy's army without catching a second breath. Her mighty exploits became a regular diet in the Sunday comics, on Saturday's cartoon dramas and even in a prime-time TV series.

Engrossing as these make-believe heroics were, everyone accepted this powerful female character for what she was—a figment of a storybook writer's imagination. No such person ever lived.

But one did—on a smaller and more realistic scale, but no less amazing in the breadth of her physical feats. Her name was Mildred "Babe" Didrickson Zaharias, and she truly was the "Wonder Woman" of the age, not colored newsprint or flimsy film but real-life flesh and blood.

"The athletic phenomenon of our time, man or woman," wrote Grantland Rice, the nation's most respected sports writer of the period, bridging the two world wars.

She was the lean, rawboned daughter of a Norwegian ship's carpenter who settled in Port Arthur, Texas. She was an All-American on a Dallas semipro women's basketball team that won three national titles. She once threw a baseball 296 feet to win a national contest. In an exhibition baseball game, she struck out Joe DiMaggio.

She competed in eight track and field events in the national Olympic trials and won five—the 80-meter hurdles, baseball throw, shot put, long jump and javelin—setting three world records. In the 1932 Olympics in Los Angeles, at age 19, she won gold medals in the hurdles and javelin and should have had a third in the high jump but was disqualified for diving over the bar, a technique later ruled legal.

There was no sport she wouldn't try. She even donned heavy pads and headgear to mix it up with the guys in football. She played tennis, bowled, fenced, skated and became adept at shooting, cycling, billiards and handball.

Later in life, she took up golf at the suggestion of Rice. The first tournament in which she played she shot a 95. After three lessons, she got her score down to 83. She could belt the ball 250 yards off the tee. She became the world's best woman golfer, winning both the British and U.S. ladies' amateur championships before turning pro to give birth to the ladies' golf tour. She won the U.S. Women's Open three times, the last in 1954, when she was dying of cancer.

BABE DIDRICKSON ZAHARIAS URGES A BALL INTO THE CUP AFTER A PUTT. DIDRICKSON ZAHARIAS WAS A THREE-TIME WINNER OF THE U.S. WOMEN'S OPEN. (AP/WIDE WORLD PHOTOS)

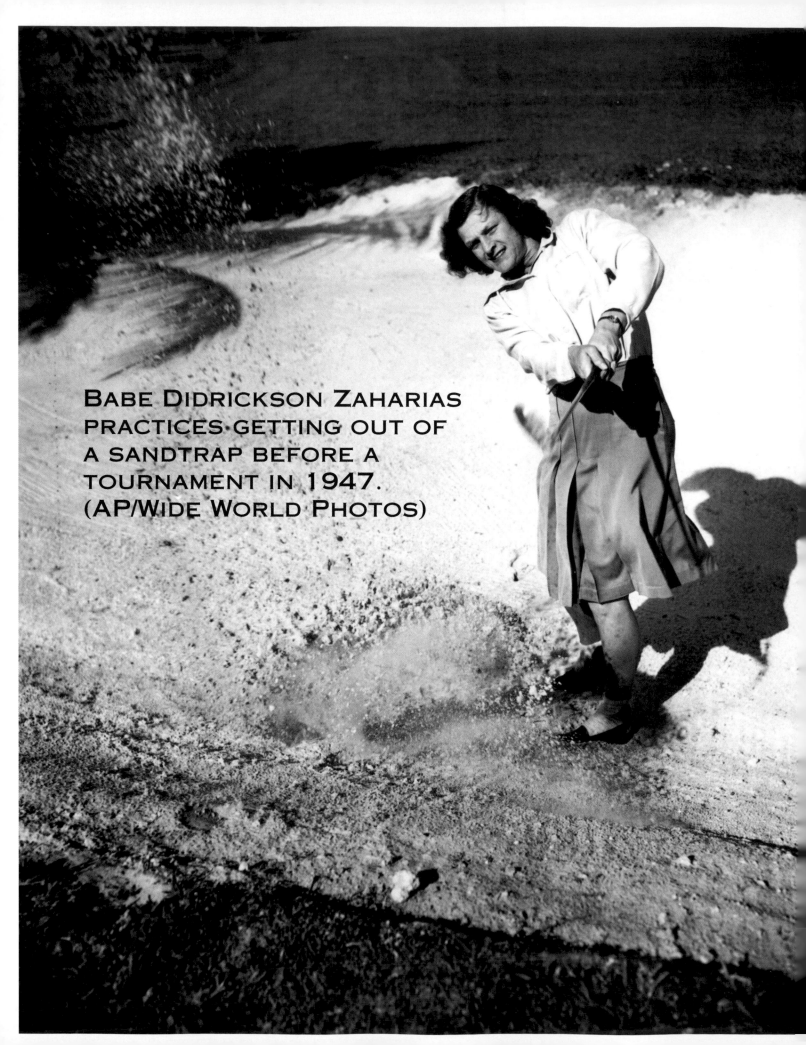

Babe Didrickson Zaharias practices getting out of a sandtrap before a tournament in 1947. (AP/Wide World Photos)

DIDRICKSON, RIGHT, IS ON HER WAY TO A WORLD-RECORD TIME OF 11.8 SECONDS IN THE 80-METER HURDLES IN A PRELIMINARY HEAT IN THE 1932 SUMMER OLYMPICS. SHE WENT ON TO TAKE THE GOLD MEDAL IN THE HURDLES AND THE JAVELIN IN THOSE GAMES. (AP/WIDE WORLD PHOTOS)

In her early years, she even boxed. She signed for a bout with the brother of heavyweight contender Young Stribling but withdrew with an apology and a vow: "I've decided I want to be a lady now."

Despite all of her achievements in realms dominated by men, the "Babe," as she became popularly known, fought to maintain her femininity.

Difficult as it was, since she was more comfortable in baggy slacks and sweatshirt, she forced herself to wear frilly dresses, have her hair coiffured and nails polished at a beauty salon and labor with high heels for formal occasions. She was good with the sewing machine. She could cook. She was proud that she could type 80 to 100 words a minute. She was a graceful ballroom dancer.

She played the harmonica, read good books, beat all her friends in gin rummy and amused herself solving difficult crossword puzzles.

"There's not a crossword puzzle I can't finish in half an hour," she once boasted.

The "Babe" was not unattractive. She had long legs and supple muscles and a strong and expressive face framed by a shock of short, dark hair. She was ebullient, admired and beloved by contemporaries, but as free and unharnessed in her public relations as in her athletic endeavors.

She disdained phoniness and was inclined to talk and act on impulse, without thought of social niceties.

In winning the British Ladies' golf title in 1947, the first American to do so, she started out by wearing a proper skirt but shifted to what she called her "lucky pants" between rounds, stunning the sensitive British galleries.

When a British journalist asked her how she managed to get so much distance on her drives, she replied, "I just loosen my girdle and let the ball have it."

Once, playing in the heat in a tournament outside Philadelphia, she called a recess in the fairway of the fourth hole, summoned some women to make a circle, removed her slip and tossed it over to her caddie.

Another time, playing an exhibition, a gentleman opponent politely offered her the honor of driving off first.

"You better hit first," she said, "because it's the last time you'll get the honor. And you better bust a good one if you don't want to be outdriven twenty yards by a gal."

The Babe's outgoing personality made her a natural show business commodity on which she capitalized after her Olympic triumphs and augmented following her sensational golf victories. She was much in demand. She played golf exhibitions with such greats as Gene Sarazen. She won a fly-casting contest over Ted Williams. She worked out with the Southern Methodist University football team. In 1947, she signed a $300,000 contract with a movie company.

A year later, she played in a golf tournament as a partner of a burly, 300-pound professional wrestler named George Zaharias, who was advertised as "The Crying Greek from Cripple Creek." It was a disaster. The two headstrong personalities barked at each other all around the course. A few months later they were married.

It was a match made in heaven. The two adored each other. Independently wealthy, Zaharias retired to help take care of the Babe's affairs. Their dream world ended tragically. In 1953, the Babe was diagnosed with terminal cancer. On September 27, 1956, at the age of 43, she died— the greatest woman athlete the world has ever known.

The legendary No. 5 at Yankee Stadium. (AP/Wide World Photos)

JOE DIMAGGIO

THE CLASSY YANKEE CLIPPER

Joe DiMaggio will be remembered by baseball buffs as the majestic outfielder of the New York Yankees who set what appeared to be an unreachable record of hitting in 56 consecutive games. To the general populace he will be forever viewed as the sports hero who married Marilyn Monroe and, in his later years, advertised coffee on television.

The man they admiringly called "The Yankee Clipper" transcended the single, cold statistic—as tremendous as it was—and the tabloid headlines of his marriages to two Hollywood beauties, first Dorothy Arnold and then the tragic Miss Monroe.

Nominal successor to the great Babe Ruth, he epitomized dignity, class and polished skills on a team that dominated the sport from the mid-1930s until he retired after the 1951 season, saying, "I want people to remember me as I was."

Author-historian Maury Allen said, "There never was a more stylish-looking, self-disciplined, and controlled baseball player."

In a nationwide poll, conducted in 1969, DiMaggio was voted "Baseball's Greatest Living Player."

He died on March 8, 1999—five months after undergoing lung cancer surgery. Joltin' Joe was 84.

An impressive athlete, 6 feet, 1-1/2 inches tall and 190 pounds, he moved like flowing water in the outfield, making the most difficult catches look easy. He was ever alert, and never threw to the wrong base. He hit for both average and power. He was a symphony in action. Quiet and retiring, he nevertheless was a tireless player and an inspiring leader among his teammates.

During the 13 years DiMaggio played with the Yankees, starting in 1936 (with three years out for service in World War II), the club won 10 pennants and nine World Series. Joe had a career batting average of .325, hit 361 home runs, knocked in 1,537 runs and scored 1,390. He forged his 56-game hitting streak—a record regarded as least likely ever to be broken—from May 15 to July 17 in 1941, hitting at a .408 mark during that stretch. He was selected for the All-Star Game in all the 13 seasons he played.

The marks are all the more remarkable because they were made in the original Yankee Stadium with its awesome "Death Valley" in spacious left-center and center field, where Joe's right-handed pull power was normally aimed. The distances were later shortened.

DiMaggio had a classic upright batting stance with feet planted far apart. He waited until the last instant to unleash his swing, whipping the ball with powerful wrists. He refused to change tactics and try hitting to the opposite field.

JOE DIMAGGIO GETS A HIT IN THE 56TH STRAIGHT GAME ON JULY 16, 1941 WITH THIS SINGLE AGAINST THE CLEVELAND INDIANS. (AP/WIDE WORLD PHOTOS)

JOE DiMAGGIO THROWS OUT
THE FIRST PITCH ON OPEN-
ING DAY AT YANKEE STADIUM
IN 1994.
(AP/WIDE WORLD PHOTOS)

JOE DIMAGGIO AND MARILYN MONROE AT A PREVIEW OF MONROE'S MOVIE "THE SEVEN-YEAR ITCH."
(AP/WIDE WORLD PHOTOS)

"I get paid to hit the long ball," he said. "If I started trying to punch the ball to right, I would lose my rhythm and not hit anything." He hit eight World Series home runs—tying a record for a righthanded hitter.

Born November 25, 1914, in Martinez, California, Joe was the most famous of three ball-playing brothers, sons of an Italian fisherman. Since no one spoke English in his home, Joe became self-conscious about his speaking ability in school and developed a timidity that he never lost.

Joe began his professional career with the San Francisco Seals of the Pacific Coast League in 1932, following his older brother, Vince. He had his contract purchased by the Yankees after the 1934 season but, because of an injury in an automobile accident, didn't see major league action until 1936. He batted .323 as a rookie.

He was an instantaneous diamond hero.

His remarkable aura of greatness and mystique, celebrated in prose and song while he was a player, seemed to expand after he retired, although baseball, the game he had honored so nobly for 13 years, was derelict in never recognizing his hold on the public and capitalizing on his image.

"When he walked into the clubhouse," former teammate Billy Martin said, "it was like some senator or president walking in there."

DiMaggio was strictly a loner. Always pleasant and soft-spoken, he never participated in locker-room high jinx. Off the field, he had his own small circle of friends. He defended his privacy fiercely. Friends always said he was basically shy.

He retained his athletic figure, paying close attention to diet and exercise. He loved golf. He was flat-bellied, straight as a poker, never more than 10 pounds over his playing weight. Silver-gray hair, which he was too proud to dye, softened his strong Italian features. His face remained deeply tanned, virtually free of lines.

Alan Courtney and Ben Homer wrote a song about him called "Joltin' Joe DiMaggio." The nation also tapped its toes to the beat of Paul Simon's song, "Mrs. Robinson," which had the catchy line, "Where have you gone, Joe DiMaggio?"

DiMaggio, after leaving baseball, seemed to grope for a security base in the game he loved. It never came. Charlie Finley of the Kansas City and Oakland A's hired him largely to hang around, perhaps hoping some of his luster would rub off on the players. The baseball commissioner once offered him $10,000 a year to serve as a public relations representative on the Pacific Coast—"I leave that much for tips," Joe scoffed.

Joe remained in the public eye with a network commercial for Mr. Coffee, a special brewing process, and helped what started as a small enterprise grow into a multimillion-dollar business.

Even after his 70th birthday, the Clipper was constantly on the road, much in demand, playing in celebrity golf tournaments, attending Little League and Boy Scout affairs, even sponsoring such events as a boccie tournament in Las Vegas.

He would show up at Old-Timer baseball games but was often too proud to play. He shunned interviews. Asked on one occasion what was his greatest thrill, he replied tartly: "Pulling on a Yankee uniform every day."

JOHN ELWAY SCRAMBLES
OUT OF THE POCKET
DURING HIS SECOND WIN
IN SUPER XXXIII IN
MIAMI. (AP/WIDE WORLD
PHOTOS)

JOHN ELWAY SUFFERED THREE
SUPER BOWL DEFEATS BEFORE
CAPTURING TWO STRAIGHT
SUPER BOWL VICTORIES AND
THEN RETIRING. (AP/WIDE
WORLD PHOTOS)

JOHN ELWAY

DENVER'S CAPTAIN COMEBACK

John Elway might be the best quarterback ever. Then again, he might not be. It doesn't really matter. The winningest and perhaps most durable QB in NFL history made his mark like few others.

"You don't have to rank excellence," says George Young, the league's vice president for football operations. "These guys are all five-star generals. If you want to have debates in bars, or on talk radio, that's fine. But these guys dominate their period."

Those "guys" include such quarterbacks as Otto Graham, Sammy Baugh, John Unitas, Roger Staubach and Terry Bradshaw, as well as Elway's contemporaries, Joe Montana and Dan Marino. Elway in 16 seasons with the Denver Broncos, played in a record five Super Bowls as a starting quarterback and, finally, NFL championships in his last two seasons. He belongs among the dozen or so "five-star quarterbacks" of all time.

His 51,475 passing yards are second only to Marino. And while Montana and Bradshaw each have four Super Bowl rings, Elway's two titles, in the words of former Buffalo coach Marv Levy, "were the frosting he needed."

Elway could finish games like no one else, with 47 game-winning or tying drives in the fourth quarter or overtime.

Sure, it's a manufactured figure, invented by a Denver writer. Nonetheless, it shows that Elway belongs in a class with Staubach, Montana and Unitas, three other QBs known for their heart-stopping finishes.

"When the game was on the line, he was like Michael Jordan, he wanted the ball," says Dan Reeves, who coached Elway for his first 10 seasons. "I think he thrived on pressure. In those clutch situations, I don't know of anyone who did a better job of handling that like John did."

Nothing demonstrates that better than "The Drive."

Not Montana's drive that beat the Cowboys in the 1981 NFC title game. No, the drive of the last two decades is Elway's 98-yard march in Cleveland that sent the 1986 AFC championship game into overtime and the Broncos on their way to the Super Bowl.

"I just marveled at it," said Staubach, who watched it on TV. "After that, you knew when you watched him he'd never quit, even if he was playing a bad game."

Still, the Broncos lost the Super Bowl that year, and the next year, and again two years later. When the Broncos finally broke through by beating Green Bay in the 1998 Super Bowl, he put his retirement plans aside and led the Mike Shanahan's Broncos to another Super Bowl win, this one over Atlanta.

The following May, in an emotional speech, he announced he was hanging it up on national television.

"I can't do it physically anymore," the 1999 Super Bowl MVP said. "And that is really hard for me to say."

JOHN ELWAY WITH HIS FIRST SUPER BOWL TROPHY AFTER DEFEATING THE GREEN BAY PACKERS IN SUPER BOWL XXII. (AP/WIDE WORLD PHOTOS)

ROY EMERSON RETURNS
THE BALL IN THE BACK-
GROUND OF THE TROPHY HE
EVENTUALLY WON AS THE
CHAMPION OF THE 1967
FRENCH OPEN. (AP/WIDE
WORLD PHOTOS)

ROY EMERSON

SETTING THE RECORD STRAIGHT

Roy Emerson, the winningest Grand Slam player of them all, played the largest role during Australia's domination of the tennis world in the 1960s.

A slender, quick, athletic kid, he played on a record eight Davis Cup teams between 1959 and 1967. He won 28 of the major (12 singles and 16 doubles) titles—a record for men—including two Wimbledon singles in 1964-65 and two U.S. singles in 1961 and 1964.

As a right-court doubles player he won 16 grand slam titles with five different partners, the last in 1971 at Wimbledon with Rod Laver.

He teamed with Aussie left-hander Neale Fraser to win Wimbledon in 1959 and 1961, the U.S. title in 1959-60 and the doubles of the Davis Cup triumphs of 1959-60-61.

Fitness was his trademark. He trained hard and was always ready for strenuous matches and tournaments.

Primarily a serve-and-volleyer, he was able to adapt to the rigors of slow courts, winning the French singles in 1963 and 1967, and leading the Davis Cup victory over the U.S. on clay in Cleveland in 1964. That year, he was unbeaten in eight Davis Cup singles as Australia regained the Cup.

While helping win the eight Cups, Emerson won an incredible 22 of 24 singles, and 13 of 15 doubles matches. In 1964, Emerson beat American Chuck McKinley, 3-6, 6-2, 6-4, 6-4, in the deciding match.

Emerson posted a singles winning streak of 55 matches during the summer and autumn of 1964. He became the No. 1 in the amateur game by winning 17 tournaments, and 109 of 115 matches. The only prize to elude him in 1964 was the French, when he suffered a quarterfinal loss to Nicola Pietrangeli.

Between 1961 and 1967, he won a men's record six Australian singles titles, including five straight from 1963-67.

During his Hall of Fame career, Emerson won a record 12 Grand Slam singles titles—a mark he figured would hold up forever.

Roger Maris thought the same thing about 61.

But just as Mark McGwire rewrote baseball's record bok, Pete Sampras appears on the verge of doing the same in tennis.

Sampras tied Emerson's 32-year-old record by winning Wimbledon in 1999. And at 28, Sampras seems to have a lot of opportunities remaining.

"He's going to break my record," Emerson predicted. "He has a lot of tournaments left in him. I have a lot of admiration for him, for his ability and the way he conducts himself on and off the court."

ROY EMERSON IN ACTION AT THE 1967 GERMAN OPEN. (AP/WIDE WORLD PHOTOS)

JULIUS ERVING GOES UP FOR ONE OF THE SLAM DUNKS HE MADE
FAMOUS AGAINST THE HOUSTON ROCKETS DURING THE 1977 SEASON.
(AP/WIDE WORLD PHOTOS)

JULIUS ERVING

THE DR. OF DUNK

In the spring of 1986, the year of the nation's mid-term elections, with politicians laying the base for a shot at Ronald Reagan's job in 1987, Dave Berry, a columnist with only half a tongue in cheek, proposed basketball's Julius Erving as a candidate for President of the United States.

"He is a smart, decent and articulate person and a very sharp dresser," wrote Berry, adding that the Philadelphia 76ers' ballhawk was better known that most early candidates and could intimidate Mikhail Gorbachev with a handshake.

Less in jest, others found in the 6-foot-7, 205-pound forward, the renowned Dr. J qualities exceeding his magical, almost ethereal exploits on the basketball court.

"Julius is an American treasure for the world to look at and admire," said Pat Williams, the 76ers' former general manager. "He's on a plateau that's never been attained before, with style and grace and humility and patience."

Super athlete, successful businessman, humanitarian, philosopher, Dr. J found his forum on the hardwood floor of a gym and saw it as a springboard to a future career for reaching people, possibly as an international ambassador.

"It's not something you can chart," he said. "All things I do have to fit under my spiritual umbrella."

Erving, who returned after 15 years to get his diploma from the University of Massachusetts, was awarded an Honorary Doctor of Arts degree in 1983 by Temple University, which cited his career as providing "a new dimension of fine art."

Artistry indeed was the proper description for Dr J's handiwork. If gargantuan Wilt Chamberlain was the true father of the dunk shot and was responsible for turning it into a normal basketball commodity, then it was Erving, the nice kid from Long Island, who refined it and made it pure theater. The slam dunk was Dr. J's private domain. Until he came along, no one ever executed it with such flair and flamboyance.

Sometimes it appeared Erving was going to shoot right out of the roof. Other times he flew through the air like Tinkerbell—sky walking, the sportswriters called it. He was Nureyev and Barishnikov in short pants and sneakers instead of leotards. He would take a ball in full flight, sweep down the floor in long, flowing strides and, cradling the ball in one of his massive hands, suddenly project himself at the hoop and slam the ball home.

It was decisive. It was exciting. And it was raw drama. Dr. J made it no patented maneuver. He improvised. Besides those soaring dunks, he could finesse the ball with soft bank shots and delicate finger rolls. He could go backward and sideways, twist his body like a contortionist, fake defenders out of their socks and score with a flair. There's no telling how many tickets were sold to admirers who came to the games to enjoy the Dr. J show. He left them breathless.

JULIUS ERVING MAKES HIS MOVE AGAINST LARRY BIRD IN 1987. (AP/WIDE WORLD PHOTOS)

JULIUS ERVING

JULIUS ERVING SCORES AGAINST LAKERS CENTER
KAREEM ABDUL-JABBAR IN THE 1980 NBA FINALS.
WHILE JABBAR'S TEAM WOULD WIN THE TITLE IN 1980,
ERVING'S '76ERS WOULD WIN THE TITLE IN 1983. (AP/
WIDE WORLD PHOTOS)

JULIUS ERVING SCORES HIS 9,994TH POINT IN 1975 DURING THE NEW YORK NETS' DAYS IN THE AMERICAN BASKETBALL ASSOCIATION. (AP/WIDE WORLD PHOTOS)

"For years the fans went to see Dr. J glean that one unforgettable moment," said Williams, "and he always seemed to offer it."

Dr. J was more than a showman. He was a producer and a motivator, serving as captain of his team. Only two players in history, Kareem Abdul-Jabbar and Wilt Chamberlain, scored more career points. Erving, seven times an NBA All-Star and twice Most Valuable Player in the All-Star Game, was one of only seven men to average more than 20 points and more than 20 rebounds in their careers. In 1996, he was named one of the NBA's 50 greatest players of all time.

Dr. J's full name was Julius Winfield Erving II. Born February 2, 1950, in Roosevelt, New York, on Long Island, he grew up in a broken home. His father was killed in an automobile accident when he was 11 years old and eight years later he was to lose his older brother, whom he idolized, to a disease that destroyed his immune system.

Young Julius, then called "Junior," was always big for his age, 5 feet, 6 inches tall at age 12, when he began playing with a neighborhood Salvation Army team. He attended Roosevelt High School, where he showed remarkable ability, but got little playing time until his senior year. Not highly recruited, he chose to attend the University of Massachusetts, where he gained national prominence by averaging 26 points and 20 rebounds a game.

It was this attention plus his sparkling one-man shows in the summer Rucker League on Harlem playgrounds that attracted the eyes of the emerging new pro league, the American Basketball Association. He quit college after his junior year to join the ABA Virginia Squires for $500,000.

Starting in 1971, he played five years in the ABA, two with the Squires and three with the New York Nets, spearheading the latter to two league championships. Averaging 26.3 points a game and thrilling audiences with his slam-dunk heroics, he helped keep the league alive.

He entered the National Basketball Association with the Nets when the NBA absorbed the ABA in 1976. Later that year he was sold to Philadelphia for $6 million. He was advertised as the Sixers' ticket to a long-sought league championship.

Frustration instead of immediate success greeted the Sixers and their "Six-Million-Dollar Man." While Dr. J played brilliantly and dazzled patrons with his acrobatics and sleight-of-hand, the Sixers couldn't find the proper formula. They lost to Boston in the Eastern Conference finals and to Portland and Los Angeles in championship showdowns.

It wasn't until 1983, after the Sixers had obtained a dominating center named Moses Malone for $13.2 million, that Dr. J got his championship ring. He scored seven straight points in a rally that overcame a 16-point Los Angeles lead. They let him hold aloft the title trophy for photographers.

Erving, who retired after the 1986-87 season, spent the next several years running his Coca-Cola bottling company in Philadelphia, doing charity work and providing color commentary on NBC.

Inducted into the Basketball Hall of Fame in 1993, he now serves as executive vice president of the Orlando Magic.

CHRIS EVERT WITH THE TROPHY SHE WAS PRESENTED BY THE WOMAN'S
SPORTS FOUNDATION AS THE "GREATEST AMERICAN WOMAN ATHLETE OF
THE LAST 25 YEARS" IN 1985. (AP/WIDE WORLD PHOTOS)

CHRIS EVERT

ICE PRINCESS OF THE COURT

"They keep calling me 'Little Miss Metronome,' the attractive young lady complained. "At first I didn't know what it meant. I hated it. It sounded like a disease or something."

If a metronome were indeed a disease, with its steady, sleep-inducing pendulum measuring the exact tempo in music, then there's been nobody more afflicted than tennis' ice princess, Chris Evert.

From the moment she stepped on the center grass court at Forest Hills in the autumn of 1972—a fetching, pigtailed lass of 17 who had stormed her way into the semifinals—right to 1989, Chris enthralled tennis galleries with her feminine charm, relentless patience and deadly killer instinct.

No power player like Australia's giant Margaret Smith Court, and lacking the ever-attacking verve of Billie Jean King, the effortless ease of Evonne Goolagong and the physical assets of Martina Navratilova, Chris nevertheless managed a dominant role in the game for more than a decade.

She did it the way her father, Jimmy Evert, had told her to do it back when she was a six-year-old, skinny tyke in Fort Lauderdale, Florida, swinging a racket she couldn't hold with one hand. Her strategy: run every ball down and hit it back. Don't whale away. Don't gamble. Just keep the ball in play and wait for the opponent to make a mistake. Simple. Dull, maybe, but it worked. And Chris never varied.

Chris popularized the two-fisted backhand, which she had been forced to use as a matter of necessity. Shortly after she burst upon the tennis scene, the world's courts were teeming with teenage sprites slashing at the ball in the same way as she did it.

The serve-and-volley game in tennis surfaced with Jack Kramer after World War II. It became the vogue. With both men and women, the feeling was that one could not survive without this new weapon. Chris proved it a fallacy.

Chris never mastered an overwhelming service, although she became very effective with spin and placement as she matured. She felt uncomfortable at the net and rarely moved into volleying range. Yet she managed to wear down more aggressive foes with backcourt steadiness.

She won 157 women's singles titles— 18 of them Grand Slam majors—before retiring in 1989. When she

CHRIS EVERT, RIGHT, POSES WITH MARTINA NAVRATILOVA AFTER THEIR WOMEN'S FINAL MATCH AT THE FRENCH OPEN IN 1984. IN THEIR CAREERS, THEY WOULD MEET IN OVER A DOZEN GRAND SLAM FINALS. (AP/WIDE WORLD PHOTOS)

CHRIS EVERT COULD WIN WIMBLEDON WITH HER EYES CLOSED, WHICH SHE DID IN THIS PHOTO FROM HER 1975 WOMEN'S SINGLES FINALS MATCH. (AP/WIDE WORLD PHOTOS)

THE 16-YEAR-OLD
CHRIS EVERT IN
ONE OF HER
EARLY
APPEARANCES AT
THE U.S. OPEN
IN 1971.
(AP/WIDE WORLD
PHOTOS)

defeated Martina Navratilova for her sixth French crown in 1986, it marked the 13th year she had won at least one of the Grand Slam events.

She won her 1,000th career match in the 1984 Australian Open. In 1974 she wove a streak of 55 consecutive victories, a record which lasted until Navratilova bettered it 10 years later with 74. She ran up a total of 125 straight triumphs on clay—her native surface—between August 1973 and May 1979, a mark unchallenged. She was the first woman to win $1 million in prize money. Her career total was $8,696,195, third-most all time.

At first, it was assumed that Chris and the buoyant aborigine from Australia's outback, Goolagong, were the players of the future and probably would dominate the women's game through the 1970s and 1980s. Fans looked forward to their first meeting.

It occurred at Wimbledon in 1971. Chris was 16 and Goolagong 19, the latter a happy youngster who just floated around a court like a ballerina, every movement a thing of artistic beauty. Chris was the antithesis—the grim machine, working for every point. Goolagong won the semifinal match and the championship, but later surrendered to injury and the life of a housewife. Three years later, at age 19, Chris arrived at the top, winning the Wimbledon, French and Italian titles.

Evert's competition was to come from a native Czechoslovakian, Navratilova, who defected to the United States shortly afterward as a plump teenager two years Chris' junior. Theirs was a long-running series staged on the courts of the world—grass, clay, hardwood and artificial surface.

Chris ran up a decided edge in the early meetings, but Martina, shaking off periodic attacks of nerves, evened the rivalry and pushed ahead in the mid-1980s. Chris maintained a lead in Grand Slam singles titles ,but Martina, a powerful left-hander, soared to more than $9 million—almost twice that of Evert—in official prize money.

Martina could never rest on her newly gained laurels. Chris always was lurking in the wings.

"I can beat her, and she knows it," Chris said after passing her 30th birthday, "but I have to be at my best. I have to hang tough and crack her confidence."

They gave the world some great matches—these two ladies of opposite personalities. Martina was the superb athlete, big and strong, a net-rusher but always tense. Then there was Chris, demure, very feminine, the epitome of decorum, yet on the court a cold and calculating retriever. The British press dubbed her "The Ice Lolly," for popsicle.

Twice Chris almost quit the game, insisting she was concerned about missing the normal life. Each time she returned to her racket. "It was in my blood," she said.

Chris met fiery Jimmy Connors at Wimbledon in 1972 and they fell in love. They announced their engagement and started making wedding plans. Then the wedding was suddenly cancelled. "I started having doubts about my permanent commitment," she said, "but not about Jimmy."

Six years later Chris married a handsome British Davis Cup player named John Lloyd. They were divorced in 1987 and she marreid Andy Mill, a former Olympic skier, the following year.

A.J. FOYT WAVES FROM THE WINNER'S CIRCLE AFTER WINNING THE INDY 500 FOR THE SECOND TIME IN 1964. (AP/WIDE WORLD PHOTOS)

A.J. FOYT

FEARED DEMON OF THE OVALS

A.J. Foyt was born with the scent of gas fumes stinging his nostrils and his ears pounding with the roar of racing engines. Son of a mechanic and part-time midget racer, his cradle was an oil bin and he teethed on a monkey wrench. Grease and grime were his heritage and his blood raced with the mad, frenzied excitement of Gasoline Alley.

From the very beginning, this auto-racing prodigy was pointed for greatness. He took the wheel of his own hand-made car at the age of 5 and won his first race against an adult before entering kindergarten. He quit school in the 10th grade to become a full-time racer. Since then, he almost indisputedly has driven more miles on more different tracks in more different cities and in more different types of racing machines than any man who ever lived.

In three decades of competing in the prestigious Indianapolis 500 alone, a race he won four times, he once estimated that he had driven more than 10,000 miles around the 2 1/2-mile oval. He raced midgets, sprints, hot-rods, stock cars and even motorcycles, in addition to those million-dollar turbo machines that zip around the track at better than 200 miles per hour.

At the peak of his career he even took a stab at the Grand Prix road circuit, the pride of Europeans, teaming with Dan Gurney to win the 1967 24 Hours of LeMans race in France in his first try. Foyt became the first man ever to win both the Indy and LeMans classics.

He earned close to $6 million in prize money and a bundle more in endorsements. But money and security were not the driving force behind this rugged Texan who continued to challenge racing's young daredevils past his 50th birthday.

"There never has been a driver with such an absolute urge to excel, the absolute necessity to win," said one associate. Author Bill Libby wrote, "His cars seem to challenge him. He drives them so hard they sometimes fall apart." A rival, Mario Andretti, said, "He thinks himself such a superior being that he can't think of himself fighting anyone. It's got to be a breeze or nothing."

Foyt, who won a record 67 Indianapolis-style championship events, hung up his racing helmet in 1993 to concentrate on his efforts as a car owner.

In May 1999, his driver, Kenny Brack gave him his first Indy 500 title as an owner.

Said Foyt: "I didn't drive it, but I worked awfully hard sitting on the sideline watching it."

Foyt will switch gears next year, when he'll field a team in NASCAR's Winston Cup circuit.

A.J. FOYT RELAXES IN HIS CAR BETWEEN QUALIFYING RUNS. (AP/WIDE WORLD PHOTOS)

A.J. FOYT

Lou Gehrig wipes a tear during a tribute to him at Yankee Stadium during his final season in 1939. (AP/Wide World Photos)

LOU GEHRIG

PRIDE OF THE YANKEES

His story was the kind that was read by millions in those 10-cent paperbacks featuring Frank Merriwell and the rags-to-riches dramas of Horatio Alger. It had all the ingredients—the poor kid, son of a janitor, who waited tables to pay his way through college. The superb athlete, shy and of impeccable character, plucked from a college campus by the greatest team in baseball to play in the shadow of the great Babe Ruth. Wonderful deeds on the playing field, home run power and a record for durability, climaxed by a debilitating illness and premature death.

It was a story that only Gary Cooper could play in the movies and people by the millions would turn out, thrilling to the moments of glory but dabbing their eyes with handkerchiefs at the film's tragic ending.

Such was the true odyssey of Lou Gehrig, the fabled "Iron Horse." "Larrupin' Lou," who had to play the role of secondary Crown Prince to the King of Swat and, even when the king's reign ended with Ruth's retirement, had to share his star with an emerging new hero named Joe DiMaggio.

It was Lou Gehrig's unfortunate lot to bridge the two most successful eras of the New York Yankees' history and to dress in the same locker room with a couple of the most charismatic and popular players who ever lived. Yet he never complained. He quietly went about the business of hitting the ball out of the park and winning ball games.

"I'm not a headline guy," he once apologized.

While Ruth and DiMaggio may have dominated the headlines, Gehrig was a powerful contributing force to a Yankee dynasty that won nine American League pennants and eight World Series during his 15-year career, scoring four-game sweeps in five of the postseason showdowns.

Lou batted .300 or better in 13 of those years, dropping off the pace only when his ailment began taking its toll on his strength in his final two years. He hit 493 home runs and had a lifetime batting average of .340. He led the league in home runs twice and a third time, in 1931, tied Ruth with 46.

That was the year he had 184 runs batted in, the league record topped in baseball only by Hack Wilson's National-League mark of 190. On June 3, 1932, he hit four consecutive homers in a game. In 1934, he recorded the prestigious Triple Crown in batting with a .363 average, 49 home runs and 165 RBIs. He repeatedly battled the great Ruth for the home-run lead and batting honors in the World Series. He was named the league's Most Valuable Player in 1927 and 1936.

Certainly his greatest achievement—the one for which he was most remembered—was that of playing in 2,130 consecutive games, a record which baseball buffs thought would never be broken—until Cal Ripken Jr. came along.

LOU GEHRIG AT BAT DURING HIS ROOKIE SEASON WITH THE YANKEES IN 1923. (AP/WIDE WORLD PHOTOS)

LOU GEHRIG SITS ON THE BENCH IN 1939 AFTER PLAYING IN 2,130 CONSECUTIVE GAMES FOR THE NEW YORK YANKEES. (AP/WIDE WORLD PHOTOS)

LOU GEHRIG IS COMFORTED BY HIS FORMER TEAMMATE, BABE RUTH, AFTER GEHRIG WAS HONORED AT YANKEE STADIUM DURING GEHRIG'S FINAL SEASON AS A PLAYER IN 1939. (AP/WIDE WORLD PHOTOS)

On June 1, 1925, he was sent to the plate as a pinch-hitter. The next day he replaced Wally Pipp at first base in the lineup. He didn't miss a game for the next 14 years. His record stood until September 6, 1995, when Baltimore's Ripken played in his 2,131st game.

Henry Louis Gehrig was born June 19, 1903, in Manhattan, the only child of German immigrant parents. His father worked as a janitor in a fraternity house. His mother was a cleaning woman. Lou was a big, strapping boy who starred in both football and baseball at Commerce High School and who, as a combination pitcher-outfielder, was regarded as the best high school baseball prospect in the New York area.

Because of his talent, he was awarded a scholarship to Columbia University. But, before he began his studies as a freshman, he naively accepted an offer from John McGraw, the New York Giants' manager, to play minor league baseball during the summer with Hartford in the Eastern League under an assumed name. He played only a few games before Columbia officials learned of the situation and had his contract abrogated on the grounds he was under age.

At 6-foot-1 and 212 pounds, Gehrig was a hard-running football fullback as a sophomore in 1922. In the spring of 1923 he played baseball. As in the case of Ruth, he started out as a pitcher but, because of his batting power, was quickly converted into a daily player.

He was in his second year of college when Paul Krichell, the famous Yankee scout, offered him a cash bonus of $1,500 and a $37,000 salary for the remainder of the season to play pro baseball. It seemed like a fortune. Lou signed.

Ironically, Hartford by this time had become a Yankee farm club and Gehrig was sent there for seasoning. Although a bit awkward around first base, he demonstrated enough power to be recalled by the parent club in the final weeks of the 1923 and 1924 seasons.

Manager Miller Huggins placed the big slugger on his roster in 1925 but used him only periodically as a pinch-hitter. Pipp complained of a headache. Gehrig was sent in as a replacement. Pipp never got his job back.

Gehrig and Ruth were teammates but never close friends. They were men of contrasting personalities—the Babe, a big, outgoing man with a thirst for fun and a flair for the dramatic; Lou, the straight arrow, low key, shy and allergic to the limelight.

Yet Lou always presented a challenge to the Babe, both in the home-run races and in World Series batting honors. In 1927, when Ruth hit his record 60, Gehrig had 47. The Babe hit the ball for great distances. Gehrig overpowered it. "No man ever hit the ball harder," said teammate Bill Dickey.

Gehrig began slowing down in 1938, and later examination showed he was dying of a nerve-destroying type of paralysis which now carries his name. He took himself out of the lineup on May 2, 1939. The Yankees staged a day for him at Yankee Stadium. A crowd of 61,808 attended and heard a tearful Gehrig say, "Today, I consider myself the luckiest man on the face of the earth." He died June 2, 1941 at the age of 38.

STEFFI GRAF DISPLAYS HER TROPHY AFTER WINNING HER FIFTH U.S. OPEN WOMEN'S SINGLES TITLE IN 1996. (AP/WIDE WORLD PHOTOS)

STEFFI GRAF TAKES AIM AT THE 1999 GERMAN OPEN. (AP/WIDE WORLD PHOTOS)

STEFFI GRAF

"END OF THE ROAD"

1999 will forever be remembered as the Year of the Retirement.

Michael Jordan. Wayne Gretzky. John Elway. Barry Sanders. Boris Becker.

And on August 14, Steffi Graf.

"I have done everything I wanted to do in tennis," Graf said, becoming the latest star to call it a career, during an emotional farewell speech in Heidelburg, Germany.

Few women's tennis players have ever done more than Graf, who retired young at 30.

A dominating force for more than a decade, she's one of just five players to complete the tennis Grand Slam in one year.

During her 17-year career, she used powerful forehand shots to win 22 Grand Slam singles titles— second only to Margaret Smith Court's 24—and 107 tournaments on the WTA Tour.

She spent a record 377 weeks as the No. 1 player in the world, including an unmatched 186 in a row, and won a WTA-record $21.8 million in prize money.

In her final comeback, Graf stunned top-ranked Martina Hingis to win the 1999 French Open, a victory she called her "best win ever." She then dropped the Wimbledon final to Lindsay Davenport.

Graf's career was marred by a string of injuries, but that's not why she said she hung it up.

"I have nothing left to accomplish," she said. "The weeks following Wimbledon weren't easy for me. I'm not having fun anymore.

"After Wimbledon, for the first time in my career, I didn't feel like going to a tournament."

She strained her left hamstring and was forced to retire from a second-round match against Amy Frazier at the TIG Classic in Carlsbad, California, weeks before her retirement announcement.

At the time, Graf said she didn't believe the injury would prevent her from playing in the U.S. Open in New York the next month. But that turned out to be her final match.

"After that, the decision (to retire) was very easy, maybe too easy," Graf said. "I was pulled back and forth, but when I made my decision I didn't think about it one minute afterwards."

Graf, who'd been linked romantically to men's tennis star Andre Agassi days after her retirement, planned to concentrate on her marketing company and developing young German talent.

She also wanted to do some traveling—without a tennis racket.

STEFFI GRAF'S POWERFUL GROUND STROKES HELPED HER WIN EACH OF THE GRAND SLAM EVENTS AT LEAST FOUR TIMES. (AP/WIDE WORLD PHOTOS)

STEFFI GRAF

93

STEFFI GRAF WAVES TO THE CROWD AT THE 1999 FRENCH OPEN. IT WAS HER FINAL APPEARANCE AT THE EVENT, WHICH SHE WON FOR THE SIXTH TIME. (AP/WIDE WORLD PHOTOS)

ONE OF STEFFI GRAF'S FIERCEST RIVALS WAS MONICA SELES. GRAF AND SELES MET IN SIX GRAND SLAM FINALS, INCLUDING THE 1996 U.S. OPEN WOMEN'S FINAL, LEFT. (AP/WIDE WORLD PHOTOS)

OVER HER CAREER,
ONE OF STEFFI
GRAF'S MOST
EFFECTIVE WEAPONS
WAS HER SERVE.
(AP/WIDE WORLD
PHOTOS)

"On the plane coming back from San Diego, I just started poring through these magazines and thinking of all the places I could go," Graf said.

"Steffi is a class act," said Bart McGuire, chief executive officer of the WTA Tour. "As a motivated, well-conditioned, disciplined and competitive athlete, she has been a role model for women athletes in all sports. ...

"Steffi is leaving, characteristically, on her own terms. We wish her well."

She turned professional in 1982, when she was 13 years and four months old. She won her first tournament in April 1986, beating Chris Evert in Hilton Head. Graf beat Evert again 11 months later in Key Biscayne, becoming the youngest player to pass $1 million in earnings.

She won her first Grand Slam in June 1987, beating Martina Navratilova at the French Open, and in August of that year, Graf earned the No. 1 ranking for the first time.

Nicknamed "Fraulein Forehand" for her devastating trademark shot, Graf won more than $20 million in her career. In 1988, she won all four majors—the Australian, French and U.S. Opens, and Wimbledon—and completed a "Golden Slam" with the women's singles title at the Seoul Olympics.

Graf, Court and Maureen Connolly are the only women to complete the slam. Rod Laver twice swept all four majors, and Don Budge did it once.

Graf won Wimbledon seven times, the French Open six times, the U.S. Open five times and the Australian Open four times.

In the early '90s, she met her match in the young Monica Seles. But Seles was stabbed by a deranged fan during a tournament in 1993 in Hamburg, interrupting her career for two years.

Becker and Graf were responsible for making tennis one of the most popular and lucrative sports in Germany. Becker also retired in 1999, playing his last match at Wimbledon.

Graf endured personal setbacks late in her career. Her father, Peter, spent time in prison after being convicted for evading taxes on her earnings. A long list of injuries hindered her in the last few years. Graf spent long spells off the circuit and began losing to lower-ranked players she would normally beat with ease.

In later years, Graf's fragile body found it hard to keep pace with the teenage generation of Hingis and others. After winning three Grand Slams in 1996, the eight-time WTA Player of the Year won only one tournament in 1997 and four more in 1998.

OTTO GRAHAM AND HIS COACH, PAUL BROWN, HOLD GRAHAM'S MOST VALUABLE PLAYER TROPHY AFTER HE WON IT IN 1950. (AP/WIDE WORLD PHOTOS)

OTTO GRAHAM SPINS AROUND A TACKLE TO SCORE A TOUCHDOWN IN 1954. (AP/WIDE WORLD PHOTOS)

OTTO GRAHAM

CLEVELAND'S GOLDEN GRAHAM

For one sublime decade, from 1946 to 1955, no professional football team did more than the Cleveland Browns. Playing the first four years in the old All-America Football Conference and the next six in the National Football League, the Browns won a conference title each of those 10 years and a league title during seven of the 10.

A major contributor to this success was Otto Graham, probably the most dominant quarterback of his day.

Paul Brown, the owner and coach of the Browns, had built his powerful team around this artistic player from Northwestern, and Graham became one of the brightest stars of his league and one of the most successful football players of all time.

"The test of a quarterback is where his team finishes," Brown said. "By that standard, Otto Graham was the best of all time."

Almost from the time he began organizing the Browns for the AFC, Brown had ticketed Graham for his team, which opened operations with the new league in 1946. Graham had been a star at Northwestern as a single-wing tailback who specialized in the run-pass option play. He passed as much as he ran, however, setting Big Ten records for completions, attempts and yards, and this led Brown to believe that Graham could be a good T-formation quarterback in the pros. He was even more impressed with Graham after the quarterback, while in military service, led the powerful North Carolina Pre-Flight eleven at Chapel Hill to an upset of Navy during World War II in 1945.

As soon as the war was over, Graham took over the controls in Cleveland, where his No. 14 has been retired.

OTTO GRAHAM PICKS UP A FIRST DOWN FOR THE
CLEVELAND BROWNS IN THE 1950 NFL CHAMPIONSHIP
GAME. (AP/WIDE WORLD PHOTOS)

RED GRANGE
DURING HIS PLAY-
ING DAYS WITH
THE
UNIVERSITY OF
ILLINOIS.
(AP/WIDE WORLD
PHOTOS)

RED GRANGE

THE GALLOPING GHOST

Back in the so-called "Golden Twenties," a zany age when the nation was obsessed with speakeasies, flappers and sports heroes, it's said that a letter simply addressed to the number "77" would find its way into the hands of a ball-carrying demon named Harold "Red" Grange.

Dubbed the "Galloping Ghost" by the flamboyant phrasemakers of the period, Grange was the gridiron wonder in a cast of sports giants accorded almost superhuman stature by writers and an adoring public. That group included Babe Ruth, the "Bambino of Swat," Jack Dempsey, the "Manassa Mauler," Helen Wills, "Little Miss Poker Face," and the incomparable Mildred Didrikson, known only as "The Babe."

The "77," Grange's jersey number first at the University of Illinois and later as a member of the professional Chicago Bears, and the feats the number represented have been passed down from generation to generation and ingrained in the country's consciousness.

Great football ball carriers have come and gone, but there are not very many enthusiasts of the sport who don't know that Grange wore "77" and that he made it a permanent part of American lore.

Red Grange was football's first dazzling breakaway runner who scored touchdowns in clusters and, if not the greatest, certainly was the one against whom succeeding whirling dervishes and line-cracking thunderbolts such as Jim Brown, O. J. Simpson, Gale Sayers, Walter Payton and Eric Dickerson had to be measured.

It was Grange's magnetism which, when he turned pro upon his graduation from college against the advice of his coaches and friends, catapulted the professional game from an impoverished, ragtag operation into a marketable enterprise that was destined to spawn the National Football League. He became the game's foremost celebrity, the first $100,000 player and the first to capitalize on his commercial value. He endorsed everything from meat loaf to ginger ale, candy bars to haberdashery.

When he played, both in college and as a professional, people hugged their radios and devoured their sports pages to absorb every ounce of the drama he generated.

Born June 13, 1903, Grange grew up in Wheaton, Illinois, a small town near Chicago where his father was chief of police. As a youngster, nicknamed "Red" because of his flame-colored hair, he excelled in basketball and track as well as football but his heart belonged to the gridiron. He scored 74 touchdowns at Wheaton High School and attracted the attention of college scouts. Long an admirer of Coach Bob Zuppke, he gravitated naturally to Illinois.

On October 18, 1924, Grange was a halfback on the Illinois team that

---

RED GRANGE ON THE BENCH DURING HIS FINAL PROFESSIONAL FOOTBALL GAME IN 1933. AT LEFT IS GREEN BAY PACKERS COACH CURLEY LAMBEAU. (AP/WIDE WORLD PHOTOS)

RED GRANGE IN A POSED ACTION PHOTO IN THE MID-1920S. (AP/WIDE WORLD PHOTOS)

RED GRANGE IN ACTION AGAINST MICHIGAN IN 1924. GRANGE SCORED FIVE TOUCHDOWNS IN THE GAME AND PASSED FOR A SIXTH. (AP/WIDE WORLD PHOTOS)

met the awesome University of Michigan in a game dedicating Illinois' Memorial Stadium. The Wolverines, under Fielding H. "Hurry Up" Yost, had been unbeaten in three years and were the most feared power in college football.

Grange received the opening kickoff and—slashing, whirling, dodging, weaving, shedding tacklers—scampered 95 yards for a touchdown. Within the next 10 minutes, throwing phantom hips at frustrated defenders, he peeled off runs of 67, 56 and 44 yards before being given a rest with three minutes remaining in the first quarter.

Sportswriter Grantland Rice compared Grange's moves with those of ring champ Dempsey, adding, "He moves almost with no effort as a shadow flits and drifts and darts." Others called the performance "the most fabulous 12 minutes in college gridiron history." Grange scored a fifth touchdown in the second half from 12 yards away and then passed 20 yards for another touchdown, as Illinois popped the Michigan bubble of invincibility, 39-14.

The next year Grange was introduced to the skeptical East, the nerve center of mass communication, when Illinois played Pennsylvania before a crowd of 63,000. Was the "Galloping Ghost" for real or a Midwest myth?

Grange swivel-tripped for a 60-yard touchdown the first time he got the ball, leaving his closest pursuer 25 yards behind, and added two more on a slippery, muddy field that brought a standing ovation from the partisan spectators.

In an era of defensive football, when scoreless ties were more the norm rather than a rarity, Grange had a three-season total of 31 touchdowns, 3,637 rushing yards and 643 yards passing. The Air Game still was young. He helped draw 738,555 to Illinois games.

The day after he completed his Illinois career against Ohio State, November 21, 1925, Grange signed a contract with Promoter C.C. "Cash and Carry" Pyle, guaranteeing him $100,000 to play football for George Halas' professional Chicago Bears. Zuppke pleaded with him not to make the move.

Pro football was a dirty word at the time. College games were drawing 40,000 to 60,000 into the big stadiums. Pro games were lucky to attract 10,000, even with an aging Jim Thorpe as a drawing card.

Thirty-six thousand fans braved a snowstorm to watch Grange make his debut with the Bears before a capacity crowd of 36,010 at Wrigley Field on Thanksgiving Day, 1925. Then followed a whirlwind tour in which the team played 10 games in as many cities in 18 days, traveling 3,000 miles and giving the South and East a first look at the relatively new game. The tour drew more than 400,000.

Grange and Pyle formed a maverick league in 1927 but it was short-lived. Grange rejoined the Bears in 1929 and took part in the NFL's first title playoff game in 1933, as Chicago beat the New York Giants 23-21.

The four-time all-NFL halfback retired in 1935, became a charter member of pro football's Hall of Fame in 1963 and settled down to a peaceful life of boating and fishing from his lakeside ranch house in Florida.

He died in 1991 at the age of 87.

WAYNE GRETZKY WAVES GOODBYE TO HOCKEY FANS AFTER HIS FINAL NFL GAME IN MADISON SQUARE GARDEN ON APRIL 18, 1999. (AP/WIDE WORLD PHOTOS)

WAYNE GRETZKY IN ACTION DURING HIS FINAL SEASON IN 1999. (AP/WIDE WORLD PHOTOS)

WAYNE GRETZKY

GREAT IN ANY HOCKEY ERA

Wayne Gretzky looked like anything but a player who has completely devastated the National Hockey League's scoring record book.

He was skinny (barely 6 feet and barely 170 pounds). He didn't skate like a blur—he moved with an awkward, elbow-waving style—and his shot was not the hardest among NHL players.

Even youngsters, who watched Gretzky play from afar couldn't believe that the baby-faced center was the greatest scorer in the league's history when they met him close up.

A perfect example occurred once when Gretzky visited the Edmonton Children's Hospital while playing for the Oilers. As he signed autographs with his uniform number "99" beneath his name, one youngster with thick glasses gave him a quizzical stare. Finally, the boy said courageously, "No way you're Wayne Gretzky."

"I can't believe you're the one who's got all those goals," another youngster said.

"I know what you mean," Gretzky said. "Sometimes I can't believe it either."

Believe it!

It was no dream that Gretzky lived. He continually surpassed scoring feats established by the game's most revered players, such as Gordie Howe, Bobby Hull, Maurice "The Rocket" Richard, Phil Esposito and Bobby Orr.

In 1,486 games with teams in Edmonton, Los Angeles, St. Louis and New York, Gretzky had 894 goals and 1,963 assists for 2,857 points.

That's 1,007 more points than Hall of Famer Howe scored in his career.

Before retiring at age 38 following the 1998-99 season, Gretzky owned roughly 60 NHL records. He'll go into hockey's Hall of Fame in 1999, way ahead of schedule after the selection committee voted unanimously to waive the three-year waiting process for potential inductees.

Some oldtimers contended that Gretzky played in an overexpanded league partially stocked with inept players who never would have made the NHL before expansion in 1967. However, former greats appreciated his talents.

"I have now seen Gretzky enough to say that in whatever decade he played, he would be scoring champion," Rocket Richard said about the player who tied for the scoring title in his rookie season in the NHL in 1979-80 and led the league 10 times.

"He's a born, natural scorer—just like I was," Richard added. "He's moving all the time, and it seems like the players trying to check him can't catch him."

AN ELEVEN-YEAR-OLD WAYNE GRETZKY (RIGHT) MEETS HOCKEY GREAT GORDIE HOWE. GRETZKY WOULD ONE DAY REPLACE HOWE AS THE ALL-TIME SCORING LEADER IN THE NHL.

WAYNE GRETZKY

WAYNE GRETZKY HOISTS THE STANLEY CUP ABOVE HIS HEAD AFTER HE WON IT IN 1984 WITH THE EDMONTON OILERS. (AP/WIDE WORLD PHOTOS)

GRETZKY CELEBRATES A GOAL IN THE 1983 NHL ALL-STAR GAME WHERE HIS FOUR GOALS LED TO A VICTORY FOR THE CAMPBELL CONFERENCE. (AP/WIDE WORLD PHOTOS)

WAYNE GRETZKY CELEBRATES HIS RECORD-SETTING 802ND CAREER GOAL. (AP/WIDE WORLD PHOTOS)

"He plays more like the old days—the way he handles the puck, the way he handles himself," said Howe, whose pro career spanned five decades, from 1946-80. "When he has to hurry, he hurries; otherwise, he thinks it through. He would have been just as great in any day."

Gretzky's hockey instincts were instilled in him at an early age by his father, Walter.

When Gretzky was only 3, his father, who never advanced beyond Junior B hockey, had his son skating on a rink in the family backyard in Brantford, Ontario, a town about 60 miles southwest of Toronto.

Gretzky's father placed tin cans on the ice for him to swirl between. He dropped sticks for the boy to hop over as he received passes—as if in heavy traffic in front of the goal. He strung up lights so Wayne could practice at night. And he made the targets smaller and smaller—so his son's shots became more accurate.

Later he would throw the puck into a corner and tell his son to get it. After young Wayne had chased several pucks around the boards, his father would say: "Watch me."

He would throw it again and skate to a spot, where he could intercept the puck as it caromed around the boards.

"I always told him, 'Skate to where the puck is going to be, not to where it has been,'" the elder Gretzky said. "The thing that I drilled into Wayne most was concentration. That's what gave him his edge."

By age 6 Gretzky was playing in a league with 10-year-olds. When he was 10, he scored 378 goals in 68 games. At 15, he had an agent. By 17, he was a pro, signing a four-year, $875,000 contract with the Indianapolis Racers.

After Gretzky had played eight games with the Racers, owner Nelson Skalbania sold his contract to the Oilers.

Edmonton owner Peter Pocklington reworked Gretzky's contract into a landmark deal that ran through 1999. The contract, however, paid Gretzky only $280,000 a year, a small sum for the game's greatest player. So, in January 1982, Pocklington renegotiated the contract, giving "The Great Gretzky" more than $1 million a year.

After winning four Stanley Cups in a five-year span from 1984-88, the unthinkable happened: Gretzky was traded to the Los Angeles Kings in a cost-cutting move.

He made hockey popular there, was dealt to St. Louis in 1996, then signed a free-agent deal with the Rangers, for whom he played three seasons and finished his career.

Despite all the money he made and all the fame he accumulated, Gretzky remained humble.

"When I'm compared with the greats of the past, it's an honor and a pleasure," he said. "But nobody will ever duplicate Howe, Orr, Esposito, Richard, Jean Beliveau—any of them. Nobody can play like those guys played. I am me.

"The really great players play at the same level year after year. That's why Gordie Howe is the greatest player in the history of the game. The year-after-year consistency, the records he set, the Stanley Cups he won… The important thing to me now is consistency."

Everyone in the NHL—and all those connected with the game—agree that Gretzky more than lived up to his end of the bargain. His skills, combined with his personality, made him the game's No. 1 ambassador.

FLORENCE GRIFFITH-JOYNER CELEBRATES HER VICTORY IN THE 100-METER DASH AT THE 1988 OLYMPIC GAMES IN SEOUL. (AP/WIDE WORLD PHOTOS)

FLORENCE GRIFFITH JOYNER

MISSED BY MANY

Florence Griffith Joyner's flowing black hair, skintight outfits and glittering 6-inch fingernails brought a model-like presence to track and field, where she left still-unequaled marks as the fastest and most fashionable woman sprinter in history.

A decade before her tragic death on September 21, 1998, "FloJo" won the first of her three gold medals at the Seoul Olympics, where her sister-in-law, six-time Olympic medalist and world heptathlon record-holder Jackie Joyner-Kersee, also starred.

She still holds world records in the 100- and 200-meter dashes.

She set the 100 mark of 10.49 seconds in the quarterfinals of the 1988 Olympic trials at Indianapolis, and since then no one has even broken 10.60. At Seoul, she won the gold medal in a wind-aided 10.54.

Griffith Joyner then smashed the world 200 record in the Olympic final, clocking 21.34. American Marion Jones, with a 21.62 at the 1999 World Cup in South Africa, is the only other woman to run the 200 in under 21.70.

She also won a gold medal in the 400 relay and just missed a fourth gold medal when the U.S. team finished second in the 1,600 relay, which Griffith Joyner anchored.

"It's an amazing legacy. Many have tried and all have failed in terms of her records," said nine-time Olympic gold medalist Carl Lewis. Her death "is something that impacts the sport when the sport is hurting very, very bad."

Griffith Joyner died at her home in Mission Viejo, California. Coroner's experts say she suffered a seizure in her sleep—probably triggered by a brain lesion—and suffocated.

She was 38.

Joyner-Kersee praised her sister-in-law as "a woman of substance."

Track and field had never seen such an exotic creature as Griffith Joyner. At the 1988 trials, she stunned fans and competitors by running in a purple bodysuit with a turquoise bikini brief over it, but nothing on her left leg. She called the design a "one-legger."

"She proved a beautiful woman could go out and be a phenomenal athlete," said Dwight Stones, a two-time Olympic bronze high jump medalist.

"We won't know for a long time how many female athletes she inspired by being her own person."

Griffith Joyner's muscular physique prompted talk of steroid use, but she insisted she never used performance enhancers, and she never failed a drug test.

"She was very, very determined," former Olympic teammate Jeanette Bolden said. "There was no impossibility to anything. She really tried to live that."

FLORENCE GRIFFITH-JOYNER RACES TO A WORLD RECORD IN THE 200-METER DASH IN A SEMIFINAL HEAT IN THE 1988 SUMMER OLYMPICS. (AP/WIDE WORLD PHOTOS)

ERIC HEIDEN SKATES HIS WAY TO A GOLD MEDAL IN THE 10,000-METER EVENT AT THE 1980 WINTER OLYMPICS IN LAKE PLACID. IT WOULD BE HIS FIFTH GOLD MEDAL. (AP/WIDE WORLD PHOTOS)

ERIC HEIDEN

THE OLYMPIC SPEED SKATING MARVEL

Eric Heiden, a zephyr on silver skates, streaked to five gold medals in the 1980 Winter Olympics at Lake Placid, New York, in a dazzling one-man performance that marked him as one of the premier athletes of the age.

Participating in a sport with very little recognition in the United States, although popular in Europe, he did on an oval ice rink what Czechoslovakia's Emil Zatopek did on Helsinki's red clay running track in 1952 by sweeping the three long-distance races and came close to what Mark Spitz accomplished with seven swimming golds two decades later in Munich.

Before Heiden, no one had ever won five gold medals in the Winter Games. At age 21, the handsome Wisconsin collegian established himself as the unquestioned king of speed skating, while sister Beth, a year younger, also won a medal and turned the Games into a royal family affair.

The Heidens shared their moments of glory with a group of countrymen who also wore skates—the gutsy U.S. hockey team that beat the Russians and won the gold medal, triggering a wave of unharnessed nationalist fervor.

Both Heidens were swarmed by admirers. In Oslo, U.S. Ambassador Louis Lerner appointed Eric honorary ambassador to Norway.

Norwegians adopted Eric, then a pre-med student at Wisconsin, as a folk hero. He had to be sneaked in and out of hotels through garages to avoid admirers. His picture appeared on milk cartons. Songs and books were written about him.

In dramatic succession, he won his first four gold medals—in the 500, 1,000, 1,500 and 5,000 meters, surpassing the 1972 record of Holland's sensational Art Schenk. Then he went out the next day and won the 10,000 in record time.

While both the Associated Press and *Sports Illustrated* chose the hockey team for "Athlete of the Year" honors, European sportswriters gave that award to Heiden.

The private Heiden turned down thousands of dollars in commercial offers.

"Put my face on a cereal box? No thanks," he said. "I didn't get into skating to be famous. If I had, I would have played hockey."

ERIC HEIDEN RAISES HIS ARMS IN TRIUMPH AFTER WINNING THE U.S. PROFESSIONAL CYCLING CHAMPIONSHIP IN 1985. (AP/WIDE WORLD PHOTOS)

SONJA HENIE PUTS ON
A SKATING EXHIBITION
AT NEW YORK'S
ROCKEFELLER CENTER
IN 1937. (AP/WIDE
WORLD PHOTOS)

SONJA HENIE

"PAVLOVA OF THE SILVER BLADES"

In the 1930s, with the nation climbing out of a terrible Depression and seeking to bury its problems in the exciting exploits of sports idols such as Joe DiMaggio and Joe Louis, families would crowd into the neighborhood theater to watch a petite Nordic beauty glide and pirouette through romantic scenes in a setting of a winter wonderland.

Those in larger metropolitan areas would pour into arenas such as New York's Madison Square Garden and the indoor forums of Los Angeles, Chicago and Dallas to watch the same ice ballerina, in lavish costumes, spin through similar routines in a Ziegfeld-style follies.

Mothers sighed. They rushed out to buy their daughters ice skates. If they lived in the colder climes of the North, they sought out the nearest frozen pond. Others subscribed to ice rinks wherever available. Their purpose was the same:

"My daughter is going to be another Sonja Henie."

The impact on American culture was monumental. Little girls found Sonja Henie dolls and silver skates under their Christmas trees. Ice rinks mushroomed all over the country. In Canada, a little girl named Barbara Ann Scott laced on her first skates. In Boston, the parents of Tenley Albright put her on ice to combat a slight case of polio. A mother in Los Angeles sewed dresses for daughter Peggy Fleming. A humble baker in Queens, New York, hocked his shop to finance ice skating lessons for his daughter, Carol Heiss. Similar sacrifices were made for New England's Dorothy Hamill.

All became figure skating champions, giving the Americans dominance in a sport that previously had been reserved for those Alpine and Scandinavian countries with a heritage of ice and snow. All unquestionably could trace this ascendancy to the swan-like Norwegian described by a *New York Times* critic as "a transfigured Degas ballerina" and those old movies of winter chill and romance.

Sonja Henie was a real, live doll—only 5 feet, 2 inches, blonde, with a round, dimpled face that seemed to glow in the sparkle of lights and glistening ice.

Unlike the skaters who came along in later years, with their acrobatic leaps and triple spins in mid-air, Sonja was a symphony on ice—smooth, graceful, flowing, with never a hitch in her routines. No one ever recalls seeing her take a spill. She performed before royalty—England's King George and Queen Mary, as well as the ruling monarchs of Sweden, Belgium and Norway—and thrilled them all.

A child prodigy, she won 10 consecutive world ladies' figure skating championships, starting in 1927, and Olympic gold medals in 1928, 1932

SONJA HENIE SKATES ON THE RINK IN ST. MORITZ, SWITZERLAND, WHERE SHE WON THE GOLD MEDAL IN 1928, IN THIS 1932 PHOTO. (AP/WIDE WORLD PHOTOS)

SONJA HENIE PRAC-
TICES FOR THE EURO-
PEAN FIGURE SKATING
CHAMPIONSHIP IN
1934. (AP/WIDE
WORLD PHOTOS)

SONJA HENIE AND
FELLOW OLYMPIC
CHAMPION FIGURE
SKATER DICK BUTTON
DURING AN
IMPROMPTU WORKOUT
IN 1954. (AP/WIDE
WORLD PHOTOS).

and 1936. No one else has won more than one. After the 1936 Games, she turned professional and organized the first of her extravagant ice spectaculars, the Hollywood Ice Revue, with which she toured leading American cities and Europe.

They said she became the richest athlete of all time.

Sonja was born April 8, 1912, in Oslo, daughter of a well-to-do wool merchant who had won trophies in cycling. Both Wilhelm Henie and his wife recognized artistic talents in their daughter and started giving her ballet and snow-skiing lessons when she was 4 years old.

She started collecting trophies almost immediately. At 5, she won a copper medal for capturing a 40-meter foot race while the family was vacationing in Grenen, Denmark. She won a junior skiing trophy when she was 7.

A year later, she was disappointed when she opened her Christmas gifts and found only a doll and a kitchen stove, while her brother, Leif, received a pair of racing skates. When the elder Henies saw tears in their daughter's eyes, they rushed out, persuaded a merchant to open his closed store and bought some junior skates. Sonja was ecstatic. She hurried to join Leif on the frozen pond.

Sonja lived on the ice, getting counsel from her parents. She was only 9 years old, a mere strip of a lass of 79 pounds when she won the Oslo junior and senior ladies' figure skating crowns, and only 10 when she captured the first of her 11 Norwegian national championships.

At only 12, Sonja found herself competing in the 1924 Olympic Games. It was immaterial that she finished last. She was hailed as "Des Wunderkind," the "Wonder Child," and she was never to lose on the ice again.

Shortly afterward, Sonja saw a performance by the famous Russian ballerina, Anna Pavlova, in London and acknowledged that the experience had a significant influence on her skating routines.

The Norwegian teenager easily won her first Olympic title at St. Moritz, Switzerland, in 1928, and in 1932 repeated at Lake Placid, New York, her first visit to the United States. She was intrigued by the country and admittedly smitten by "the movie bug."

In 1936, Sonja swept overwhelmingly to her third Olympic gold at Garmish-Partenkirchen, Germany, moved on to Paris for her 10th world championship, then launched her professional career in the United States. Billed as "Pavlova of the Silver Blades," she drew 90,000 in four shows at Madison Square Garden and later had tea with President and Mrs. Roosevelt at the White House.

She made numerous movies for 20th Century Fox, including "One in a Million," which grossed $25 million. She became a naturalized U.S. citizen in 1941 and married the first of her three husbands—Dan Topping, owner of the New York Yankees. Divorcing Topping in 1947, she married wealthy Winthrop Gardiner Jr., a merger dissolved in 1956. The same year she was wed to Niels Onstadt, a Norwegian shipping magnate. She had no children.

In 1969, Sonja collapsed on a Paris holiday and died at age 57, leaving a legacy on ice that may never be duplicated.

Ben Hogan, with an uncharacteristic smile on his face, holds his trophy after winning the 1948 PGA Championship. (AP/Wide World Photos)

BEN HOGAN

GOLF'S "WEE ICE MON"

Ben Hogan battled early adversity, critics who advised him to give up the game, a crippling automobile accident and dire predictions he would never swing a club again to become the greatest golfer of his day—the period spanning and following World War II.

"People were always telling me what I couldn't do," he related years later after his putting nerves had failed him and he transferred his golf interests into the successful manufacture of clubs and balls bearing his name. "I found myself always having to prove they were wrong."

It was an inner battle that left lasting scars more damaging to his personal image than the physical ones he carried after his broken body was pulled from the wreckage of his car on a lonely Texas highway in the winter of 1949.

Always a grim competitor, a dour man who eschewed social contact and defended his privacy with a deep passion, he mellowed only slightly in his retiring years and maintained a crusty, do-not-disturb exterior. Hogan, who died in 1997 at the age of 84, rarely attended a tournament. He became the only Masters winner to shun the gathering of the exclusive green-coat clan at the Masters "Champions Dinner," on the eve of this great tournament. He avoided personal interviews and steadfastly refused efforts to cooperate in a biography.

Introverted and impenetrable as he was in private life, he was a dramatic and imposing figure on the golf course as he trod the fairways, a white cap pulled low over chiseled features, his lips a vise of determination, hitting the ball with machine-like precision and dropping half-smoked cigarettes and deadly putts on every green.

Scots, who adored him as they did the pleasant, gentlemanly Bob Jones, dubbed him "The Wee Ice Mon" after he won the only British Open in which he competed at Carnoustie in 1953.

Hogan's icy, defensive personality was understandable when one considers the barriers he had to overcome to win all four of the major professional championships—a feat accomplished by only three other players, Gene Sarazen, Gary Player and Jack Nicklaus—and establish the late 1940s and the early 1950s as definitely "The Hogan Era."

He was born August 13, 1912 in the little town of Dublin, Texas, son of the village blacksmith who moved the family to Fort Worth when Ben was 10 years old. The boy sold papers on street corners to help provide food for the family. At the age of 12, he became a caddie at Fort Worth's Glen Garden Country Club for 65 cents a round. A fellow caddie was Byron Nelson, later one of his strongest rivals.

Ben was 15 when he won his first title, a Christmas caddie tournament at Glen Garden. At 19, he turned pro and, with $100 in his pocket, headed to the West Coast to join the pro tour. He lasted a month. He had to return to Fort Worth and save

BEN HOGAN WATCHES HIS TEE SHOT DURING A PRACTICE ROUND PRIOR TO HIS VICTORY IN HIS ONLY BRITISH OPEN APPEARANCE IN 1953. (AP/WIDE WORLD PHOTOS)

BEN HOGAN

BEN HOGAN THINKS OVER A SHOT ON HIS WAY TO HIS FOURTH U.S. OPEN
TITLE IN 1953. (AP/WIDE WORLD PHOTOS)

1949 RYDER CUP TEAM CAPTAIN BEN HOGAN, CENTER, WITH TEAM MEMBERS LLOYD MANGRUM, LEFT, AND SAM SNEAD. (AP/WIDE WORLD PHOTOS)

additional money before setting out again in 1933 at age 20. Again he failed, returning home with his confidence shaken by the well-meaning pros.

A converted lefthander, Hogan was plagued by an atrocious hook. "Look, son," the pros said to him, "Why don't you go home and get a good job working in a store? With a hook like yours, you'll starve to death on the tour."

Hogan was not so easily deterred. He spent three years slaving to refine his game and received encouagement when he qualified for the 1936 U.S. Open at Baltusrol in Springfield, N.J., although he failed to make the cut.

In 1937, newly married to a demure sweetheart named Valerie Fox and with $1,400 as a stake, he headed West again. "I know I can make it," he assured friends. The stakes began to dwindle as Hogan moved from Pasadena to Los Angeles to Sacramento. He was down to $85 when he and Valerie reached Oakland for the next stop. Meanwhile, adding to their misery, a thief jacked up their second-hand car and made off with the two rear wheels.

Hogan acknowledged that at this point he was at rope's end. It was live or die. Ben and Valerie decided that if their fortunes did not turn at Oakland they would return to Texas and he would seek another career.

The tide turned. Ben shot an opening-round 66, ultimately tied for third and collected $385. He never looked back. He won $4,150 in 1938 and $5,600 in 1939—enough to keep his head above water. He won his first tour title in the North and South at Pinehurst in 1940, was leading money winner in 1941 and 1942, finished third in the U. S. Open in 1941 and tied Byron Nelson for the Masters crown in 1942 before losing in a playoff.

World War II intervened at the time Hogan reached his peak. Hogan joined the Army's Special Services program and played sporadically in tour events which were being dominated by Byron Nelson, who was unable to enter the military because of medical reasons, but won 19 tournaments in 1945.

Hogan captured his first U.S. Open in 1948 at Los Angeles' Riviera Club, which became known as "Hogan's Alley." His future seemed now assured.

But on February 2, 1949, while he and Valerie were driving on a lonely Texas highway en route to Phoenix, Arizona, a huge truck lunged out of the haze and skidded into their car. Instinctively, Hogan flung himself over to Valerie's side to protect her just as the impact drove the steering wheel through the driver's seat.

Valerie sustained minor injuries. Hogan suffered a double fracture of the pelvis, a broken collarbone, a fractured left ankle and a smashed rib. Hogan's life hung in the balance. Doctors saved the plucky golfer's life but warned that he might never walk, much less swing a club again. The golf world thought it was the end of an era. But they reckoned without the grit and determination from the man they called "Little Ben."

Fiercely determined, Hogan not only walked but played again and went on to his greatest triumphs in 1953, when he won the Masters, U.S. Open and British Open and missed adding the match-play PGA, perhaps because he chose not to play in it.

From Britain, he returned home to a ticker tape parade up New York's Broadway. As Hogan stood on a platform with thousands lining the streets and leaning out skyscraper windows, the world saw the icicle melt for the first time — even if only temporarily.

"I owe it all to Valerie and to God," he said, wiping a tear from his eye.

ROGERS HORNSBY ON HIS FIRST DAY OF PRACTICE AFTER
BEING TRADED TO THE NEW YORK GIANTS IN 1927. (AP/WIDE
WORLD PHOTOS)

ROGERS HORNSBY

THE ARROGANT, ABRASIVE RAJAH

Rogers Hornsby may have been the greatest right-handed hitter of all time—old-timers insist he was—as well as the worst manager and one of the most fascinating and controversial characters baseball has ever known.

He was a veritable Dr. Jekyll and Mr. Hyde—at bat, a bold, grooved swinger who hit rocket-like line drives, but who also could propel the ball out of the park; on the field, a slick, poised performer who played shortstop, second or third base; a fierce competitor respected but only tolerated by teammates, feared and disliked by his rivals. Off the field, he was an independent person who marched to his own drummer—arrogant, abrasive, often downright nasty.

A man's man, close to six feet and 175 pounds with good looks, he nevertheless became the idol of women. Debutantes bought seats near the dugout in order to catch his eye. He had an unusual lifestyle, frankly admitting he never cared for books, music or social activities. He couldn't dance or make speeches. He abhorred parties.

In his advancing years, he advised young players, "If you want to be a great hitter, don't go to the movies. It ruins your eyes."

He was an inveterate gambler, with a fetish for cards and race tracks, and those vices led to his repeated failures as a manager with the Cards, Braves, Cubs, Browns and Reds. He had difficulty relating to young players because he thought everyone should be as good as he was.

Hornsby played for five clubs and managed five in a volatile major league career that spanned 23 years. He earned close to a half-million dollars and blew most of it before he was 45 years old.

Called "the Rahah" by the press, he had a batting average of .358. He collected 3,030 hits in 8,173 times at bat and hit 303 home runs. Three times he batted over .400, setting a modern record in 1924 with .424. Between 1920 and 1925, he reeled off averages of .370, .397, .401, .384, .424 and .403 to lead the National League in batting for six consecutive years. He added a seventh batting title in 1928 with a .387 average. Twice he was the most valuable player in the National League.

Baseball historian Maury Allen reported that, during spring training in 1962, Hornsby, then coach with the Mets, was asked by a photographer to pose with home run king Roger Maris of the Yankees. "If he wants to come over here," Hornsby snapped, "I'll pose with the busher."

On January 5, 1963, Hornsby, recovering form cataract surgery, died of a heart attack in Chicago.

ROGERS HORNSBY AT BAT AT TRAINING CAMP IN 1934. (AP/WIDE WORLD PHOTOS)

GORDIE HOWE IN 1956. (AP/WIDE WORLD PHOTOS)

GORDIE HOWE

THE GREATEST OF THE HOCKEY GREATS

The great Gordie Howe.

How else could one describe a player who lasted through 32 professional hockey seasons, skated on the same team as his sons, led the world in goals, assists, points, games and respect when he retired and has become one of the sport's finest ambassadors?

When Wayne Gretzky speaks of Howe, it is with a reverential tone. Gretzky has met Howe dozens of times, yet he still feels in awe in Gordie's presence.

"If people someday compare me to Gordie Howe, it will be the biggest compliment they could pay me," Gretzky says. "If you ask me about my idol, there has been just one, Gordie."

Howe's Hall of Fame career began inauspiciously in 1946-47, when he scored only seven goals and 22 points in 58 games for the Detroit Red Wings. He did, however, quickly establish a reputation for toughness that he would hold onto.

"No one in their right mind ever wanted to tangle with him," said Red Wings' teammate Ted Lindsay. "Gordie had a lethal pair of elbows, was strong as a moose and knew every angle. He never let himself get into a bad position."

Phil Esposito, yet another Hall of Famer who idolized Howe, recalled the first time he lined up alongside Gordie.

"I was with the Chicago Blackhawks, and we were getting ready for a faceoff," Esposito said. "I looked up at him and he said something like, 'Hi, kid.' I felt like a million."

Then, after the puck was dropped, Howe planted an elbow in Esposito that cost the rookie several teeth.

"I learned my lesson right away," Esposito said.

The lesson that Howe taught was that age never should matter as long as you have the drive and desire to succeed. Howe already was one of hockey's all-time greatest stars in 1971, when he retired after 25 years with the Red Wings. He had 786 goals, 1,809 points and six MVP awards. Howe also won the scoring title six times, including four straight from 1950-51 through 1953-54.

He still was performing well as a 43-year-old when he left the Red Wings following a 23-goal, 52-point campaign.

GORDIE HOWE RAISES HIS STICK HIGH AFTER SETTING A NEW NHL SCORING RECORD OF 545 CAREER GOALS. (AP/WIDE WORLD PHOTOS)

GORDIE HOWE AT
AGE 41 AFTER 23
NHL SEASONS.
(AP/WIDE WORLD
PHOTOS)

GORDIE HOWE, CENTER, WITH SONS MARTY, LEFT, AND MARK, RIGHT, IN THEIR NEW UNIFORMS AFTER ALL THREE SIGNED WITH THE HOUSTON AEROS IN 1973. (AP/WIDE WORLD PHOTOS)

"I didn't feel I couldn't play anymore," he said. "I felt I didn't *want* to play anymore."

What more could the man do? He had been on four Stanley Cup winners, collecting 68 playoff goals and 160 points. He made a dozen All-Star teams. Offensively, he was the most productive player in history until Gretzky came along.

"I felt fulfilled as a player," he admitted. "I never would have come back if not for the chance to skate with the boys."

The boys, sons Mark and Marty, signed with the Houston Aeros of the World Hockey Association in 1973. At first, convincing Gordie to return to play with them seemed like a publicity stunt. But the youngsters, particularly Mark, proved themselves immediately, and Gordie still was Gordie. He averaged 30 goals a year for four seasons in Houston, scoring 100, 99, 102 and 68 points.

When the Aeros folded, the Howes moved to New England, and Gordie scored 34 goals and 96 points in his first season with the Whalers.

"It was good, high-quality hockey," Howe said. "There was nothing to be ashamed about in the WHA."

In 1979, four WHA teams entered the NHL. The Whalers, then representing Hartford, were one of them, and at 51, Howe again was playing in the league he once dominated. He scored 15 goals that season, lifting his NHL career total to 801.

"Playing with my sons is something I'll always remember," he said. "Returning to the NHL for that one season was just another dream come true—the three Howes playing together in the NHL."

Howe's marvelous NHL tenure nearly ended before it began, then almost ended in tragedy. When he was 14, Howe was sent to a New York Rangers' tryout camp in Winnipeg, 500 miles from his Saskatchewan home. But Howe was so homesick that he left the camp. Two years later, a more mature Howe made it through a similar camp run by the Red Wings in Windsor and became Detroit property.

In a 1950 playoff game, a collision with Ted Kennedy of Toronto sent Howe reeling head-first into the sideboards. He fell unconscious and emergency brain surgery was performed hours later.

"It looked pretty bad," Red Wings' boss Jack Adams said. "When they got him into bed, he started to bleed from the nose and mouth."

"I did awake and realize something was going on," Howe recalled. "Then they started shaving my head and I thought, 'Hell, no,' then I remember the drilling to relieve the pressure."

The 90-minute operation saved Howe's life. He was allowed to attend the seventh game of the Stanley Cup finals, which the Red Wings won in double overtime. When the Cup was being presented to the Wings, the home crowd shouted for Howe, who came on the ice and accepted the trophy.

He would do so three more times.

Even in retirement, Howe has carried an aura of being special. At All-Star games and league meetings, he is swamped by fans seeking autographs and by players anxious to meet the great man, talk hockey with him or just stand nearby in admiration.

In October 1997, Howe skated the first shift with the Detroit Vipers in their International Hockey League opener against the Kansas City Blades, becoming the only professional in his sport to compete in six decades. The 69-year-old Hall of Famer did not handle the puck in his 47 seconds of action.

BOBBY HULL IN ACTION IN 1964. (AP/WIDE WORLD PHOTOS)

BOBBY HULL

THE POWERFUL GOLDEN JET

Has anyone ever fit a nickname better than Bobby Hull? The Golden Jet, indeed.

Hull had the power, the speed and the majesty of a jet. He soared above the opposition. Or he went through it with his strength. The blistering slapshot, launched from the prototype curved stick, made goalies shudder. The flowing blond hair made female fans swoon.

He made 50-goal seasons commonplace. His ability to change the flow of a game with one burst made other teams seek out one-dimensional skaters whose only job was to try to prevent Hull from scoring.

Few athletes have had the impact on their sport that Hull had on hockey in the early 1960s. The slapshot still was an oddity that only a few players, notably Montreal's Bernie Geoffrion, were using. Hull not only changed the way the slapshot was regarded by coaches and players, he changed the way it was used.

"His shot once paralyzed my arm for five minutes," Hall of Fame goalie Jacques Plante once said.

"The first time I saw that thing," added Glenn Hall, the star goalie for the Chicago Blackhawks and, luckily, a teammate of Hull's, "I said a prayer of thanks that I didn't have to worry about it."

Perhaps the incident with the most impact regarding Hull's howitzer came in 1966, at the height of his superb career. The opposing netminder was Eddie Giacomin of the New York Rangers.

"He was flying down the wing and started winding up at the red line," Giacomin said. "There was no way I was going to see the shot. You hardly ever did. I just hoped he was off target."

Hull wasn't. His rising bullet struck Giacomin in the midsection. The force of the shot carried the goaltender backward into the net. With the puck.

Putting pucks into the net was a habit for Hull, who was named the Player of the Decade in the '60s. In 1966, he became the first player to break the 50-goal barrier, scoring 54. Two seasons later, he hit for 58.

A three-time NHL point-scoring champion, Hull also took league MVP honors twice. For many of his years in Chicago, he and Stan Mikita earned an inordinate load, skating as much as 40 minutes a game and working on all special teams.

"I was only 18 when I came to the Hawks, so anything they wanted me to do was fine by me," Hull said. "I sort of got used to playing a lot of time and I liked it."

What the fans liked most was seeing Hull come streaming down left wing, ready to unleash the fury of his 100-plus mph slapshot. But there was more to his game.

BOBBY HULL, LEFT, WITH JACK EVANS IN THE DRESSING ROOM WITH THE STANLEY CUP AFTER THE BLACKHAWKS WON IT IN 1961. (AP/WIDE WORLD PHOTOS)

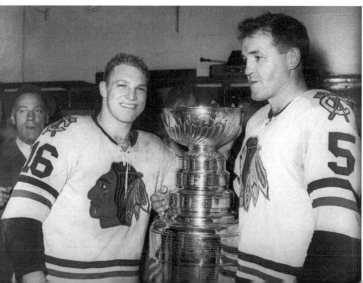

125

BOBBY HULL TAKES A SHOT ON BOSTON BRUINS GOALIE ED JOHNSTON IN 1964. (AP/WIDE WORLD PHOTOS)

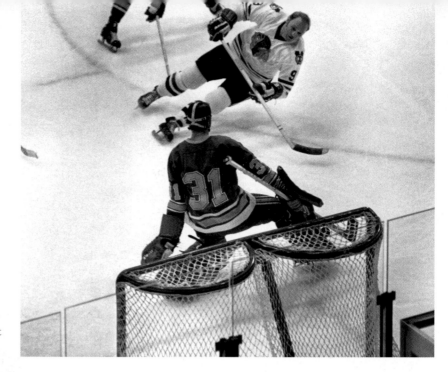

BOBBY HULL
SHOOTS ON
ST. LOUIS BLUES
GOALIE ERNIE
WAKLY IN THE 1972
GAME WHEN HE
SCORED HIS 601ST
CAREER GOAL.
(AP/WIDE WORLD
PHOTOS)

People forget that Bobby was one of the most physical players in hockey," John Ferguson, once a tough Montreal forward, said. "He wouldn't back away from anyone and he knew how to hurt you."

Hull and Ferguson were involved in one of the bloodiest fights in NHL history, a battle which made its way into *Life Magazine*, complete with photos of both players dripping red.

At 5-10, 195, Hull had a body that looked like it was sculpted from granite. His muscles bulging beneath the Indian on his jersey, Hull in full flight was a special sight.

"When I was eight years old, I started going out into the woods with my grandfather," he said. "I chopped down trees with an ax and that helped develop my arm and back muscles. I also walked to and from school four miles a day, and during the winter, I shoveled snow from morning until night."

When Hull was 14, the Blackhawks found him playing outdoor hockey in Belleville, Ontario, and signed him to their organization. By 1957, Hull had been invited to the Blackhawks' training camp.

"I don't think they expected me to make the team then," he said. "But they also realized when I got there that I was ready."

Ready to make history. But not immediately.

"I had a lot to learn about the game," he said. "I really was a raw player. I had the skills but I didn't really know how to use them. It took me a few years to get going."

In his third full season as a Blackhawk, Hull scored 39 goals and had 81 points, leading the league. He was a perennial All-Star the rest of his career and one of the most feared scorers the game had known.

For Hull, life on the ice never was without company.

"I made Bryan Watson famous," Hull once joked of the man who was called "Super Pest" for his ability to shadow the Golden Jet. "I can't remember a game where there wasn't one guy assigned to check me. Even if he had a chance for a breakaway, he might forget it and just stick with me."

How did Hull handle such treatment?

"I tend to ignore those guys, not let them get to me," he said. "You couldn't show them they were getting to you. That would just give them confidence in what they were doing."

What was Hull's best way to frustrate the frustrators?

"With a goal or two," he said. "Scoring goals always did the trick."

Hull didn't limit his contributions to the ice. In 1972, he became the cornerstone of the World Hockey Association. The new league, seeking someone to give it instant credibility, found, in Hull, a willing pioneer. The Blackhawks haggled with Hull about his salary and the length of a new contract for several years, with Hull twice threatening to retire.

When the Winnipeg Jets of the WHA offered him a $2.5 million contract as a player-coach at the age of 33, Hull flew from the Blackhawks' coop. A sticky lawsuit couldn't halt him from playing in the WHA, where he scored a then-record 77 goals in 1974-75.

Perhaps more importantly, Hull's move meant other NHL stars would consider the new league. The WHA-NHL bidding war didn't help the sport, but the players' salaries skyrocketed.

Almost every player in the game today can thank Bobby Hull for that, including son Brett, a perennial All-Star who helped lead Dallas to the 1999 Stanley Cup title.

Don Hutson during his days at the University of Alabama in 1934. (AP/Wide World Photos)

DON HUTSON

THE MAN WHO CHANGED THE NFL

Don Hutson was ahead of his time in the early days of the NFL and is generally credited with devising pass patterns as the greatest receiver of that era.

Named to the NFL's All 50-Year Team in 1970 and then to the league's 75th anniversary team in 1994, Hutson also played safety and was a kicker for the Green Bay Packers from 1935-45. He was inducted into the Pro Football Hall of Fame in 1963.

"To me, he made the passing game what it is today, and I don't think anybody can argue with that," said Tony Canadeo, a teammate of Hutson's with the Packers. "Pass patterns and routes we ran were modeled after him."

"He most certainly was the greatest player in the history of this franchise. In the era he played in, he was THE dominant player in the game, not just as a receiver, but as a kicker and with his ability to play defense," Green Bay Packers general manager Ron Wolf said.

One opposing coach, Greasy Neale of the Philadelphia Eagles, said, "Hutson is the only man I ever saw who could feint in three different directions at the same time."

A half-century after his retirement, Hutson still held 11 NFL records in 1997. He scored 99 career touchdowns, a mark that stood until Steve Largent broke it in 1989. Largent broke many of Hutson's marks, which since have been surpassed by Jerry Rice.

Rice's success did not bother Hutson at all. He said in a 1994 interview that Rice is the best receiver ever.

"Including everybody," he said. "I've watched a lot of football on TV. A lot of these people are still missing passes trying to catch it with the arms. Rice catches with the hands, and that's that.

"He's No. 1 as far as I'm concerned."

Hutson, who once scored 29 points in a quarter, led the Packers to NFL championships in 1936, '39 and '44. He was the league's MVP in 1941 and '42, when he caught a then-unheard-of 74 passes for 1,211 yards and 17 touchdowns. He led the NFL in receiving eight times.

After an All-America career at Alabama, where Hutson became known as the "Alabama Antelope," he signed with two pro football teams, the Packers and the Brooklyn Dodgers. The Packers' contract arrived at the league offices in New York the following morning and the Dodgers' contract got there in the afternoon. So NFL president Joe Carr ruled Hutson would play in Green Bay.

When Hutson retired in 1945, he was earning $15,000 a year.

In 1994, Hutson returned to Green Bay to dedicate the Packers' new indoor practice facility that was named in his honor. He died in June of 1997 at age 84.

DON HUTSON, IN THIS 1951 PHOTO, WAS THE GREATEST RECEIVER OF THE EARLY DAYS OF THE NFL. (AP/WIDE WORLD PHOTOS)

DON HUTSON

MAGIC JOHNSON REJOICES AFTER RECEIVING HIS GOLD MEDAL IN THE 1992 SUMMER OLYMPICS AS PART OF THE DREAM TEAM. (AP/WIDE WORLD PHOTOS)

MAGIC JOHNSON

A REMARKABLE COURT WIZARD

When her son was given the flashy nickname of "Magic"' in high school, Christine Johnson was the first to consider its practical consequences.

"When you say 'Magic,' people expect so much," she said. "I was afraid that it would give him a lot to live up to at some point." However, few basketball players have matched their nickname with more expression and panache than the ebullient Earvin "Magic" Johnson, perhaps the most remarkable athlete of his generation in the National Basketball Association. Johnson's improvisational skills inspired not only applause from fans, but acclaim from contemporaries.

"I'd pay to see Magic play," said his old rival, Larry Bird. "I think he's the best player in the league. Magic plays the game the way I like to see it played."

Like Bird, Johnson was a player around whom a game flowed. With the Los Angeles Lakers, Johnson was the motivating force, from the time he came into the NBA in the 1979-80 season to the time he left for good in 1996.

With ballhandling and passing abilities rarely seen in a player of his height, 6-foot-9, Johnson made an auspicious debut in the NBA, when he triggered the Lakers to the league championship.

The success of the Lakers with Johnson should have surprised no one, however. He had always had a habit of turning teams into champions, as far back as high school.

In Johnson's senior year at Everett High in Lansing, Michigan, 1976-77, the team won the state championship with a 27-1 record.

In his first year at Michigan State, Johnson helped the Spartans win the Big Ten title after a losing season; and in his sophomore year, he led them to the NCAA title with a rousing victory over Bird's previously undefeated Indiana State team.

It would not be until his later years in the pros that his latent scoring abilities would blossom; it was, rather, as a playmaker that Johnson first expressed his genius on a basketball court: his flair for ballhandling and those fabulous, no-look, thread the-needle passes that inspired applause. Not only did they make Johnson look good, but others as well.

Johnson's abilities, when first recognized on a national level at Michigan State, began changing the face of basketball in America, according to Spartan coach Jud Heathcote. Johnson not only had a great impact on Michigan State, he said, but on basketball in general. Heathcote saw Johnson's imprint on high school players who made the pass prologue. "If these kids growing up have their sports idols and they can identify with them

EARVIN "MAGIC" JOHNSON CELEBRATES WITH HIS MICHIGAN STATE TEAMMATES AFTER WINNING THE 1979 NCAA CHAMPIONSHIP. (AP/WIDE WORLD PHOTOS)

MAGIC JOHNSON GOES UP FOR A REBOUND AGAINST THE DALLAS MAVERICKS DURING THE 1986 REGULAR SEASON. (AP/WIDE WORLD PHOTOS)

and emulate what they do best, that's how they'll play," Heathcote said. "If it's Earvin, they'll start thinking 'pass.'"

The 6-foot-9 Johnson left the game with the second highest assist total in league history, behind Utah star John Stockton. He could do it all, though, averaging 19.5 points, 7.2 rebounds and 11.2 assists in 906 regular-season games.

He also holds the all-time marks for most All-Star Game assists (127) and three-point baskets (10).

"Magic is head and shoulders above everybody else," Bird once said. "I've never seen anybody as good as him."

And he didn't just make magazine covers for his exploits. He was a neon advertisement for basketball, ever eager, bristling with enthusiasm and always smiling.

"One thing I'm going to do is have fun," he once said. "There is a time for business and a time for fun. Basketball is fun."

MAGIC JOHNSON LOOKS UP AT THE SCOREBOARD DURING A PLAYOFF LOSS TO THE HOUSTON ROCKETS IN 1996. (AP/WIDE WORLD PHOTOS)

Voted one of the NBA's 50 Greatest Players of All Time, Johnson stunned the world by announcing he was retiring just before the start of the 1991-92 season after learning he had tested positive for the virus that causes AIDS.

He returned to play with Bird on the U.S. team that won gold at the 1992 Olympics. Then he tried a brief comeback with the Lakers, but quit again during the 1992-93 exhibition season after several players expressed concerns about playing with him for health reasons.

Johnson coached the Lakers for the final 16 games of the 1993-94 season, going 5-11, and purchased a five-percent ownership interest in 1994. He sold his stake back to owner Jerry Buss before returning as a player in 1996.

He played the remaining half of the 1995-96 season, retiring once and for all, at age 37, after the Lakers were eliminated in the first round of the playoffs by Houston.

Now a successful businessman, Johnson opened a chain of movie theaters in minority neighborhoods in the Los Angeles area in 1995, an enterprise he later took to other U.S. cities.

One legacy he left with the game was an enlightened attitude toward players who might be HIV-positive. During his second comeback, that never seemed to be an issue.

WALTER JOHNSON WARMING
UP FOR ACTION IN 1924.
(AP/WIDE WORLD PHOTOS)

WALTER JOHNSON

THE BIG TRAIN WAS QUICK

On December 10, 1946, the obituaries of two of America's most prominent personalities passed across the desks of the nation's newspapers—those of Walter Johnson, the great right-handed pitcher, and Damon Runyon, a sportswriter turned-author whose colorful characters were to be immortalized in books and the movies.

How should the two stories be played—on Page 1 or back in the sports section?

The answer was both intriguing and significant: Johnson's death was played prominently on Page l by most newspapers, while Runyon's was relegated to the inside.

The big, rawboned farmer's son out of Humboldt, Kansas, christened "The Big Train" by sportswriter Grantland Rice in comparing the pitcher's fastball to the whine of a locomotive passing over the countryside, had grown into a legend, more popular than presidents, movie stars and industrial tycoons.

He was indeed "King of the Hill"—that small hump of dirt comprising the pitcher's mound—in the swinging, pre-Depression era, when defense and the dead ball predominated and the game was a national fever.

For the entire 21 years of his career, Johnson pitched for one of the sorriest teams in baseball—the Washington Senators, chided as "first in war, first in peace and last in the American League"—yet compiled records that were to endure for generations.

Johnson won 416 games, a total exceeded only by Cy Young; completed 531 of the 666 games he started; hurled 113 shutouts; struck out 3,508 batters; and once had a string of 56 consecutive scoreless innings. He had a dozen seasons with 20 or more victories, 10 in a row. His career earned run average was 2.17.

A big man at 6 feet, 1 inch and 200 pounds, he never resorted to subtlety or tried to confuse opposing batters with off-speed stuff. Utilizing a sidearm delivery, he reared back and fired hard.

His speed was awesome, perhaps the fastest of all time.

"You always knew what was coming—always just raw speed, blinding speed," Ty Cobb said. "You were lucky to see it."

Johnson was a soft-spoken, easy-going man described by *Washington Post* columnist Shirley Povitch as "everybody's country cousin, a big handsome, modest hick." He didn't drink, smoke or swear. He purposely avoided brushback pitches for fear he might hurt someone.

One of five original inductees into baseball's Hall of Fame, in 1936, he went on to a managerial career after baseball. He led the Senators for four seasons and the Cleveland Indians for two and a half before being fired and retiring to a farm in Maryland.

He died in 1946 at the age of 59.

WALTER JOHNSON IN A 1924 PHOTO. (AP/WIDE WORLD PHOTOS)

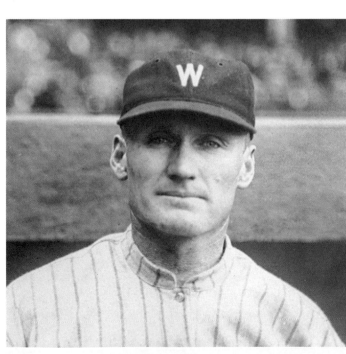

BOBBY JONES TEES OFF DURING THE 1941 MASTERS. (AP/WIDE
WORLD PHOTOS)

BOBBY JONES

KING OF GOLF'S GRAND SLAM

Bob Jones made the term "Grand Slam" a part of the lexicon of golf. An expression originating with the card game of bridge, it meant taking all the tricks. Baseball borrowed it to describe a home run with the bases loaded. It carried the same connotation in golf—a sweep, winning all of the big ones, clearing the board.

Jones became its symbol. In 1930, he scored the first and only Grand Slam in golf history, winning the U.S. and British Amateur, and the U.S. and British Open championships in a single season. Not only has the feat never been equaled, it has not been seriously challenged. Nor will it ever be, in the judgment of the game's finest minds.

The achievement is all the more remarkable because it was fashioned by a young amateur who proved himself master not only of his amateur contemporaries but of the sport's greatest professionals. No more worlds to conquer, Jones retired from competition at age 28, leaving an unattainable goal for generations that followed.

Jones' departure marked a change in the character of the game. There was a sharp shift from the amateurs, the blue ribbon competitors in sports' Golden Age, to the professional tour with its mushrooming purses and television exposure. One man who made the changeover was Jack Nicklaus, a two-time U.S. Amateur champion who turned pro in 1961 and went on to win 20 major championships, seven more than Jones, and establish himself as the all-time monarch of professional golf.

The pros set up their own version of the Grand Slam, bracketing the Masters, U.S. and British Opens and the American PGA as the four major events, but none has packaged them neatly in a single year. Ben Hogan came closest, winning the Masters, U.S. and British Opens in 1953 but passing up the PGA. Others, including Nicklaus and Arnold Palmer, have won two.

Students of the game say there is no telling how many championships Jones might have won had he not retired at such an early age. Hogan was 35 before he won the first of his four U.S. Opens. Nicklaus, who substantially had two careers, won the Masters at age 41.

Jones also had two careers— seven years of want as a teenage phenomenon before his seven years of plenty.

Born Robert Tyre Jones II, son of a well-to-do Atlanta lawyer and named for his grandfather, he grew

A MULTIPLE-EXPOSURE PHOTOGRAPH OF BOBBY JONES DRIVING A GOLF BALL IN 1938. (AP/WIDE WORLD PHOTOS)

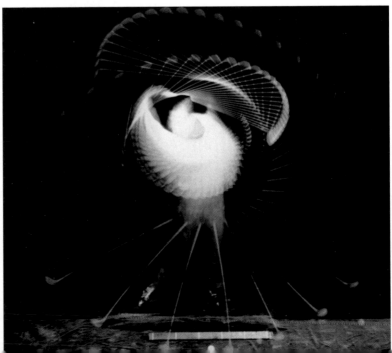

BOBBY JONES DURING A PRACTICE ROUND BEFORE THE 1936 MASTERS. (AP/WIDE WORLD PHOTOS)

BOBBY JONES HITTING HIS FIRST GOLF SHOT ON THE WEST COAST PRIOR TO A TOURNAMENT IN 1929. (AP/WIDE WORLD PHOTOS)

up in a country club atmosphere, getting his first baptism in the sport by following his parents around the East Lake course.

After acquiring his first golf club at age 5, little Bobby built a hand-made course on the family's front lawn, and he and his friends played for hours.

Bobby was 6 when he won his first tournament—a six-hole event for neighborhood kids at a birthday party. At 9, he won a junior tournament at the Atlanta Athletic Club, and at 13 he captured two club championships and two invitation events against some of the South's top amateurs.

Bobby was only 14 when he played in his first National Amateur Championship at the Merion (Pennsylvania) Cricket Club. Spectators were awed by the smooth swing of the husky youngster who led first-day qualifying and won two matches before blowing up. The press criticized his ungovernable temper.

He lost in the final of the 1919 U.S. Amateur. In his National Open debut in 1920, he was in contention until he blew himself out of it in the final round. That same year he won the qualifying medal in the National Amateur but lost to Francis Ouimet in the semifinals.

In 1922, having lost his baby fat and developed into a handsome, trim man, Jones made his first trip to England, helping the United States beat the British in their Walker Cup matches. However, he lost in the fourth round of the British Amateur at Holylake and picked up in disgust in the third round of the British Open.

By this time, the young American was getting a lot of attention throughout the world. A favorite almost every time he teed up the ball, he continually found a way to lose.

"That Jones boy," they said. "Great talent but can't go in the clutch."

During his so-called seven years of famine, a Biblical reference, Jones played in 11 major tournaments, often as the favorite, and won none. He acknowledged that he had begun to wonder if he ever could win a big one.

In 1923, the tide turned. Playing in the National Open over the Inwood course on Long Island, Jones tied Bobby Cruickshank after 72 holes, then defeated the little Scottish pro in a dramatic playoff.

Thus began his seven years of plenty. During that period, he amassed 13 national titles—five U.S. Amateurs, four U.S. Opens, three British Opens and one British Amateur. In the last nine years of his career, he played in 12 Open championships, nine American and three British, and finished first or second in 11 of them. Jones considered the latter feat superior to his Grand Slam, which the world followed with feverish interest and for which he will be forever known.

The 1930 sweep began with the British Amateur, where Jones beat Roger Welhered in the final 7 and 6, continued in the British Open and U. S Open, and culminated with the U.S. Amateur at Merion, outside Philadelphia.

Still a young man at 28, he announced his retirement from competitive golf. He and his financier friend, Cliff Roberts, collaborated on building a course in Augusta, Georgia, where he would play each spring with friends. Thus the Masters was born. Jones, the soft-spoken Southern gentleman who was the epitome of the amateur spirit, refused to turn pro. He continued to play informally until stricken with a paralyzing spinal ailment that led to his death in 1971.

MICHAEL JORDAN FLIES UNDER THE BASKET AGAINST THE PHILADELPHIA 76ERS' RON ANDERSON IN A 1991 GAME WHERE JORDAN WOULD SCORE HIS 15,000TH CAREER POINT. (AP/WIDE WORLD PHOTOS)

MICHAEL JORDAN

SIMPLY THE BEST

The real wonder of Michael Jordan was this: He always kept score.

Not just in his head, not just on a basketball court, and not just some nights, but every minute of every day.

The first week Jordan played for the Bulls, official scorer Bob Rosenberg looked up to find him studying the scorebook every time he reported to the table to re-enter the game. It didn't take long to figure out why. By knowing everybody's point and rebound totals, Jordan knew how the newspaper stories the next day would begin. Then he took the floor and made sure they always began the same way: "Michael Jordan ..."

Fourteen years later, the playing and promoting had not dulled his competitive edge. Even in the last days of what Bulls coach Phil Jackson called "The Last Dance," Jordan could turn the walk from the hotel lobby to a waiting bus into an event.

What people who saw him sweep by in an elegant suit didn't know was that Jordan practiced for even those few seconds, trying on his clothes the night before.

It was that obsession, his father once said, that made his son special even as a child. From the moment he started playing games, Michael had to win, and just as important, there had to be something riding on the outcome.

He is restless in a way the rest of us are not.

Jordan traveled everywhere and anywhere for a competitive fix, a modern-day Ulysses roaming the world in sneakers and baggy shorts.

His journey started in his own front yard, against an older brother on a makeshift court of caked dirt. It detoured through the University of North Carolina, where he won a national championship ... through Barcelona, Spain, where he won a second Olympic gold medal ... through minor-league ballparks in the South, where he ran from the ghost of a murdered father ... and through corporate boardrooms, where he helped sell more of everything–hot dogs and hamburgers, Wheaties, sunglasses, calling cards, underwear and the Internet.

It ended in June 1998 in Salt Lake City, where the drama of Jordan's sixth NBA championship came down to one last heart-stopping shot swishing through the net and sucking every last bit of air out of the state of Utah.

Afterward, as everyone else struggled to catch their breath, he said: "Hopefully, I've put enough memories out there for everybody to at least have some thoughts about what Michael Jordan did."

He was never bigger, never better, even at 35, nor was there a more perfect time for him to take his leave. His statue already stands guard outside the United Center, where thousands come to have their picture taken each year—in the shadow of the $175 Million House That Jordan Built.

It was the second time he walked away from the game he loved. The first time, in the fall of 1993, Jordan said the thrill of playing was not so much gone as sated. Besides, living like Elvis had him positively spooked. He was 30.

AS A FRESHMAN, MICHAEL JORDAN LED NORTH CAROLINA TO THE 1982 NCAA TITLE. (AP/WIDE WORLD PHOTOS)

MICHAEL JORDAN HOLDS THE
BALL AWAY FROM THE SEATTLE
SUPERSONICS' GARY PAYTON
DURING THE 1996 NBA FINALS.
(AP/WIDE WORLD PHOTOS)

MICHAEL JORDAN RETURNS TO
FLIGHT AGAINST THE INDIANA
PACERS ON MARCH 19,1995.
JORDAN HAD RETURNED TO
PROFESSIONAL BASKETBALL AFTER
RETIRING AND ATTEMPTING A
SECOND CAREER IN PROFESSIONAL
BASEBALL. (AP/WIDE WORLD
PHOTOS)

FIVE-TIME
NBA MVP,
JORDAN LED
THE BULLS
TO SIX
CHAMPIONSHIPS
AND LEFT AS
THEIR ALL-
TIME LEADING
SCORER.
(AP/WIDE
WORLD
PHOTOS)

"The one thing that's weird about Michael," good friend Charles Barkley said at the time, "is that whenever we're together, we're in a hotel room, because he doesn't ever go out."

Going out wasn't high on Jordan's list. He said he wanted to see his kids more. What he really wanted, though, was time to grieve, time off from basketball, time away from the spotlight.

In September, 1994, he played in teammate Scottie Pippen's charity basketball game; only, Jordan said, to pay his respects to Chicago Stadium before the 65-year-old building fell to the wrecking ball. He wound up scoring 52 points. And Gen-X kids like Anfernee Hardaway and Isaiah Rider, who knew him only by reputation, were stunned to find out Jordan was even better in person.

When the game ended, he walked to the center jump circle, knelt and kissed the hardwood bull in the middle goodbye, then left. But something inside him stirred.

A few months later, after playing as much golf as he wanted and then playing as much baseball as pride would allow, after one entire basketball season passed and a second was nearly complete, his competition problem surfaced.

The announcement of his return was faxed from his agent's office to media across the country.

"I'm back," was all he said.

It was hard to say who was happiest—NBA commissioner David Stern or Bulls owner Jerry Reinsdorf. Or maybe it was the CEO at Nike or NBC or Coke or General Mills or Wilson or McDonald's or one of the other companies Jordan represented.

After his retirement, *Fortune* magazine totaled what it called "The Jordan Effect." It put his impact on the economy since joining the NBA in 1984 at $10 billion. If that number seems high, consider that even a bad movie like "Space Jam"—in which Jordan played himself saving the earth from evil cartoon characters—grossed $230 million worldwide.

Just because he was in it.

"He was like the rising tide," Harvard professor Stephen Greyser told the magazine, "raising all boats."

The six-time world champ put up some amazing numbers on the court. He was a five-time MVP, a three-time NBA Finals MVP, a three-time All-Star Game MVP. He won 10 scoring titles, was named to the All-Defense first team six times and averaged a league-record 31.5 points per game in his career.

"I've got three words," former teammate Will Perdue once said, "Thank you, baseball."

JACKIE JOYNER-KERSEE MAKES HER FIRST JAVELIN THROW DURING THE HEPTATHLON IN THE 1992 SUMMER OLYMPICS IN BARCELONA. JOYNER-KERSEE WENT ON TO WIN HER SECOND CONSECUTIVE GOLD MEDAL IN THE HEPTATHLON. (AP/WIDE WORLD PHOTOS)

JACKIE JOYNER-KERSEE

"SHE'S A LEGEND"

For Jackie Joyner-Kersee, it began in poverty-stricken East St. Louis, Illinois. From that hardscrabble environment, she emerged not only as one of the greatest athletes in track-and-field history, but in all of sports.

It ended 15 miles down the road—in Edwardsville, Illinois, where Joyner-Kersee made her final competitive appearance on July 25, 1999.

The IAAF Grand Prix meet was billed as "track and field's farewell to Jackie."

Some found it hard to say goodbye.

"She'll always be one of the greatest who ever was," said Jane Frederick, former world-record holder in the heptathlon who owns the 12th, 18th and 19th best multi-event scores in U.S. history; the other 17 in the top 20 belong to Joyner-Kersee. "She's a legend."

Bob Kersee couldn't agree more.

"Even if she wasn't my wife, I would still say she's the greatest athlete I've ever coached," said Kersee, whose protégés have included the late, great Florence Griffith Joyner, Valerie Brisco-Hooks, Gail Devers and Greg Foster.

"But she always said, 'I don't want to be just a great athlete, I want to be a great human being.'"

Since becoming a world-class athlete in 1981, Joyner-Kersee won six Olympic medals—two golds and one silver in the heptathlon and one gold and two bronzes in the long jump—and four World Championship golds—two each in the heptathlon and long jump. She also won eight U.S. long jump titles and six heptathlon championships, and probably would have added to that total had injuries not cost her a couple of seasons.

"Fifty or 100 years from now, people will still be talking about athletes like Wilma Rudolph, Wyomia Tyus, Babe Didrickson, FloJo and Jackie," said Martha Watson, former Olympic long jumper who competed against Joyner-Kersee during the early 1980s.

"She and Wyomia had similar personalities. They were both quiet, but they did their jobs. When they were in a race or an event, you were usually going for second place.

"We have a lot of great people coming up, like Marion Jones, but they've got to earn the respect that Jackie did over the years. She really earned it."

She earned it with the help of a strong family, including older brother Al Joyner, the 1984 Olympic triple jump champion, and lots of neighborhood friends. And, of course, Bob Kersee.

"Jackie was very ambitious, but when her relationship with Bobby solidified, that's when she became unbeatable," Frederick said. "He completed a certain part she didn't have. With his

JACKIE JOYNER-KERSEE SMILES AFTER WINNING THE LONG JUMP AT THE 1988 SUMMER OLYMPICS. (AP/WIDE WORLD PHOTOS)

JACKIE JOYNER-KERSEE RAISES HER HANDS IN VICTORY AFTER THE WOMEN'S HEPTATHLON 100-METER HURDLES IN THE 1998 GOODWILL GAMES. (AP/WIDE WORLD PHOTOS)

JOYNER-KERSEE NARROWLY CLEARS THE HIGH-JUMP BAR DURING THE 1998 GOODWILL GAMES. (AP/WIDE WORLD PHOTOS)

JACKIE JOYNER-
KERSEE TAKES TO THE
AIR WHILE COMPETING
IN THE LONG JUMP AT
THE 1997 WORLD
TRACK AND FIELD
CHAMPIONSHIPS.
(AP/WIDE WORLD
PHOTOS)

screaming, his yelling ... both of them together became the complete package."

The complete package made Joyner-Kersee track and field's most versatile athlete.

She holds the world record in the heptathlon with 7,291 points at the 1988 Seoul Games. She held the world record in the long jump and still owns the American record of 24 feet, 7 inches, a distance she reached twice, first at New York in May 1994, then at Sestriere, Italy, less than three months later. And she shared the U.S. record in the 100-meter hurdles with Gail Devers, her training partner and close friend, and now is the No. 2 performer, behind Devers, with a best of 12.61 seconds at San Jose, California, in 1988.

"She was one in a million," former heptathlete Cindy Greiner said. "She was like Michael Jordan. You just couldn't beat her."

Joyner-Kersee did not lose a heptathlon in which she finished for 12 years, from the time she lost the 1984 Olympic gold medal by five points to Australia's Glynis Nunn until the 1996 Olympic trials, where she was runner-up to Kelly Blair-Labounty.

"To show the type of person she is," Blair-Labounty said, "I remember after the 800 meters (the final event), they were counting up the points. Before the final scores were announced, she put her arm around me and congratulated me. I didn't even know I had won. But she was the first to offer congratulations, and that showed a lot of character."

Joyner-Kersee always had a close camaraderie with her competitors, especially with Germany's Heike Drechsler, the 1992 Olympic gold medalist and 1983 and 1993 world champion in the long jump, and former world-record holder.

She has transferred that engaging personality into helping youngsters in East St. Louis. Her Jackie Joyner-Kersee Youth Center Foundation, in which she takes a very active part, provides recreational and educational activities for area kids.

"Just as Mary Brown had a dream to improve the lives of young people and everyday citizens, Jackie has that dream today," said Nino Fennoy, Joyner-Kersee's high school track coach.

The foundation is one of many activities that will occupy Joyner-Kersee's time following her retirement. She is a popular guest on television shows. She conducts the JJK Relays in East St. Louis. She is a sports agent, one of the few women in the business, working under Elite International Sports Marketing, Inc., her and her husband's agency.

And as an asthmatic, she will continue to educate parents and children about the ailment.

One thing she won't do is return to playing basketball, in which she starred for four years at UCLA and played one season in the American Basketball League with the Richmond Rage.

JEAN-CLAUDE KILLY RACES DOWN
THE GIANT SLALOM COURSE IN THE
1968 WINTER OLYMPICS IN
CHAMROUSSE ON HIS WAY TO A
SECOND STRAIGHT OLYMPIC GOLD
MEDAL. (AP/WIDE WORLD PHOTOS)

JEAN-CLAUDE KILLY

FRANCE'S OLYMPIC HERO

He is one of the most glamorous skiers of all time, a French national hero named to the Legion of Honor.

Jean-Claude Killy is probably the only French athlete many people in the world can name—years after he won his last big race.

And that fame, along with years of hard work, played a big part in bringing the 1992 Winter Olympic Games to France.

A triple gold medalist in skiing at Grenoble in 1968, the last time France hosted the Olympics, he helped bring the Games back to the French Alps as co-president of the organizing committee. He was the first gold medalist to run an Olympics, and proud of it.

Killy grew up in the village of Val d'Isere, where his family moved when he was two. He took to the slopes at three, and in his heart has never left.

In those days in Val d'Isere there were few things to do besides ski. Killy would shun school for the slopes—he eventually left school at 15—and remembers being chased by a priest, on skis, for cutting Bible class.

Coaches and friends remember him as a risk-taker driven by a motivation to win. Killy did win various junior and national championships, though he had mixed results: a couple of broken legs before important championships, and hepatitis and amebic dysentery resulting from French compulsory military duty in Algeria in 1962.

Those ailments plagued him at the 1964 Olympics in Innsbruck where he placed fifth in the giant slalom, the only race he finished.

But his stardom was sealed with a fantastic 1966-67 season when he won 23 of 30 races, including a record six straight, and then his three victories at the 1968 Olympics.

He took the downhill, slalom and giant slalom when he was half his current age. That feat was accomplished by only one other, Austrian Toni Sailer the 1956 Olympics in Cortina.

"Jean-Claude is a very romantic guy who was a great skier, plus he is French, which made it even more perfect," former figure skating star Peggy Fleming once said. "Every girl fantasized about Jean-Claude."

So did corporate executives. Killy has plugged Rolex watches, Bic pens, United Airlines and Chevrolet cars. Even Hollywood got him —he starred in the movie "Snow Job" as a jewel thief on skis.

He runs a chain of sporting goods shops and his company Veleda makes upscale skiwear popular in Europe and Japan; his business and sports empire has been estimated at $725 million.

JEAN-CLAUDE KILLY ON HIS WAY TO THE GOLD MEDAL IN THE MEN'S DOWNHILL IN THE 1968 WINTER OLYMPICS. (AP/WIDE WORLD PHOTOS)

BILLIE JEAN KING SMILES AS SHE HOLDS HER TROPHY AFTER WINNING HER SIXTH
AND FINAL WIMBLEDON SINGLES TITLE IN 1975. (AP/WIDE WORLD PHOTOS)

BILLIE JEAN KING

LONG LIVE THE KING

In the mid-1970s, an informal survey was made of tennis players and followers of the game on this theoretical question: If one were facing a highly pressured situation with a crucial point that probably would determine victory or defeat, who would you most prefer to play that point?

Of all the great players, male and female, considered in this hypothesis, one name dominated: Billie Jean King.

This bouncy, tomboyish daughter of a California fireman left a legacy of grit and determination, of an unbreakable will and tenacity not fully reflected in the scores of her court triumphs carved in the record books.

She wasn't the storybook idea of a female superstar. She was a chubby, girl-next-door type with 140 pounds distributed over a 5-foot-6 frame with short-cropped hair, harlequin spectacles and a face full of freckles.

If she had chosen baseball instead of tennis (and she always regretted that gender had made this impossible), she would have resembled Ty Cobb or Pete Rose in style of play. If she had been a boxer, she would have been like a little Dempsey.

She played the game with a dynamic gusto, scurrying around the court, leaping, bouncing, rushing the net. She didn't know what it was to temporize. She attacked every ball as if it were a mission. As she battled for points, she glowered and screamed at herself:

"Keep your eye on the ball, stupid!"

"You've got the touch of an ox. Think, think, think!"

She left a lasting impression on the game with not only her racket but her tongue. She was the Susan B. Anthony of her day, in the forefront of the feminist movement, an early crusader for open tennis and equal prize money for women players. She was once described by *Life* magazine as one of the "100 Most Important Americans of the 20th Century."

She and Rosemary Casals once walked out of their final match in a Pacific Southwest tournament, run by Jack Kramer, in protest of unequal pay. She threatened to lead a boycott of Wimbledon unless ladies' purses were raised to the level of the men's. Most of these inequities were changed.

She helped organize the women's pro circuit, and with husband, Larry King, was co-founder and chief sponsor of Team Tennis, an intercity project. She helped form both the Women's Tennis Association and the Women's Sports Federation. She published a magazine called *WomenSports* and in 1994 received *Family Circle*'s "Player Who Makes a Difference" award.

BILLIE JEAN KING IN ACTION DURING THE 1983 WIMBLEDON TOURNAMENT. (AP/WIDE WORLD PHOTOS)

BILLIE JEAN KING IN ACTION DURING THE 1968 WIMBLEDON IN WHICH SHE WON FOR HER THIRD CONSECUTIVE TITLE. (AP/WIDE WORLD PHOTOS)

BILLIE JEAN KING AND
BOBBY RIGGS MET IN
THE "BATTLE OF THE
SEXES" IN HOUSTON IN
1975, WHICH KING WON
HANDILY. (AP/WIDE
WORLD PHOTOS)

Billie Jean, although both knees carried scars of repeated operations, was ranked No. 1 in the world four times and inducted into the International Tennis Hall of Fame in 1987. She became the darling of Wimbledon, where on July 7, 1979, she won her 20th title—a record for both men and women—by capturing the women's doubles with Martina Navratilova. She won six Wimbledon singles titles and four American crowns.

Her greatest triumph, however—the one for which she probably will be most remembered—came in the "Battle of the Sexes" against feisty Bobby Riggs in the Houston Astrodome on September 20, 1973.

Riggs, a 55-year-old former Wimbledon and U.S. champion who had turned con man in his later years, taunted Billie Jean for her strong feminist views and insisted that even an old, rundown codger like him could beat the best of the women players. Billie Jean spurned his challenge until Bobby finally convinced Margaret Smith Court to meet him on Mother's Day in a remote California resort and then shamed the nervous Australian with a straight-set victory.

That was more than Billie Jean could take. She threw down the gauntlet. The match struck a national chord. The buildup was tremendous. They set up training camps, which were covered like a big heavyweight title fight. The slick news magazines featured Bobby on their covers, surrounded by a bevy of Hollywood starlets, and revived tales of Riggs' hustling days. While Bobby gulped vitamin pills and soaked up the fanfare, Billie Jean trained with a passion.

In a circus setting with all the trimmings, the largest crowd ever to see a tennis match—30,472—jammed into the Astrodome to watch a cold-eyed, tight-lipped King gag the obstreperous court jester with a 6-4, 6-3, 6-3 shellacking.

Born Billie Jean Moffitt on November 22, 1943, King grew up in a sports atmosphere. Her father played baseball and basketball. Her mother was a crack swimmer. A younger brother, Randy, was good enough to pitch for the San Francisco Giants. So Billie Jean wound up with a $9 racket because her father was determined that she not be a tomboy.

As a kid, Billie Jean played football and baseball with the boys. At firemens' picnics, she was always one of the first chosen for softball games. She was a natural athlete.

Besides her successes at Wimbledon and Forest Hills. She won national singles titles in Australia, France and Italy. She captured 29 Virginia Slims tour events and became the first woman to win $1 million in prize money.

She fared better at Wimbledon than at home, playing 100 matches on the storied English grass, winning nine doubles and five mixed doubles titles besides her six singles crowns.

"I love Wimbledon," she said. "It is a tournament for players. Forest Hills is a tournament for officials."

The bouncy Californian always was as free-swinging with her rhetoric as with her slashing topspin shots.

Discussing President Ford's Commission on Olympic Sports, she said, "Our sports system is a colossal joke. Amateur athletics stink."

On professionalism: "If a person wants to dedicate himself to sport, he should get paid. People relate to it."

She chided the establishment for its stuffy traditions such as all-white attire and complete silence during play.

"You picture people sipping mint juleps under an umbrella," she said. "Tennis must get away from that country club atmosphere. In basketball and football, the players cuss like sailors. At tennis matches, you can't breathe."

SANDY KOUFAX PITCHES IN THE 1965 WORLD SERIES AGAINST THE MINNESOTA TWINS. (AP/WIDE WORLD PHOTOS)

SANDY KOUFAX

A SHORT BUT SWEET CAREER

Sandy Koufax is considered by many the greatest left-handed pitcher to ever step on the mound.

He was the best pitcher in baseball for five seasons. From 1962 to 1966, he was 111-34 with 100 complete games, 33 of them shutouts. He led the NL in ERA all five years, in wins and strikeouts in 1963, 1965, and 1966, and won the Cy Young Award all three years.

Koufax, who pitched the last several years with an arthritic condition that finally forced him to quit, received accolades from old and young in a career that spanned 12 seasons and saw him pitching for the Dodgers on two coasts, in Brooklyn and Los Angeles.

Frank J. Shaughnessy, the late president of the International League, who saw such great pitchers as Christy Mathewson, Grover Cleveland Alexander and Walter Johnson, flatly said about Koufax:

"He comes closer to being unhittable than any other pitcher I ever saw."

In a different generation and a different vein, Bob Oldis, a catcher with the Philadelphia Phillies, said: "When Koufax is pitching the batter should get four strikes and three balls."

Despite retiring in his prime at the age of 30, Koufax distinguished himself with the following achievements:

• Pitched four no-hitters, at a one-a-year pace, from 1962 through 1965, a feat unmatched in baseball history.

• Struck out a major-league record 382 batters in 1965, which has since been broken.

• Led the league in strikeouts in a period spanning four seasons (1961, 1963, 1965 and 1966), as well as having the lowest ERA from 1962-1966.

• Won 27 games in 1966, a modern NL record for a left-hander, since tied.

• Led the NL in ERA a record five consecutive seasons, from 1962 through 1966.

• Won the Cy Young Award in 1963, 1965 and 1966, and won the Most Valuable Player Award in addition, in 1963.

In late August of 1964, Koufax was forced to stop pitching with a record of 19-5 and an ERA of 1.74. On medical orders, he didn't throw between starts in 1965 and went 26-8, crowning the regular season by pitching a perfect game against the Cubs on September 9.

Koufax was the World Series hero for the Los Angeles Dodgers in 1965, pitching a shutout in Game 5 and then coming back on two days rest to pitch another one in Game 7 against Minnesota.

He went 27-9 and led the league in ERA for a fifth straight season the next year, his last in baseball.

In 1972, he became the youngest player ever elected to the Hall of Fame.

SANDY KOUFAX DELIVERS THE FIRST PITCH OF THE 1963 WORLD SERIES AGAINST THE NEW YORK YANKEES. (AP/WIDE WORLD PHOTOS)

ROD LAVER HOLDS HIS TROPHY AFTER WINNING HIS SECOND U.S. OPEN IN 1969 TO COMPLETE HIS SECOND GRAND SLAM. (AP/WIDE WORLD PHOTOS)

ROD LAVER

TENNIS' FIRST MILLIONAIRE

In 1938, when America's Don Budge was sweeping the Australian, French, Wimbledon and U.S. championships for an unprecedented tennis Grand Slam, a cattle rancher and his wife in remote Queensland, Australia, celebrated the birth of their third son. The boy, like Budge, had a shock of red hair. But who in his wildest fancies could imagine that the infant would grow up not only to match the American's role as the world's best player but also would duplicate the coveted Grand Slam?

The Aussie redhead, born Rodney George Laver, later nicknamed "The Rocket," not only repeated the sweep of the four biggest crowns in the game, but did it twice, first as an amateur and later as a professional. That put him one up on Budge. Furthermore, many astute observers of the time, the 1960s, went so far as to hail him as perhaps the greatest tennis player who ever lived.

To look at him, one would not have thought it possible. Laver was a puny, skinny kid with a sunken chest, long nose and bandy legs. Even when he grew to maturity, playing before royalty, a king of his own court, he lacked the looks and the demeanor of a great sports champion. He stood five feet, eight inches and weighed less than 150 pounds—the antithesis of Budge, a robust six-footer.

He was shy and unassuming. Only when he took a racket in his left hand—a left forearm inches bigger around than his right and wrists of steel—did the Herculean image emerge.

He was no stylist. He was light and quick in movements, unleashing sudden bombardments of shots, heavy with spin, that neutralized his opponents. He didn't have a cannonball serve but relied on a high-bounding drive that he could spin in the corners or down the line.

He was spectacularly aggressive, usually catching the ball on the rise and whacking it across the net for repeated winners. Perhaps no other player attacked as relentlessly or as effectively. Against such rivals as Ken Rosewall and Pancho Gonzales, he never temporized. He grabbed the net advantage quickly and volleyed with a swordsman's fury. He turned tennis into a new game.

Young Laver emerged at a time when Australia, as big as the United States in size but with a population only a little larger than New York, was at its zenith as a tennis power. From 1956 through 1971, Aussies won 13 of 16 Wimbledon men's singles titles and 12 American crowns, while dominating the Davis Cup under a wily, old captain named Harry Hopman, who personally took Laver under his wing.

The first time Hopman laid eyes on Laver, he blinked and remarked, "My, he's a little one. We're going to have to do something about that

ROD LAVER MAKES A BACKHAND AT AN INDOOR TOURNAMENT IN 1969. (AP/WIDE WORLD PHOTOS)

ROD LAVER LEAPS IN ACTION ON HIS WAY TO WINNING THE 1962
WIMBLEDON MEN'S SINGLES TITLE. (AP/WIDE WORLD PHOTOS)

ROD LAVER MAKES
A BACKHAND
RETURN IN HIS
SEMIFINAL MATCH
OF THE 1960 U.S.
OPEN. (AP/WIDE
WORLD PHOTOS)

sunken chest." Actually, Rod's father, a tennis enthusiast, had more confidence in two older sons, Trevor and Bob. But Charlie Hollis, a coach in Laver's hometown of Rockhampton, favored Rod from the beginning.

"Trevor's got beautiful strokes," Hollis told the father. "They're better than Rodney's, but he's got an explosive temper like you. Rodney's like his mother, quiet and determined. He'll make it."

Rod began playing at age 10, using his mother's racket, on the family's lighted court in the backyard. He hung around Hollis' tennis shop, stringing rackets and absorbing the coach's wisdom.

When Laver was 18, Hopman took time off from his other duties to chaperone Rod and another promising junior, Bob Mark, on a five-month world tour, financed by Australian millionaire Arthur Drysdale. At 19, Laver was named a sixth member of the Davis Cup team.

Americans first became aware of Laver's potential in 1960 when, at Forest Hills, he gained both the men's singles and doubles final in the U.S. Championships. He lost in the singles final to Neale Praser.

The flashy left-hander won his first major crown—the Australian—in 1960. He won Wimbledon in 1961 but lost in the finals of the Australian and U.S. championships. They served as tune-ups for his Grand Slam years.

Laver began his 1962 campaign by beating a fellow Queenslander and chief rival, Roy Emerson, in the Australian final. The two crossed rackets again in Paris, Rod winning a five-setter for the second leg of his Slam. At Wimbledon, seeded No. 1 and nervous, he fell behind Spain's Manuel Santana 9-11, 1-5 in the quarterfinals but survived and beat fellow Aussie Marty Mulligan for the title. Only the U.S. remained.

Laver recalled that Budge called him aside prior to the Forest Hills tournament and advised, "Play the game the way you can, don't worry about the Slam."

"It made me more nervous," Laver said, but he persevered, beating Emerson for the second Grand Slam ever achieved in tennis.

Rod turned professional in 1963, signing a $100,000 contract for three years of one-night stands. He started shakily, losing his Australian debuts to Lew Hoad and Ken Rosewall. But in 1966 and 1967 he compiled the best won-lost record on the pro tour and reestablished himself as the game's undisputed No. 1, solidified when he repeated his Grand Slam in 1969 as a pro, a year after the game had gone open.

His trophy cache includes four Wimbledon crowns, three Australian, two French, two U.S., plus Italian and German singles championships and numerous titles in doubles and mixed doubles.

He retired to California as tennis' first millionaire.

In July 1998, the 60-year-old Laver suffered a moderate stroke while taping a television interview. He was discharged a month later.

MARIO LEMIEUX SHOOTS THE PUCK BETWEEN HIS LEGS AGAINST THE OTTAWA SENATORS IN THIS 1997 GAME. (AP/WIDE WORLD PHOTOS)

MARIO LEMIEUX GETS PAST MARK MESSIER OF THE NEW YORK RANGERS DURING A GAME IN THE 1995 REGULAR SEASON. (AP/WIDE WORLD PHOTOS)

MARIO LEMIEUX

"I DID IT MY WAY"

Mario Lemieux could not say the word never. They said a team as bad as the Pittsburgh Penguins could never win the Stanley Cup. Lemieux proved them wrong.

They said a hockey player could never be as revered as a Roberto Clemente or a Terry Bradshaw in a city that tolerated hockey but never took to it. He proved them wrong.

They said an athlete could never undergo debilitating cancer treatment in the morning, then be his game's best player that night. He proved them wrong.

They said a relatively young athlete such as Lemieux could never retire happily. And, again, Lemieux proved them wrong.

Weary of all the clutching and grabbing that has reduced his scoring average, Lemieux had enough. He quit on his terms following the 1997 season, not those of some team owner or commissioner.

"I did it my way," Lemieux said.

The last comparable Hall of Fame-caliber athlete to leave on his own volition, rather than injury, while still at the top of his game was former Cleveland Browns star Jim Brown.

Like Brown, Lemieux is his own man, a loner unwilling to follow the status quo. Lemieux didn't just win three MVP awards while leading a once-dreadful franchise to two Stanley Cups, he elevated the act of scoring goals into an art form. He also beat two career-threatening back operations and Hodgkin's disease.

Through 13 seasons Lemieux cared not about everyone else's expectations, just his own. Perhaps that is the burden of a last name that translates, in French, into "the best."

Along with Wayne Gretzky, Lemieux was the dominant scorer of this era. He finished with 613 goals, 1,494 points, three league MVP trophies and two playoff MVP trophies in a career that was interrupted by Hodgkin's disease, which caused him to sit out the 1994-95 season.

One can only imagine what Lemieux might have accomplished had he played as long as Gretzky.

"He made hockey in Pittsburgh," former teammate Mark Recchi said.

He still is. In September 1999, Lemieux became the first retired player to own a major sports team he played for when he purchased the Penguins.

MARIO LEMIEUX CELEBRATES AFTER HE SCORES A GOAL AGAINST THE PHILADELPHIA FLYERS IN THE 1997 STANLEY CUP PLAYOFFS. (AP/WIDE WORLD PHOTOS)

SUZANNE LENGLEN IN
ACTION IN THIS 1926
PHOTO. (AP/WIDE
WORLD PHOTOS)

SUZANNE LENGLEN

FRANCE'S PHENOMENON

It is hard to visualize Suzanne Lenglen, the graceful, floating court vision of the 1920s in her high silk stockings and calf-length skirts, trying to match her delicate strokes against the riveting serve of Martina Navratilova.

Yet in a poll in the early 1980s, with the aggressively overpowering styles of the modern players fresh in their minds, the world's tennis writers and commentators voted the talented but tormented French mademoiselle the greatest woman tennis player of all time.

Certainly, no other court figure in history exerted such influence on her times. For more than a decade she was the darling of the sports world. Thousands packed arenas just for the privilege of seeing her strike a ball. She was a Wimbledon favorite. She was fawned over by royalty. Her exploits were front-page news on every continent.

She was a complex and tragic figure. Pushed by doting parents, she gave the impression of being a prima donna. She demanded limousines when other players rode trains. She had costumes made by top designers who fought for the privilege of dressing her without charge. She often sulked and sometimes petulantly pulled out of a match, disappointing huge crowds.

Yet on the court, while the epitome of grace and style, she was a relentless killer. Tense and high-strung, she resented every point scored against her, never giving an inch.

Born in 1899, Suzanne grew up in Nice, daughter of humble and provincial parents who early saw her tennis potential and were determined to mold her into a world tennis champion.

Small and sallow-complexioned as a girl, she was forced to practice hours upon hours on hard courts. She was denied a normal childhood.

Literally, she became so precise in her shot-making that she could put the ball on a dime. Her father would place a coin on the court and have Suzanne practice hitting it.

Mama and Papa Lenglen were never satisfied. They constantly yelled criticism.

"Stupid girl! Keep your eye on the ball!"

Certainly, this stern discipline paid dividends, yet it ultimately had a devastating effect on her health and psyche. She didn't live a happy life. She was plagued by chronic illnesses and died prematurely, at age 39, of pernicious anemia. But she left an indelible mark.

She won the ladies' singles title in the first Wimbledon in which she played, at age 20 in 1919 and went on to capture six Wimbledon and seven French championships in the space of seven years. In her honor, the women's singles winner at the French Open is presented with the Suzanne Lenglen trophy.

SUZANNE LENGLEN IN ACTION IN 1923. (AP/WIDE WORLD PHOTOS)

Carl Lewis celebrates after crossing the finish line to win the 4 x 100-meter relay in the 1992 Summer Olympics in Barcelona. (AP/Wide World Photos)

CARL LEWIS

AN ENIGMA TO THE VERY END

For all the fantastic achievements that make him perhaps the greatest Olympian ever, Carl Lewis forever seems tinged by controversy and self-aggrandizement.

So it seemed fitting for him to leave the Olympic stage after winning another gold medal, stirring up nearly a week of controversy, then disappearing.

At the end of the 1996 Atlanta Games, he was merely a spectator, watching from a VIP booth high atop Olympic Stadium while the 400-meter relay team, his baby, ran without him and lost. No one will ever know if having Lewis in the relays would have altered the result and given him a record 10th gold medal.

The lingering impression of Lewis should be his winning leap in the long jump during those same Games, the last of his record-tying nine golds covering four Olympiads. The sight of an aging warrior extracting a jump for the ages from his 35-year-old legs was the defining moment of Lewis' career.

Or was it?

The next day, Lewis began lobbying for a spot on the 400 relay team.

Never mind that he had finished last in the 100 at the U.S. trials and didn't bother to show up for a pre-Olympic training camp.

When his erstwhile teammates complained about King Carl trying to horn his way onto the track one more time, he claimed he was merely speaking for the fans who wanted him on the relay squad.

"Winning 10 gold medals would be tremendous," Lewis said.

"But after the other night, you go through your career and realize there is a time when you hang up your spikes and call it a day. ...That night (winning the long jump) was so special, I don't know if I can match it."

He never got the chance.

U.S. coach Erv Hunt passed over Lewis for a spot on the relay team, even when his training mate and close friend Leroy Burrell was injured. When Burrell's replacement, Tim Harden, struggled to grasp the baton and made a sloppy handoff after the second leg, the Americans were beaten outright in the 400 for the first time in Olympic history.

Lewis watched from his private suite, then slipped out of the stadium without uttering a word to the media.

CARL LEWIS LANDS THE GOLD MEDAL IN THE LONG JUMP IN THE 1992 SUMMER OLYMPICS. (AP/WIDE WORLD PHOTOS)

CARL LEWIS ON HIS WAY TO WINNING HIS NINTH GOLD MEDAL IN THE LONG JUMP IN THE 1996 SUMMER OLYMPICS IN ATLANTA. IT WAS LEWIS' FOURTH OLYMPICS. (AP/WIDE WORLD PHOTOS)

CARL LEWIS TAKES THE BATON FROM THE TEAMMATE CALVIN SMITH DURING A SEMIFINAL OF THE 4 x 100-METER RELAY IN THE 1984 SUMMER OLYMPICS. THE U.S. TEAM WENT ON TO WIN THE GOLD MEDAL. (AP/WIDE WORLD PHOTOS)

"He said, 'This has all become a big mess,'" said Carol Lewis, his sister. "He got sucked into this whole big mess and he got tired of it."

Lewis is used to big messes.

He created a furor at the '84 Olympics when he refused to take his final four attempts in the long jump, saying he wanted to save himself for the 200 final later in the day. Right in his home country, he was booed by the fans who wanted to see him go for the world record.

Seven years later, in the greatest series ever for a long jumper, Lewis soared 29 feet or beyond three times at the world championships, only to be beaten by Mike Powell's world record of 29-4 1/2.

Instead of praising Powell's performance, Lewis scoffed at it, proclaiming it a once-in-a-lifetime effort that paled in comparison to his own great day. Lewis was right when he said of Powell, "He may never do it again," but the public image of King Carl took another blow.

On the track, though, the whims of public opinion couldn't diminish Lewis' greatness.

Not since Jesse Owens dominated track and field during the mid-1930s has there been an athlete with the speed and explosiveness of Carl Lewis. And no one performed so well, for so long.

Lewis' nine golds and one silver include four golds at the 1984 Los Angeles Olympics, matching Owens' feat of four golds at the '36 Berlin Games. Lewis also equaled discus thrower Al Oerter's record of winning the same event (the long jump) in four straight Olympics.

For more than a decade, no one beat Lewis in the long jump. No one ran more sub 10-second clockings in the 100. Only Michael Johnson has run more sub-20 clockings in the 200. No one has run on more 400-meter relay teams that have broken 38 seconds. And no one has soared farther than 28 feet more often in the long jump.

In all, Lewis set or helped set 10 world records.

"Carl is the greatest athlete I've ever seen," said 1992 Olympic coach Mel Rosen, "and he proves it time and time again."

Yet the man himself remained an enigma to the very end.

"None of you," he once said, "will ever know who I really am."

A QUIET MOMENT IN 1984 FOR GREG LOUGANIS. (AP/WIDE WORLD PHOTOS)

GREG LOUGANIS

IN A LEAGUE OF HIS OWN

In diving, there were two eras: Before Greg and After Greg. After was definitely better.

Greg Louganis, who absorbed taunts as a child for the color of his skin and who coped with dyslexia and sexual confusion, found refuge in the grace and power of his sport.

He took it to heights never seen before, and maybe never again.

His dives cut water like a jet-propelled knife, leaving barely a ripple but stirring all who watched.

"I've never seen anyone come close to what he did," said Steve McFarland, president of U.S. Diving and one of Louganis' former coaches.

Louganis, who disclosed that he has AIDS, was the only man to sweep the diving gold medals in two consecutive Olympics. But those accomplishments in 1984 and '88 were only part of the story.

He became the first diver ever to top the 700 barrier in platform, with a 710.91 to win at the 1984 Los Angeles Olympics.

He was the only diver to score consecutive perfect 10s in an international competition. He also held five world championships, four Pan American championships and 47 national titles at one point.

Born on January 29, 1960, Louganis was adopted at nine months. His natural father was Samoan, his mother European; both were 15 when he was born. In addition to being taunted as a child because of the color of his skin, he said he didn't learn he was dyslexic until he was a freshman at the University of California-Irvine. He told Barbara Walters he was so sad it hurt."Three times he tried to commit suicide.

At age 12, a year after scoring a perfect 10 in the AAU Junior Olympics, he began concentrating on diving.

Dr. Sammy Lee, an Olympic gold medalist, began coaching Louganis and took him to the 1976 Montreal Olympics. There, he won a silver medal at the age of 16. It was also there that he came to terms with something he had long suspected—he was homosexual.

"I knew I was different, and I didn't understand what that difference was," he told ABC News' "20-20" in an interview.

Asked if other people on the team knew, he said: "I didn't try to hide it, you know, I didn't try to have any false life or anything like that, but I mean, on some of the trips it was really hard."

Asked if he was shunned, Louganis said, "Yeah, nobody would room with me. I mean I was lucky to find one person on the team that would room with me."

GREG LOUGANIS HITS HIS HEAD ON THE END OF THE SPRINGBOARD DURING THE PRELIMINARIES OF THE 1988 SUMMER OLYMPICS. HE WENT ON TO WIN THE GOLD MEDAL IN THE SPRINGBOARD. HE WAS THE FIRST TO WIN BOTH THE PLATFORM AND SPRINGBOARD EVENTS IN TWO CONSECUTIVE OLYMPICS. (AP/WIDE WORLD PHOTOS)

JOE LOUIS IN A 1940 PUBLICITY PHOTO. (AP/WIDE WORLD PHOTOS)

JOE LOUIS

THE DESTRUCTIVE BROWN BOMBER

He was a shuffling, unschooled product of America's slave and ghetto conclaves, born in a sharecropper's shack in Alabama and thrust onto the assembly lines in teeming Detroit—a man people would least imagine could become one of the greatest heavyweight boxing champions of all time and help change the social conscience of a nation.

Joe Louis had all the credentials—a lithe, panther-like figure, 6 feet, 2 inches and 200 pounds, with fists of devastating power. But he was black, and when he emerged as a raw but exciting fighter in the mid-1930s, the country was not ready to accept a black man as its heavyweight king.

The Jim Crow laws were prevalent throughout the South, where Louis was born. Black people could not drink water from a public fountain, eat in the best restaurants or go to the main schools in town. They had to ride in the back of buses and say, "Yes, suh" to their white benefactors.

Black baseball players were barred from playing in the major leagues. Pro football was lily white. Blacks could carry the clubs but couldn't play in the pro golf tournaments. The all-white rule in tennis also applied to the people wearing the attire. A black jockey hadn't had a mount in the Kentucky Derby since the early part of the century.

There hadn't been a black heavyweight contender since Jack Johnson, who hammered his way to the title just after the turn of the century, then offended the public with his arrogance and flaunting of white women.

Louis was different. Born Joe Louis Barrow on May 13, 1914, son of a sharecropper and the seventh of eight children, he was 12 when his family moved to Detroit, where he dropped out of school to take a job in a Ford plant. He boxed as an amateur, winning AAU and Golden Gloves titles while dropping the name "Barrow."

Although shy, he attracted the eyes of the pros and fell into the hands of two affluent black men connected with the rackets, Julian Black and John Roxborough. They immediately began fashioning him to fit society's mold.

"After you beat a white opponent, don't smile," they said.

"Never have your picture taken with a white woman."

In his 17 years as a professional, 12 as the heavyweight champion, Louis posted a 68-3 record with 54 knockouts. Louis' two most dramatic fights were against a beetle-browed German named Max Schmeling. Hitler was just beginning to make waves with

JOE LOUIS IS DIRECTED TO A NEUTRAL CORNER AFTER HE KNOCKED DOWN MAX SCHMELING THE FIRST OF THREE TIMES IN THEIR 1938 TITLE FIGHT. (AP/WIDE WORLD PHOTOS)

JOE LOUIS CONNECTS WITH A JAB AGAINST CESAR BRION IN THEIR BOUT. (AP/WIDE WORLD PHOTOS)

JOE LOUIS STANDS OVER MAX SCHMELING AFTER A FIRST-ROUND KNOCKOUT TO WIN THE HEAVYWEIGHT TITLE IN 1938. (AP/WIDE WORLD PHOTOS)

his military aggressiveness and Nazi philosophy. Louis was 22, a threat to one of sports' proudest titles. Ironically, the first fight, June 19, 1936, was more black vs. white than Uncle Sam vs. Nazism.

Louis was heavily favored, but he was inadequately prepared and overconfident. He built an early lead, but Schmeling surprised him with a right to the jaw in the fourth round that sent him to the canvas. Dazed, Louis rose and hung on until the 12th round, when he was dropped again and counted out.

In many places, the South mainly, people danced in the streets. Women named new-born babies for the German victor. "What we thought was tremendous calm" one columnist wrote of Louis, "was nothing more than lack of fire and spirit."

Louis was shamed by the defeat. But he resumed his quest for the heavyweight crown and gained it by knocking out 35-year-old Jim Braddock in the eighth round in Chicago's Comiskey Park on June 27, 1937. "I won't be happy 'til I get that Schmelin'," he told his handlers.

The opportunity came June 22, 1938, by which time Hitler was spouting Aryan supremacy and threatening to conquer the world. Seventy thousand fans crammed Yankee Stadium in New York. When the bell rang, the seething Louis leaped out like a raging bull, fists flying. Two minutes and four seconds later, Schmeling lay on the canvas in a battered, bleeding heap. The American nation celebrated wildly. The black warrior from Alabama had crushed the Nazi monster. Blacks throughout the country found in their hero a new pride and hope which might some day lead them out of their wilderness.

Boxing writers reached for new hyperbole and clichés: Joe Louis the "Brown Bomber," "Dark Destroyer," "Sepia Slasher."

He lived up to all of his nicknames. A classic stand-up fighter with a left jab that shot out like a cobra's tongue, he stalked his foes like a jungle cat, backed them into a corner of the ring, after which he unleashed a series of short, jolting blows. Then he would step back nonchalantly and watch his victim fall.

It happened often. Of the three opponents who were able to go the distance with him after he became champion—Tommy Farr, Ariuro Godoy and Jersey Joe Walcott—Godoy and Walcott were stopped in rematches. Walcott and Billy Conn gave the champ the most trouble, but Conn, who led for 12 rounds in 1941 before being knocked out, was KO'd in eight in a rematch after World War II.

The Brown Bomber volunteered and spent almost four years' service in the Army during the war. A gentle, easygoing man, he further endeared himself to the American public by risking his title in a Navy Relief bout against Buddy Baer in 1942, sacrificing money he badly needed to offset the back tax pressures of the IRS.

Louis reportedly earned $5 million during his career and squandered it all on golf course wagering and alimony to former wives. He twice married and divorced his first wife, Marva Trotter, followed with Rose Morgan and, finally, Martha Malone, a Los Angeles attorney who mothered his adopted children and nursed him in his final days as a public relations representative for Caesars Palace in Las Vegas.

He died of a massive heart attack on April 11, 1981.

MICKEY MANTLE SIGNS AUTOGRAPHS BEFORE A 1965 EXHIBITION GAME IN PUERTO RICO. (AP/WIDE WORLD PHOTOS)

MICKEY MANTLE

THE MOST POWERFUL SWITCH-HITTER

The New York Yankees realized early that to maintain the tradition of "The House That Ruth Built," it was necessary that Yankee Stadium should always try to have a Ruthian personality—a ballplayer who could hit with power and fire the imagination of the fans.

They found such a commodity in Joe DiMaggio, who filled Babe Ruth's void in 1936 and kept the Bronx baseball temple rocking for more than a dozen years. But, entering the second half of the century, DiMaggio was showing signs of wear and tear and there was concern over who could step into his shoes.

The answer lay in a sleepy, little town in the northeastern corner of Oklahoma where a doting father was carefully fashioning a son for baseball stardom. Elvin "Mutt" Mantle named his eldest son "Mickey" after one of his baseball heroes, Mickey Cochrane. He put a baseball in the infant's crib and, by the time the youngster was two, had him in the backyard swinging a bat from both sides of the plate.

Mickey Mantle pulled on his Yankee pinstripes for the first time in 1951, a 19-year-old switch-hitter with power and amazing speed. He had arrived, not unknown but in the wake of a tremendous buildup campaign, as a possible successor to Ruth and DiMaggio.

"He's got it in his body to be great," rasped Manager Casey Stengel, the first time he saw Mickey at bat.

Mantle didn't disappoint, going on to become the greatest switch-hitter in baseball history. He hit 536 home runs (373 lefthanded, 163 righthanded) and a record 18 in the World Series, including a grand slam in 1953.

A three-time American League MVP, 20-time All-Star and 12-time World Series participant, Mantle was inducted into baseball's Hall of Fame with pal Whitey Ford in 1974.

He died from liver cancer in August 1995 at age 63, still one of the nation's most endearing heroes.

Later, the dark side came out. He became addicted to alcohol and his association to gambling got him kicked out of baseball for two years.

But in his later years, Mantle realized his flaws and reinvented his image, letting everyone know he was an alcoholic and urging others to sober up.

A month before he died, he warned children, "Don't be like me."

MICKEY MANTLE TAKES A SWING FOR THE PHOTOGRAPHERS AT YANKEE STADIUM IN 1961. (AP/WIDE WORLD PHOTOS)

MICKEY MANTLE

ROCKY MARCIANO REACHES THROUGH EZZARD CHARLES' GUARD
TO CONNECT WITH A RIGHT IN THEIR 1954 HEAVYWEIGHT TITLE
BOUT. (AP/WIDE WORLD PHOTOS)

ROCKY MARCIANO

THE BROCKTON BLOCKBUSTER

Down through the years one of the most hotly contested arguments is that involving heavyweight boxing champions. Who was the greatest of them all—the swarming Jack Dempsey, Joe Louis, rugged Rocky Marciano or the float-like-a-butterfly-sting-like-a-bee kid, Muhammad Ali?

It is a debate without end because there is no way to bring the eras together. Or is there? An ingenious entrepreneur of the 1960s sought to solve the problem through modern science. The records, styles and techniques of the great champions were fed into a computer for an imaginary film series and the intricate machine produced the two finalists, Ali and Marciano, with Marciano winning by a knockout in the 13th round.

A lot of hardened, experienced fight observers would not argue with the result. The "Brockton Blockbuster," as the stumpy New England pulverizer was called, left a brief but imposing legacy that brooks little dispute.

Marciano knocked out an aging Joe Louis to set up a title victory over tough Jersey Joe Walcott in 1952 at age 28, defended the crown six times and retired in the spring of 1956 while at the peak of his career. As a professional he won 49 straight fights, 43 by knockout, never lost and was knocked off his feet only twice—once by Walcott and later in his career by Archie Moore. Both indignities were properly avenged by knockouts. Of his title defenses, only Ezzard Charles managed to last 15 rounds but fell in a return bout.

Marciano was hardly the Hollywood version of a boxing hero. At 5 feet, 11 inches and 185 pounds, he was one of the lightest and shortest of all heavyweight champions and his reach was the shortest, only 68 inches.

But that didn't bother Rocky, a swarming, brawling gladiator willing to take half a dozen punches to deliver one.

Marshall Smith, writing in *Life Magazine* in 1952, marvelled at Rocky's calm, relaxed composure before big fights, remarking that he was "nervous as a fire hydrant."

He also cited what other fight journalists learned at the time, writing, "Marciano is a real live edition of the comic strip character, Joe Palooka—unassuming, clean living, a humble guy with a heart of gold who uses his God-given strength to slay ogres and flatten city slickers."

Rocky got his fighting start in elementary school, when a bigger kid beat him up and sent him home crying. A few days late, his uncle built him a punching bag in the backyard.

Soon, the kid left Rocky alone.

He fought until he was 33, winning $1.7 million in prize money and defending his title six times.

A family man, he engaged in several business enterprises and was active in civil work. In 1969, flying home to celebrate his 36th birthday with his family, he died in a plane crash.

ROCKY MARCIANO DELIVERS A BLOW TO ARCHIE MOORE.(AP/WIDE WORLD PHOTOS)

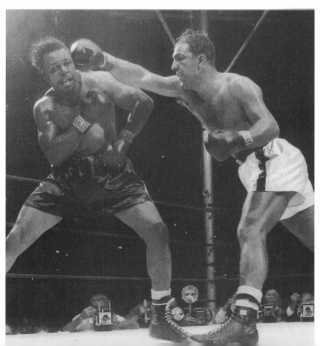

BOB MATHIAS MAKES A DISCUS TOSS TO TAKE THE LEAD IN THE DECATHLON IN THE 1948 SUMMER OLYMPICS IN LONDON. MATHIAS WOULD GO ON TO TAKE THE GOLD MEDAL IN THE DECATHLON. (AP/WIDE WORLD PHOTOS)

BOB MATHIAS

THE DECATHLON'S SCHOOLBOY PHENOM

He could have been the model for those soft-cover Frank Merriwell books that our fathers and grandfathers read with such relish as kids—the genuine American hero; young, handsome, talented, too good to be true.

Robert Bruce Mathias of Tulare, California, was all of those things, and no star in the galaxy appeared too distant for his reach. He was a football star at Stanford University, all-around track athlete, winner of the demanding Olympic decathlon at age 19, repeater four years later, two and a half years in the Marine Corps, motion picture and TV celebrity, finally U.S. Congressman and whisperings in the back rooms: Presidential material? Maybe. Certainly, he had all the ingredients.

Then came Watergate.

President Richard Nixon, caught up in a web of White House political shenanigans and found guilty of a cover-up, was forced out of office. Many Republicans—including Mathias—went down the drain with him.

"I was not personally involved," Mathias said later. "But I was a Republican and, like Mr. Nixon, was from California. They remandered my district. As a result of the scandal, there was great apathy among Republicans. They didn't turn out for anybody."

Mathias' political balloon burst, but nothing could destroy the impact the young Californian made in winning consecutive Olympic gold medals for the decathlon in 1948 and 1952 in the toughest, most rigorous event in the Games.

When Mathias returned home from Helsinki in 1952, he got a reception matched only by that tendered Jesse Owens in 1936. Track historians hailed his feat as comparable to the all-around brilliance of Jim Thorpe. Mathias was named The Associated Press' "Male Athlete of the Year."

Mathias took the world by storm at the 1948 London Games, wining the decathlon gold at 19. London newspapers heralded the feat as the feature of the Games. He became the "Schoolboy Phenom."

Four years later, he soared to a new world record score of 7,887. It got top billing in "The Bob Mathias Story," one of five movies he went on to star in when his athletic career was over.

Married to his childhood sweetheart, Mathias served eight years in Congress and then became director of the Olympic Training Center in Colorado Springs.

BOB MATHIAS, RIGHT, TAKES THE 110-METER HURDLES ON HIS WAY TO THE GOLD MEDAL IN THE DECATHLON IN THE 1948 SUMMER OLYMPICS. HE WON THE GOLD AGAIN IN 1952. (AP/WIDE WORLD PHOTOS)

A POSED ACTION SHOT OF WILLIE MAYS DURING HIS DAYS WITH THE SAN FRANCISCO GIANTS. (AP/WIDE WORLD PHOTOS)

WILLIE MAYS

THE DYNAMIC "SAY HEY" KID

A ball is hit to deep center field and almost at the crack of the bat, Willie Mays sets out in pursuit, scampering like a flushed-out rabbit. His cap flies off his head. He wheels simultaneously as the ball reaches near the end of its parabola, cups his hands below his chest and cradles the pellet as he might a fragile baby.

The crowd screams in delight. "Say Hey, Willie!"

Later he comes to bat and, with hysteria in the stands heightening, with one mighty swing, propels the ball out of the park.

"Oh, you Willie!" Another deafening roar.

Such, in thumbnail, is the baseball profile of the man many diamond historians rate, if not actually the greatest all-around player who ever pulled on a uniform, certainly worthy of ranking with such giants as Babe Ruth, Ty Cobb and Hank Aaron for consideration in that unsolvable debate.

When he was inducted into the Baseball Hall of Fame, after a sparkling 22-year career with the New York and San Francisco Giants and the New York Mets, Willie was asked who was the best baseball player he ever saw.

"Me," Willie replied without a second thought.

He wasn't being cocky, simply naively honest. It was an assessment shared by baseball buffs, teammates and rivals.

"He could do everything," said his first major league manager, Leo Durocher. "Joe DiMaggio is the only other player I've seen who could do it all. Willie was a natural."

"When it comes down to needing a run," said Walt Alston, longtime manager of the Dodgers, "Willie is the greatest."

There was always a small-boy quality about the superb black athlete out of Alabama. He radiated energy and desire. He acted as if he couldn't wait to get onto the field and, once there, to play with a contradictory mixture of fierce pride and schoolboy enthusiasm. He loved to put on a show.

Once explaining how he kept losing his hat while running down fly balls in the outfield, he said, "Early in my career, my cap came off while I was chasing a ball. The crowd went wild. So I always kept my cap loose to please the crowd."

Actress Tallulah Bankhead, an admirer, wrote, "Willie does everything with a flourish. He has the spectacular…a theatrical quality. In the terms of my trade, he lifts the mortgage five minutes before the curtain falls."

Mays was the ultimate ballplayer. He hit for both percentage and power. He ran the bases as daringly as a Pepper Martin or Jackie Robinson. Flawless in the field, he had a fine arm, good instincts and rarely made a mental error.

WILLIE MAYS GETS HIS 3,000TH CAREER HIT AGAINST THE MONTREAL EXPOS IN 1970. (AP/WIDE WORLD SPORTS)

Willie Mays at bat during his days with the New York Mets. (AP/Wide World Photos)

WILLIE MAYS MAKES HIS FAMOUS CATCH OF A 450-FOOT SHOT BY VIC WERTZ IN THE 1954 WORLD SERIES OPENER. MAYS' NEW YORK GIANTS DEFEATED WERTZ'S CLEVELAND INDIANS IN FOUR STRAIGHT GAMES. (AP/WIDE WORLD PHOTOS)

He hit 660 home runs, batted .302 for his career and had 1,903 runs batted in. He played in four World Series and was a participant in all All-Star Games from 1954 through 1973. He was named the NL's Most Valuable Player in 1954 and 1956. In 1981, baseball author-historian Maury Allen ranked baseball's all-time top 100 and placed Mays on top, saying: "If not for two years in service, Mays would have outdistanced Babe Ruth in career homers…was the best, most exciting, No. 1."

Willie was born May 6, 1931, in Westfield, Alabama, a mill town just outside Birmingham, and given the little-boy name of Willie (not William) Howard Mays, Jr. He grew up in the neighboring town of Fairfield, where he starred in several sports in high school and played sandlot baseball with his father, a former outfielder in the pro Negro League. Papa played center field, Willie left field.

Mays joined the Birmingham Black Barons of the Negro National League when he was just 17, and it was there in the spring of 1950 that he was spotted by Giants' scout Eddie Montague and signed a contract for $5,000. Willie stayed with the Black Barons until he finished high school, however, and then reported to Trenton in the Class B Interstate League.

At Trenton, he batted .353 in 81 games— "It was like playing in the Little League after the Negro League," he said—and earned promotion the next spring to the Minneapolis Millers of the Triple A American Association.

That stop was brief. In New York, the Giants were struggling early in the 1951 season. In Minneapolis, Mays was hitting .477. Willie was summoned to the Polo Grounds, given number 24 and thrust onto the field—a raw kid just turned 20, making his debut in the majors four years after Jackie Robinson had crossed the color line.

"They said I was scared and nervous," Willie said. "It was not true. My father worked in the steel mills and later as a railroad porter. I never had it bad. And the crowds didn't bother me. I was used to crowds in the Negro League."

Willie opened his major league career in Philadelphia and got off to an inauspicious start, hitless in his first 12 times at bat, and was becoming discouraged until the team returned to New York for a series with the Boston Braves. Facing All-Star left-hander Warren Spahn, he poled the first pitch over the left-field roof for a home run.

He became an immediate idol of the fans. They called him the "Say Hey Kid" because that was the way he greeted people whose names he didn't remember. His rookie season was climaxed by the Giants' dramatic playoff victory over the Dodgers for the National League pennant and a losing effort against the New York Yankees in the 1951 World Series. He was named his league's Rookie of the Year.

Willie missed most of the 1952 season and all of 1953 because of military service, but returned in 1954 to share in the Giants' World Series victory over the favored Cleveland Indians, marked by his unforgettable running catch of a Vic Wertz shot which the Indians said "broke our backs." Mays was the league's MVP and the Associated Press' Athlete of the Year.

He accompanied the Giants in their move to San Francisco but was never as appreciated as he was in New York. He was traded to the New York Mets in 1972, retiring June 15, 1973, at age 42.

Willie left with a profitable real estate investment business, public relations jobs with an Atlantic City casino and two other firms, condos in New York, Birmingham, Tampa and Reno and eight cars, all bearing "Say Hey" plates.

JOE MONTANA SETS TO PASS AGAINST THE ATLANTA FALCONS DURING HIS DAYS
WITH THE KANSAS CITY CHIEFS IN 1994. (AP/WIDE WORLD PHOTOS)

JOE MONTANA

NO ORDINARY JOE

What made Joe Montana special?

Precision. Instinct. Timing. Leadership.

"He had all of that," said Seattle coach Mike Holmgren, the San Francisco 49ers' quarterback coach during the late 1980s.

Montana had all of those elusive qualities and he combined them into a brilliant package that made him the NFL's best quarterback ever. Even more, he could convince his teammates that he could do the impossible.

"He had a great ability to relax and relax his teammates," Holmgren said. "In practice, he was a little bit of a jokester. Yet they knew how hard he worked at it. And when it came down to crunch time, he always came through. They saw that. He was a great leader that way. By example."

The examples are legendary, an almost endless succession of plays that astounded opponents and 30 times brought his team from behind to victory in the final quarter.

And he was at his best in the biggest games.

Late in the 1990 season, the San Francisco 49ers' linebackers were shown tapes of a spectre they were lucky enough not to have to encounter in person.

"The coaches pulled out Joe's touchdown pass to John Taylor that beat the Giants," recalled Matt Millen. "Then they asked us where we'd aim the ball in order to put it where Joe threw it and most of us said at the 'R' or the 'S' where '49ers' was written in the end zone.

"It turned out that he threw it at the '4,' 10 yards away."

That was Joe Montana, 10 yards better than everybody else in his quest for perfection. If he wasn't perfect during his 16 NFL seasons, he was probably closer to perfection than any quarterback has ever been, his career a series of benchmarks with a "THE" in front of them—"The Catch," "The Drive," "The Comeback."

Bill Walsh didn't really want Montana when he left Notre Dame in 1979, preferring instead Phil Simms of Morehead State. Simms was an NFL prototype—big, tall, strong armed. Montana was a little too short, listed at 6-foot-3 but more like 6-1 1/2, and there were doubts about his arm strength.

But Walsh's predecessor, Joe Thomas, had traded the first pick in the draft for an aging O.J. Simpson. So he had no shot at Simms, who went to the Giants seventh overall.

Walsh was inclined to take Steve Dills, whom he'd coached at Stanford. But Tony

JOE MONTANA TRIES TO SHAKE OFF A TACKLER IN ACTION AS QUARTERBACK AT NOTRE DAME. (AP/WIDE WORLD PHOTOS)

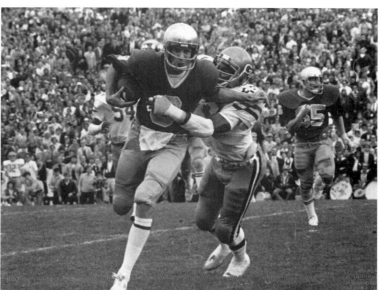

JOE MONTANA DROPS BACK IN A 1989 DIVISION PLAYOFF GAME AGAINST THE MINNESOTA VIKINGS. (AP/WIDE WORLD PHOTOS)

JOE MONTANA PASSES IN SUPER BOWL XIX IN CALIFORNIA. HE WAS NAMED THE GAME'S MVP IN THE 49ERS' 38-16 WIN. (AP/WIDE WORLD PHOTOS)

JOE MONTANA CELEBRATES HIS SECOND OF FOUR SUPER BOWL VICTORIES WITH SAN FRANCISCO 49ERS HEAD COACH BILL WALSH AFTER DEFEATING THE MIAMI DOLPHINS IN SUPER BOWL XIX. (AP/WIDE WORLD PHOTOS)

Razzano, 49ers chief scout, convinced Walsh that Montana was a born winner and worth taking when the 49ers made their first pick of the draft, in the third round.

He was right. But it took a while.

He struggled as a rookie, but took over for Steve DeBerg toward the end of the 1980 season and finished with a completion percentage of 64.5, best in the NFL. The 49ers had found their quarterback and were about to find themselves.

He was the top-rated quarterback in the NFC in 1981, completing 63 percent of his passes. The 49ers finished 13-3, and won the Super Bowl, beating Cincinnati 26-21 in a game in which Montana won the first of three Super Bowl MVP trophies.

But that was anticlimactic to the NFC title game—a 28-27 victory over Dallas that included "The Catch" at the end of the first of many Montana productions known as "The Drive."

"The Catch" was pulled in by Montana's buddy, Dwight Clark, on a 6-yard play with 51 seconds left. Montana threw the ball so the only player who could catch it was Clark, leaping over Everson Walls at the back of the end zone.

Memorable because of the circumstances, but no different from dozens of other throws over Montana's 16 spectacular seasons.

In 1984, Montana led what many consider to be the best of the San Francisco Super Bowl winner. In 1988, he pulled out a last-second Super Bowl win over Cincinnati, in 1989, he won his third Super Bowl MVP award throwing five TDs against Denver.

In four Super Bowls, he put up super numbers: 83 for 122, 11 TDs, no interceptions.

The 49ers turned to Steve Young in 1991 when Montana was injured, and Young has stayed the starter ever since. On April 20, 1993, San Francisco shipped Montana and David Whitmore to Kansas City for a first-round draft pick.

Montana led the Chiefs to the AFC title game that year, but never made it any further. He called it a career at 38 after two years in Kansas City.

ANNEMARIE MOSER-PROELL
WON THE 1971 WORLD CUP
INCLUDING THIS WIN IN THE
FOEMINA CUP GIANT SLALOM.
(AP/WIDE WORLD PHOTOS)

ANNEMARIE MOSER-PROELL

AUSTRIA'S QUEEN OF THE SLOPES

Annemarie Moser-Proell is the greatest woman alpine skier of all time.

In 12 years she won 62 races, which is still considered untouchable.

In 1971, the Austrian won her first of six Women's World Cup titles at age 17. She dominated that decade, winning her last World Cup title in 1979.

She won 36 downhills, including an unprecedented sweep of the eight women's downhills in 1973. Those eight wins were part of a record 11 consecutive downhills between December 1972 and January 1974.

She posted 10 victories in a season twice during her career, including a record 11 times in 1973. Vreni Schneider of Switzerland surpassed that single-season record of 11 for women in 1989. Schneider also has come the closest to capturing Moser-Proell's career victory record. She had 55 wins before retiring in 1995.

In Olympic competition, Moser-Proell twice was a frustrated silver medalist in 1972. She missed the 1976 Olympics because of a one-year retirement.

She stepped down after complaining about strife inside the Austrian team and for personal reasons. During her one-year hiatus she opened a cafe in the Austrian village of Kleinarl.

Moser-Proell appeared in a television commercial with her husband, advertising a detergent. Later, she sent her fee to the Austrian Ski Federation and returned to the World Cup circuit.

Emerging from retirement, Moser-Proell continued her winning ways, winning six consecutive downhills. She fell in the final downhill.

There was a fear that she would be barred by the International Olympic Committee on charges of professionalism, but a probe by Olympic officials cleared her of all charges.

She finally capitalized in 1980 winning the downhill gold medal at Lake Placid. She retired again shortly after the Olympics and continued running her cafe.

The cafe walls were full of photos and other paraphernalia reflecting the Austrian passion for ski racing. One trophy case set the place apart with six crystal globes inside, each representing a World Cup overall title won by "the ski queen."

ANNEMARIE MOSER-PROELL ON A TRAINING RUN BEFORE THE 1972 WINTER OLYMPICS IN SAPPORO. (AP/WIDE WORLD PHOTOS)

EDWIN MOSES ON HIS WAY TO A GOLD MEDAL IN THE 500-METER HURDLES AT THE
1984 SUMMER OLYMPICS IN LOS ANGELES. (AP/WIDE WORLD PHOTOS)

EDWIN MOSES

ONE OF A KIND

Edwin Moses was the most dominant hurdler for a decade and holds one of the greatest winning streaks in sports.

From 1977 to 1987, he posted 122 consecutive victories (107 finals) in the 400-meter hurdles. In that period, he captured two Olympic gold medals, two world titles, four world records in the event. Moses had unparalleled success in the hurdles. In addition to this amazing streak, he also won the World Championship in 1983 and 1987 and the World Cup in 1977, 1979 and 1981.

Known as the "Bionic Man" during his college days at Morehouse, Moses burst into international prominence in 1976, when he won his first Olympic gold medal in a world-record 47.64 seconds. His victory margin of 1.05 seconds was the largest in the history of the Olympic 400 hurdles.

After earning a place on the 1980 Olympic team but not competing because of the U.S. boycott of the Moscow Games, Moses collected his second gold medal in 1984, winning in 47.75 at Los Angeles.

Moses lowered the world record to 47.45 in 1977, 47.13 in 1980 and 47.02 in 1983 on his 28th birthday. The 47.02 clocking stood as a record for nine years, until Kevin Young ran 46.78 at the 1992 Olympics.

In 1983, Moses ran another overpowering race, winning by 1.11 seconds in 47.50 at the inaugural World Championships at Helsinki, Finland. He also won the 1987 World Championships in 47.46, the first three World Cups in 47.58, 47.53 and 47.37, respectively, and five national championships.

From 1976-84, he was ranked No. 1 in the world each year except 1982, when he missed the season because of illness. Moses also was ranked No. 1 in 1987, his ninth time at the top.

His remarkable winning streak began September 2, 1987. It didn't end until Danny Harris, the 1984 Olympic silver medalist, beat him June 4, 1987, at Madrid, Spain.

At the Seoul Games, he missed becoming the first athlete in Olympic history to win three golds in a running event. His third-place finish in the final was his first loss ever in a championship race.

At one time, the graceful Moses had the 13 fastest times in his event.

After retiring following the 1988 Olympics he changed gears and seasons, to concentrate on bobsledding. Moses failed to qualify for the U.S. bobsled team for the 1992 Winter Olympics, but did compete on the American four-man team in the 1991 World Championships.

Among the honors he won were the Sullivan Award and the Jesse Owens Award. He was elected to the National Track and Field Hall of Fame in 1994.

EDWIN MOSES CLEARS A HURDLE ON HIS WAY TO THE GOLD MEDAL IN THE 400-METER HURDLES AT THE 1976 SUMMER OLYMPICS. (AP/WIDE WORLD PHOTOS)

STAN MUSIAL DEMON-
STRATES HIS UNUSUAL
BATTING STANCE FOR
PHOTOGRAPHERS IN
1951. (AP/WIDE WORLD
PHOTOS)

STAN MUSIAL

THE CARDS' "MR. NICE GUY"

Stan Musial's legacy in baseball can be capsuled in two words: sock and smile. Or, if one chose to carry the alliteration further, it could be power and personality, grandeur and grace, clout and class.

If his lengthy era in the major leagues could be likened to a graduation class, Stanley Frank Musial undoubtedly would have received cascades of votes as the most talented and most successful, but would have been a runaway winner as the most popular.

He was the all-time "Mr. Nice Guy" in a sport that has bred many heroes but few gentlemen. This relaxed, outgoing athlete from the coal-mining town of Donora, Pennsylvania, became as well known for his ever-present smile and friendly handshake as for his batting records in his 22 years as a member of the St. Louis Cardinals.

Musial never raised a ruckus. He mingled with fans, was never too busy to sign an autograph and was great with kids. He was so respected by rival teams that they never badgered him from the bench.

Newspapermen loved him. No matter how busy, he never turned down an interview, after which he would politely ask: "Got enough, fellow? If not, just let me know."

It was natural that historians of the period would compare him in performance and style with the great Ted Williams of the Boston Red Sox in the rival American League.

They were contemporaries but, playing in different leagues, their only confrontations came in spring training, All-Star games, and in the 1946 World Series. They were the greatest left-handed batters of their day—many contend two of the top three of all time, bracketing them in the same breath with the incomparable Babe Ruth.

Stan the Man, as he became popularly known, compiled a remarkable record during his 22 years as an outfield and first baseman for the Cardinals, starting in 1941. He had a career batting average of .331. He set a National League record of 3,630 hits that stood for two decades before being broken by Pete Rose.

After retiring, the seven-time NL batting champion remained in St. Louis, serving the club in various capacities. He opened a popular restaurant, became director of a bank and involved himself in various charitable activities.

Once when the Cardinals were experiencing hard times, Frank Lane, the club's crusty general manager, was asked if he might trade Musial. "Trade Musial?," Lane snapped. "Hell, he's part of this town. You might as well trade the Mississippi."

STAN MUSIAL AS A ROOKIE WITH THE ST. LOUIS CARDINALS IN 1942. (AP/WIDE WORLD PHOTOS)

BRONKO NAGURSKI
DURING HIS COLLEGE
DAYS AT MINNESOTA.
(AP/WIDE WORLD PHO-
TOS)

BRONKO NAGURSKI

LIKE A RUNAWAY FREIGHT TRAIN

Legendary tales generally get embellished with years of telling and retelling, but football diehards in the Midwest insist these stories are absolutely true in the case of Bronko Nagurski.

One is that Doc Spears, the coach at the University of Minnesota, driving along a country road on a recruiting mission, stopped to ask directions of a big kid who was plowing a field without a horse just outside International Falls, Minnesota. The kid responded by picking up the plow in one hand and pointing the way.

That, so the story goes, is how Bronko wound up pursuing an education and football career at Minnesota and ultimately becoming the devastating fullback who led the Chicago Bears to the first championship of the modern pro era in 1933.

The other is that the "Bronk," in a game at Chicago's Wrigley Field, where the end zone was only nine yards deep, once scored a winning touchdown by stampeding over two opponents, leaving one unconscious and the other with a broken shoulder. Then, unable to curb his momentum, he collided with a goalpost and crashed into a brick wall.

Picking himself up, Nagurski said, "That last guy hit pretty hard."

They say that years afterward, if one looked hard enough, he could still see the crack in the wall. "I've seen it," said Fran Tarkenton, a quarterback whose deeds thrilled pro fans in a later era.

Nagurski, who died in January 1991, at the age of 81, was a massive man, 6 feet, 2 inches tall and 225 pounds heavy in an age of 175-pound tackles. He was rock-hard, all muscle and bone, without an ounce of fat. His collar size was 19 inches. The ring he received for induction as a charter member into pro football's Hall of Fame in 1963 was size 19 1/2.

Many legitimate observers contend he may have been the greatest football player of all time, surpassing the great Jim Thorpe, named to that honor in a national poll of sportswriters by The Associated Press, and the sensational Red Grange, "The Galloping Ghost," at one time his teammate on the Bears.

Bronko, showing his versatility, passed for two touchdowns in Chicago's 23-21 triumph over the Giants in the first NFL title game.

"He was a star end, a star tackle and a crushing fullback who could pass," wrote Grantland Rice. "I believe 11 Nagurskis could beat 11 Granges or 11 Thorpes."

Nagurski was a 60-minute player, performing both on offense and defense in those pre-platoon days In one single college game he played end, tackle, guard, halfback and fullback. Spears said he could have been an All-America at any position.

All-time great Ernie Nevers, said, "Tackling Bronko was like trying, to stop a freight train going downhill."

A 1943 PHOTO OF BRONKO NAGURSKI. (AP/WIDE WORLD PHOTOS)

MARTINA NAVRATILOVA BACKHANDS A RETURN DURING THE FINALS OF THE 1986 FRENCH OPEN WOMEN'S SINGLES. SHE LOST TO CHRIS EVERT IN THE MATCH. (AP/WIDE WORLD PHOTOS)

MARTINA NAVRATILOVA

WIMBLEDON'S PERENNIAL POWER

Martina Navratilova immediately fell in love with the United States during her first visit there early in 1973. It took much longer for Americans to warm up to Martina Navratilova.

"My first impression of Americans was how friendly they were," she wrote in her autobiography. "I still like that openness about Americans. You can be honest and be yourself with Americans. I always felt I could be me, the real Martina, from the first time I came to the States."

It was during that trip, in Akron, Ohio, that her first-round opponent was "America's Sweetheart," Chris Evert, almost two years her senior. That was the beginning of the longest rivalry in professional tennis, an almost unparalleled rivalry that helped put both on the list of the sport's all-time stars.

Born October 18, 1956, in Prague, Czechoslovakia, Martina Subertova was raised near the village of Spindleruv Mlyn in a ski lodge some 1,200 meters high in the Krkonose Mountains, where her father, Miroslav Subert, was a ski instructor. Later, after her parents divorced, she and her mother moved to Revnice, where she began playing tennis, a sport in which her maternal grandmother had excelled.

It was there, at the municipal tennis club, that Martina met Miroslav Navratil, who eventually became her stepfather. She later changed her name to his, adding the feminine ending "ova", becoming Martina Navratilova.

Most Americans heard about Navratilova the first time in September 1975 when, during the U.S. Open, she defected to the United States. At the time, however, she was ranked No. 5 in the world and seeded third in women's singles in the Forest Hills, N.Y., tournament.

By then, she already had won two Grand Slam titles, teaming with fellow Czechoslovak Ivan Molina to win the French Open mixed doubles title in 1974 and with Evert to capture the 1975 French Open women's doubles. And she had led Czechoslovakia to victory in the 1975 Federation Cup.

But, consumed with her love of American fast food, especially hamburgers and milkshakes, Navratilova gained weight and became known as the "Great Wide Hope." Still, the talent was there as she displayed flashes of brilliance in her aggressive serve-and-volley style.

Her first coach in Prague was George Parma, a former Czechoslovak Davis Cup player. He not only worked on her game but gave her advice.

"Work hard, Martina. Compete wherever you have the chance. Get to see the world. Sports is one way you'll be able to travel," he told her.

MARTINA NAVRATILOVA FIGHTS BACK TEARS AS SHE HOLDS HER RECORD NINTH LADIES SINGLES CHAMPIONSHIP TROPHY AFTER THE 1990 WIMBLEDON. (AP/WIDE WORLD PHOTOS)

MARTINA NAVRATILOVA SERVES
DURING HER RUN TO THE FINALS OF
THE 1994 WIMBLEDON WOMEN'S
SINGLES, IT WOULD BE HER 12TH
TRIP TO THE FINALS AND ONLY HER
THIRD LOSS THERE. (AP/WIDE
WORLD PHOTOS)

MARTINA NAVRATILOVA CELEBRATES HER FIFTH OF SIX CONSECUTIVE WOMEN'S SINGLES WIMBLEDON CHAMPIONSHIPS IN 1986. (AP/WIDE WORLD PHOTOS)

"He would tell me to set my sights on becoming a good European player—maybe, just maybe, in the top ten in the world," Navratilova wrote. "Meantime, my father was telling people I was going to be a Wimbledon champion some day and I wasn't about to disagree with him."

That day came in 1978, when she defeated Evert in the final. She went on to win a record nine Wimbledon singles crowns, including an unprecedented six straight. In 1980 she had a bad year, although she was part of the winning women's doubles teams at the U.S. Open and the Australian Open. She dropped to No. 3 in the world.

The following year was her most disappointing. After winning the Avon Championships in New York against Andrea Jaeger, she appeared ready to capture her first U.S. Open singles title. It was not to be, however, as Tracy Austin fought back to beat her. It was especially disheartening because Navratilova had received her U.S. citizenship shortly before the tournament.

Her tears of defeat, however, were wiped away when the crowd at Flushing Meadows gave her a standing ovation following the match. She was, at last, accepted by American fans, and later that year she won her first Australian Open women's singles crown.

But in December, at the season-ending Toyota Championships in East Rutherford, N.J., she again lost to Austin after winning the first set. And the following March came another major disappointment, as she was upset by West Germany's Sylvia Hanika in the final of the Avon Championships.

It was time for Navratilova to devote her every moment to tennis. She hired a full-time coach, went on a special diet, and began a physical training regimen. It paid immediately, as she won the French Open women's singles crown for the first time, captured her third Wimbledon singles title and began her domination of women's tennis. In 1982, she won 90 matches while losing only three times and earning nearly $1.5 million. The next year she went 86-1, her only loss coming in an upset to young Kathy Horvath in the fourth round of the French Open.

Beginning with Wimbledon in 1983 and lasting through the 1984 U.S. Open, Navratilova won six consecutive Grand Slam singles crowns tying Margaret Smith Court's record. And she teamed with Pam Shriver to win eight consecutive Grand Slam women's doubles titles, beginning with Wimbledon in 1983 and extending through the 1985 French Open.

When she lost to Hana Mandlikova in early 1984, it snapped a 54-match singles winning streak, only one shy of Chris Evert Lloyd's record 55 straight Navratilova's next defeat came against Helena Sukova of Czechoslovakia in the semifinals of the 1984 Australian Open, halting a consecutive match winning streak of 74.

Navratilova retired from singles play following the 1994 season with 166 titles, more than any player—male or female. She won 56 Grand Slam titles—second only to Margaret Smith Court—and spent 332 weeks ranked No. 1 in the world.

One of sport's most articulate and outspoken figures, she's never been shy about commenting on any topic, whether it be her lesbian lifestyle or her commitment to promoting gay-lesbian rights and various political issues.

That frankness has cost her millions of dollars in missed endorsements over the years, plus the embarrassment of rejection by corporate sponsors her agents have approached. Virtually all those companies have been scared away from having her promote their products because they fear the backlash of a small percentage of their companies.

But there has been a positive flip side to Navratilova's honesty: a genuine respect for her that has made her one of the world's most popular and esteemed athletes. Recently she was honored with an offer to join the U.N. 50th committee, the only athlete along with top corporate executives, diplomats and public officials who will seek to formulate broad human rights policies.

JACK NICKLAUS AND THE GALLERY WATCH HIS SHOT FROM THE ROUGH DURING THE BOB HOPE CLASSIC IN 1979. (AP/WIDE WORLD PHOTOS)

JACK NICKLAUS

THE GOLDEN BEAR WITH A GOLDEN TOUCH

In 1962, a fat kid out of Ohio, playing his second year as a pro, shook up the golf world, first by tying and then beating in a playoff the idolized Arnold Palmer for the U.S. Open championship.

The charismatic Palmer, a fast-walking, belt-tugging, go-for-broke attacker, was at the height of his game and popularity. With the aid of television, he had made the sport a universal attraction, becoming a heartthrob for women and a hero to their husbands.

Everybody knew the kid, Jack Nicklaus, blond and beefy, was a comer, but he had no right to challenge the man they called "The Charger."

In the U.S. Open playoff, over the Oakmont Club outside Pittsburgh, "Arnie's Army," defending its idol, taunted big Jack almost every step of the way.

"Miss it, Fatso!" they yelled as Nicklaus stood over a crucial putt.

An embarrassed Palmer several times stopped and pleaded for his supporters to show more restraint.

Unshaken, Nicklaus proceeded to shoot a 71 in the playoff to win by two strokes. It marked the passing of an era, and no one recognized that milestone more than Palmer himself.

"That was it," Arnie said later. "If I could have stopped that big dude out there, I might have held him off for five years. But he just took off."

That Nicklaus did.

In the ensuing years Nicklaus set records that defied belief. He completely dominated the game for the next two decades, piling up a total of 71 tour victories, 20 major championships and close to $5 million in official earnings while pursuing in later years business enterprises that grossed around $400 million a year.

He scored multiple triumphs in the four blue ribbon tournaments that comprise the professional Grand Slam, winning six Masters, four U.S. Opens, three British Opens and five American PGAs, added to two earlier victories in the U.S. Amateur.

While wild thousands scrambled for vantage positions at Augusta and millions watched on TV, Jack captured his record sixth Masters in 1986 at age 46. It was his last major title and one of sports' most miraculous achievements of the

JACK NICKLAUS PUTS ON THE TRADITIONAL GREEN JACKET AFTER WINNING THE 1963 MASTERS CHAMPIONSHIP. HELPING HIM IS THE PREVIOUS YEAR'S WINNER, ARNOLD PALMER. (AP/WIDE WORLD PHOTOS)

Jack Nicklaus and his caddie celebrate Nicklaus' birdie putt on the 16th hole at Augusta en route to Nicklaus winning an unprecedented fifth Masters Tournament in 1975. (AP/Wide World Photos)

JACK
NICKLAUS
BLASTS OUT
OF A SAND
BUNKER
DURING THE
1995
MASTERS.
(AP/WIDE
WORLD
PHOTOS)

generation. He set scoring records in both the Masters and the U.S. Open and fell only one stroke short of the British record when he lost a historic head-to-head struggle to Tom Watson's 268 at Turnberry, Scotland, in 1977.

After Jack shot a record 271 at the Masters in 1965, going one stretch of 28 holes without a bogey and having only one three-putt green, an ailing Bob Jones, who watched on a TV screen in his white cottage, commented:

"Palmer and (Gary) Player played superbly, but Nicklaus played a game with which I am not familiar."

Besides his 71 tour triumphs, Nicklaus had 51 second places or ties and 33 thirds or ties. He was runner-up in the British Open seven times, as well as three times each in the U.S. Open, Masters and PGA. His victories around the world totaled 89, including six Australian Opens.

Jack Nicklaus was moving the ball almost from the day he was born—January 21, 1940, in Columbus, Ohio, the son of a prosperous and sports-minded pharmacist. Jack was 10 when his dad, Charlie, took him to the Scioto Club and put a set of clubs in the boy's hands. They played nine holes. Jack shot 51, the highest nine he ever had. By age 12, the boy was beating adults.

Jack won the Ohio Open at age 16, beating established pros, and then set off on a brilliant amateur career, qualifying for seven National Amateur tournaments, winning two—in 1959 and 1961. As an amateur, he finished second to Palmer in the U.S. Open at Denver in 1960, then competed in the World Amateur Team Championship at Merion (Pennsylvania), where his 72-hole score of 272 was 15 shots lower than that of Ben Hogan in winning the U.S. Open over the same course.

By this time, the golf world was hailing Nicklaus as "another Bobby Jones," and traditionalists in the game were hoping that Jack would remain an amateur and thus launch a pro-amateur rivalry like the one that marked the Bobby Jones-Walter Hagen confrontations decades before.

Jones, shortly before his death, wrote a personal letter to Nicklaus and his father urging that he remain an amateur, pointing out the great contribution for golf, generally, and assuring Jack of financial security in the business world. Long an admirer of Jones, Nicklaus wrestled with his decision and finally decided in 1962 to take the professional route.

"My reasoning was," Jack explained, "that if I intended to make golf my career, and I did, I should pursue it in the arena where the best golf is played—the tour."

While he was playing once in Australia, a sports writer from that country looked at him on the green and commented, "Look at that Nicklaus—just a big 'Golden Bear.'" It was a name that stuck. He had his blond hair cut in crew-cut style. This plus his weight gave him an appearance that elicited such uncomplimentary nicknames as "Blob-o," "Whaleman" and "Ohio Fats" from some indiscreet sports writers.

Deeply offended by such treatment and fearing he was becoming complacent, Nicklaus underwent a strict diet in the early 1970s, dropped to a lean 180 pounds and let his hair grow to the popular length at the time. The change was dramatic. Jack became not only the greatest golfer in the world but one of the most admired. In 1988, he was named Player of the Century.

An astute businessman, Nicklaus set up a corporation called "Golden Bear Inc." and has been involved in golf course design and construction.

In January 1999, at 59, Nicklaus had hip replacement surgery and missed the Master's for the first time in 40 years. Nicklaus was hobbling so badly in the summer of 1998 that he pulled out of the British Open, ending his streak at 146 majors.

Paavo Nurmi lights the Olympic torch to begin the 1952 Summer
Olympics in Helsinki. (AP/Wide World Photos)

PAAVO NURMI

THE FLYING FINN

It was a dank and drizzly late summer day in Helsinki, Finland, but the vast Olympic Stadium throbbed with fanfare and pageantry as thousands of spectators awaited the climactic lighting of the torch for the 1952 Olympic Games.

Old Avery Brundage, president of the International Olympic Committee, had made a terse speech. The flag of the five rings had been raised, and the smartly clad athletes of competing nations stood at soldier-like rest in the infield.

Suddenly, through a portal, emerged a figure carrying the flame overhead. He was a stringy little man with knobby knees and a bald head, but he ran with an easy grace that was immediately recognizable.

The huge crowd gasped at first, then broke into a roar, as Finland's greatest sports hero, Paavo Nurmi, circled the track, sped up six flights of steps and put the torch to the cauldron. The athletes broke ranks.

After a quarter of a century, the Flying Finn, 55, perhaps the greatest distance runner who ever lived, was thrilling Olympic galleries again. For the proud Finns, it was a page out of history, a dramatic exercise in nostalgia.

To many, it might have seemed as if the nude Nurmi statue which stood outside the stadium as a memorial, had suddenly become flesh and blood, because the dour, reclusive racing machine, with an antipathy for crowds and public attention, had virtually hidden himself from the world in the intervening years.

Nurmi dominated distance running as no one ever did, challenged perhaps only by Emil Zatopek's sweep of the 5,000 and 10,000 meters and the marathon in the Helsinki Games. But whereas the Czechoslovakian's feat was packaged into a single Olympiad, Nurmi's conquests were spread over most of two decades.

He competed in three Olympics—1920, 1924 and 1928—and accumulated 10 gold medals, unmatched in track-and-field annals—seven individual and three in team events. He might have added to his total had he not been barred from the 1932 Games at Los Angeles by the International Olympic Committee for alleged expense-account irregularities in a German meet three years earlier.

In those days, the IOC enforced a strict, if unrealistic, amateur code, as the great American Indian athlete, Jim Thorpe, learned to his dismay when stripped of his 1912 medals for playing semi-pro baseball.

Nurmi set world records for distances from 2,000 meters to 20,000 meters. His mark for six miles lasted 18 years; for 10 miles 17 years, and for the mile eight years. In

PAAVO NURMI WINNING A 5,000-METER RACE IN 1930. (AP/WIDE WORLD PHOTOS)

PAAVO NURMI, SECOND FROM LEFT, POSES WITH OTHER DISTANCE RUNNING
LEGENDS: GLENN CUNNINGHAM, JACK LOVELOCK, AND LOUIS BECCALI IN THIS
1936 PHOTO. (AP/WIDE WORLD PHOTOS)

the 1924 Olympics, he set world records in two events—the 1,500 and 5,000 meters—in the space of an hour, a test of endurance that astounded track observers.

Contemporaries recalled that he wasn't friendly or outgoing, but was sullen and grim, rarely laughing. They attributed his cold personality to his disadvantaged youth.

He was born in Abo, Finland, on June 13, 1897. His father died when he was 12. His mother had to work and he ran errands and later got a job in a foundry to help support his mother, brother and two sisters. He reportedly became a vegetarian, not by choice but because there was no meat.

At an early age, he came under the influence of a former Olympic champion, Hannes Kolehmainen. Young Nurmi ran as much as 50 miles a week, usually alone, sometimes racing against streetcars. Drawn into military service with the outbreak of World War I, he would get up before daybreak and run for miles along icy country roads, rushing back in time for reveille. Legend is that he could run 15 kilometers (9.3 miles) in less than an hour in full military gear.

He wasn't a classic runner. He had a huge chest for such a relatively small man and he sometimes ran with both arms dangling at his side or with a stopwatch in one hand close to his chest. He ran on his toes with long strides.

He competed in his first Olympics at Antwerp in 1920, finishing second to France's Joseph Guillemot in the 5,000 meters but winning a gold in the 10,000.

Nurmi's greatest glory was reserved for the 1924 Games in Paris, where the Finns charged organizers had scheduled the 1,500-meter and 5,000-meter events within an hour of each other to thwart their champion. The so-called "Peerless Paavo" was undeterred. He won both in world-record time.

He also won gold medals in the cross country and 3,000-meter team races. He was denied a chance to run in the 10,000 meters, but that was an honor that could not be denied him in 1928 at Amsterdam, when at age 31, he repeated his triumph of eight years earlier.

Nurmi, who had made a successful tour of the United States in 1925, was deeply disappointed when he was denied a shot at the marathon in the Los Angeles Games in 1932.

"If I did something wrong," he said of the IOC ban, "why did they wait three years to take action?"

Nurmi won his last race in the Finnish national championships in 1933, capturing the 1,500 meters, then drifted into retirement. His earnings from his American tour and from other amateur expenses enabled him to launch a business career. He became a contractor and opened a haberdashery in Helsinki, where one could get an autographed tie for a princely price.

He had a brief marriage in the 1930s but it ended in divorce. Friends said Paavo's wife disapproved of her husband's stretching the feet of their infant son to condition him to become a runner.

Actually, Nurmi made few friends. He wasn't very sociable. He refused interviews and public appearances. He died in 1973 at age 76, still seething, they say, over the Olympic Committee's action in barring him from the 1932 Games.

BOBBY ORR IN FRONT OF THE NET FOR THE BOSTON BRUINS IN 1975.
(AP/WIDE WORLD PHOTOS)

BOBBY ORR

THE GRACE OF A BALLET DANCER

Prior to the 1970 National Hockey League's Stanley Cup final, St. Louis coach Scotty Bowman was asked how he planned to stop Boston's Bobby Orr.

"We practiced covering Bobby Orr for six hours today, but the only trouble is, we don't have Bobby Orr to practice against," he said.

And, neither did any other NHL team, because Orr, the greatest defenseman of all time, was unique.

The Bruins swept Bowman's Blues, 4-0, in the best-of-seven series, with the 22-year-old Orr scoring an overtime goal in Game 4 for Boston's first NHL championship since 1941.

Two years later, the Bruins won the Stanley Cup again, this time in six games over the New York Rangers. Orr played the series on a swollen left knee, but as one Ranger said: "Orr is better on one and a half legs than most people on two."

Although he was reserved off the ice, on the ice Orr gave the big, bad Bruins color. He had the grace of a ballet dancer, a blond whirling dervish who electrified crowds with his rink-long dashes—unusual for a defenseman.

Orr was just 18 when he joined the Bruins from the Ontario Hockey Association for the 1966-67 season. He had 13 goals and 28 assists, won the NHL's Calder Trophy as Rookie of the Year and was named to the second All-Star team.

When the Rangers' Harry Howell was voted the Norris Trophy as the league's top defenseman the same year, he said he was glad "because I've got a feeling from now on it's going to belong to Bobby Orr."

Howell knew what he was talking about.

From 1968 through 1975, Orr won eight consecutive Norris trophies. In 1970, 1971 and '72, he won the Hart Trophy as the league's Most Valuable Player.

In 1969-70, Orr became the first defenseman to capture the NHL scoring title, with 33 goals and 87 assists. He won another scoring crown in 1974-75, with 46 goals and 89 assists. And his 102 assists in 1970-71 are still an NHL record for a defenseman—by 12.

Following the 1975-76 season, the Bruins and Orr—then playing on two bad knees—parted over money, and he signed with Chicago where knee injuries cut short his career at 30.

On the night of January 9, 1979, Orr's No. 4 was retired and raised to the rafters of Boston Garden.

"He was a hero," Boston Mayor Kevin White said. "He's a legend."

BOBBY ORR DIVES THROUGH THE AIR AFTER SCORING THE WINNING GOAL OF THE 1970 STANLEY CUP FINALS. (AP/WIDE WORLD PHOTOS)

Jesse Owens salutes after winning the long jump in the 1936 Summer Olympics in Berlin where he won three individual gold medals. (AP/Wide World Photos)

JESSE OWENS

STAR OF HITLER'S NAZI OLYMPICS

Jesse Owens, a black man in a white man's world, started life in an Alabama cabbage patch, endured the indignities of a Jim Crow society, yet went on to become America's most celebrated Olympian and most fluent defender of his country's democracy.

In a world torn by racial ugliness and hate, he maintained a tremendous calm and sobering influence. His cache of Olympic gold medals was outshone only by a spirit of understanding that never wavered.

"I live here. It's all I know and all I have," he once said when called upon to join his race's protests against social injustice. "My job is not to complain but to try to make things better."

Owens shattered Adolf Hitler's claim of a superior Aryan race by winning four gold medals in the 1936 Nazi Olympics in Berlin. No previous athlete had won more than three.

When Hitler abruptly gathered his swastika-adorned entourage and left the royal box before Owens could complete the final event of his unprecedented sweep—a gesture the foreign press interpreted as an outright snub—Owens refused to join the chorus of condemnation.

"It was all right with me," the American speedster said later. "I didn't go to Berlin to shake hands with him anyway."

Although treated shabbily by his countrymen after returning home a hero—forced to race against horses, lead a band and do one-night stands to keep his head above water, he never displayed resentment. He took to the road, made about 200 speeches a year—all of an uplift, patriotic nature—and caught the attention of the establishment.

He became a national public relations counselor for six firms. In 1972, he moved from his home in Chicago to a sprawling ranch in Paradise Valley, Arizona. The U.S. Olympic Committee gave him an important post as a director and liaison between the committee and the athletes. It was a move that saved the Olympic Committee unending embarrassment.

In the 1968 Olympics in Mexico City— a turbulent period in American life with Martin Luther King heading up marches in Alabama, blacks destroying property in places such as San Francisco, Detroit and Cleveland and the nation sitting on a powder keg—it remained for Jesse Owens to cool the fevers of black athletes.

These black athletes forming the bulk of the U.S. team, were on the verge of a wholesale walkout after sprinters Tommie Smith and John Carlos were suspended for staging a black fist salute on the victory stand. The gesture, which would have wrecked the American effort, was avoided when Owens thrust himself into the picture. The athletes had such high regard for

JESSE OWENS IN THE PRELIMINARIES OF THE 200-METER EVENT IN THE 1936 OLYMPICS. (AP/WIDE WORLD PHOTOS)

Jesse Owens takes the baton from his teammate on his way to winning the 4 x 100-yard relay in a meet against Great Britain in 1936. (AP/Wide World Photos)

JESSE OWENS IN THE AIR IN THE BROAD JUMP IN THE 1936 SUMMER OLYMPICS IN BERLIN. (AP/WIDE WORLD PHOTOS)

Owens that they refused to go against his wishes.

"I told Tommie and John that I could understand their actions," Owens explained. "I told them they should fight their battle on the battlefield. This was the wrong one."

Owens grew up in a small cotton-growing community in Oakville, Alabama, one of nine children of a sharecropper. His memories weren't pleasant ones.

"There were no towns to go to," he recalled. "The nearest cotton gin was 10 miles away. I learned to read and write in a one-room school where I could go only when it wasn't cotton-picking time. I was picking cotton when I was seven years old. My quota was 100 pounds a day. We caught hell, and at the end of the year we still owed the boss money. We had to buy everything at the company store."

His father packed up the family and moved to Cleveland when Jesse was nine. Jesse went to school at Bolton School in Lakewood, Ohio, which had other famous alumni in Bob Hope and the great quarterback Benny Friedman. The youngster showed a fierce dedication to learn as well as to hone his physical attributes.

"I could run," he said, "run very fast. After all, in Alabama, all we kids had to do was run, so we ran." He earned a scholarship to Ohio State University.

"On campus, there was no segregation," Owens recalled. "But on campus there was no good restaurant or place I could go with friends. I got used to riding the back of the bus."

On the cinder track, however, everybody was equal but the running wizard from Alabama's cotton fields was more equal than the rest.

Although he failed to make the Olympic team in 1932, Owens was not to be denied after a spectacular one-man show in a Big Ten Conference track-and-field meet at the University of Michigan in Ann Arbor on a sultry afternoon May 25, 1935. In the space of less than an hour, he tied the world record in the 100-yard dash and shattered world marks in the long jump, 220-yard dash and 220-low hurdles.

First the runner streaked to the 100-yard dash victory in 9.4 seconds, matching Frank Wykoff's world mark. Ten minutes later, he soared 26 feet, 8 1/4 inches in the long jump. Almost immediately afterward, he won the 220-yard dash in 20.3 seconds. He had a 26-minute rest before running the 220 low hurdles in 22.6 seconds.

"I had hurt my back two weeks before in a fall at the fraternity house," Owens recalled. "Before the warmup, I couldn't even jog because my back was so stiff. I wondered if I would be able to compete at all."

In the Olympics Jesse won the 200-meter sprint in 20.7 seconds, breaking a 21-second barrier that had lasted 36 years and setting a record that stood for 20 years. He won the long jump with 26 feet, 5 3/8 inches, a foot farther than anyone had leaped in the Olympics before. The mark stood for 24 years. Owens also won the 100-meter dash and led the 400-meter relay, both in world-record times.

As his long day neared an end in Berlin's Olympic Stadium, Jesse noted that Hitler, who had personally honored German winners, began making his exit.

"The Storm Troopers were standing shoulder to shoulder like an iron fence, and then came the roar from 100,000 throats in that stiff-armed salute, 'Heil, Hitler!' 'Heil, Hitler!'" Owens said. "It was frightening, but I was too engrossed in what I had to do. I never once felt I was insulted."

Owens died of cancer at the age of 66 on March 31, 1980, but his feats, carved on the concrete wall of the Berlin Stadium, will stand for a long time to come.

In his honor, *USA Track and Field* honors its male and female athletes of the year with the Jesse Owens Award.

ARNOLD PALMER DURING A PRACTICE ROUND BEFORE THE 1986 MASTERS AT AUGUSTA NATIONAL. (AP/WIDE WORLD PHOTOS)

ARNOLD PALMER

CHARISMATIC LEADER OF "ARNIE'S ARMY"

Arnold Palmer won only one U.S. Open and failed to capture another top prize of his trade, the PGA Championship, yet no other individual had greater impact on the fabulous growth of golf.

In the 1950s and early 1960s, when this one-time rather snobbish sport spilled out of the fashionable country clubs and into the parlors of everyday society, it was Palmer, the charismatic, belt-tugging, fast-walking charger who greased the track for the transition.

Network television was just burgeoning into a giant, hungry monster that had to be fed constantly to keep the cash registers clanging. The golf tour was seen as an appealing morsel for the sports fan. The Saturday and Sunday afternoon channels became choked with live and taped golf competitions, replacing the usual fare of cowboys and Indians. The whole family watched.

It was a situation that called for a Ruthian figure, a heroic symbol such as major league baseball found in the great Babe Ruth after the credibility of the sport had been threatened by the Black Sox Scandal of 1919.

Palmer was it—the catalyst of his time. He burst upon the scene as a natural hero—the rugged, strong-faced son of a greenskeeper from the small steel town of Latrobe, Pennsylvania, about 30 miles from Pittsburgh. A sturdy 165 pounds, he was built like a middleweight fighter, with powerful, tapering shoulders, hands like ham hocks and arms like pistons.

He had a boyish, nut-brown face that ran the gamut of changing expressions. While concentrating, his brow became furrowed and his jaw tightened.

His mannerisms titillated the galleries and enthralled housewives and the teenage set who formed the major segment of what became familiarly known as "Arnie's Army."

In the midst of a tense match, he often would stop and, his nose wrinkling, stare skyward at a passing airplane. When he rolled in a long birdie putt, his face would break into a broad grin.

He carried on a running conversation with the gallery. When he was on one of his characteristic rolls, he was inclined to increase his walking pace as if eager to step in for the kill.

"With this man, it's let it go or blow it, all or nothing," said Palmer's longtime caddie at the Masters, Nathaniel "Iron Man" Avery. "He don't know what it is to play safe. When he makes one of his charges, he just tugs at his glove, jerks on his trousers and starts walking fast and tells me, 'The game is on.'"

The veteran Gene Sarazen said Arnie was most dangerous when he appeared on the ropes, "ready to be counted out."

ARNOLD PALMER RIPS OFF HIS HAT AFTER WINNING HIS ONLY U.S. OPEN TITLE IN 1960. (AP/WIDE WORLD PHOTOS)

ARNOLD PALMER
WATCHES HIS PUTT.
(AP/WIDE WORLD
PHOTOS)

ARNOLD PALMER WAVES TO HIS FANS AS HE CROSSES THE SWILKEN BRIDGE ON THE OLD COURSE AT ST. ANDREWS DURING HIS FINAL APPEARANCE IN THE BRITISH OPEN IN 1995. (AP/WIDE WORLD PHOTOS)

"He is fantastic," said contemporary Jimmy Demaret. "He just seems to will the ball into the hole."

During Palmer's heyday, the period between 1956 and 1964 when he won four Masters crowns, Arnie's Army was co-ed with no age limitations. Young ladies wore sweaters with "Arnie baby" crocheted across the chest. Other fans flaunted signs which said, "I am a member of Arnie's Army." The Army had its own air corps. Often, when Arnie was on the course, small, private planes would fly overhead, trailing streamers that read, "Go, Arnie, Go!"

Such flagrant displays of partisanship were often distracting to Palmer's rivals and an embarrassment to Palmer himself. Often galleries would break and start running to the next tee after Arnie holed out even though his playing partners were still on the green with putts remaining.

Although he won only one U.S. Open, Palmer tied for the title on three other occasions, only to lose in playoffs, and was also runner-up a fourth time. Meanwhile, he was racking up a total of 61 tour victories, including his four Masters; capturing consecutive British Open crowns in 1961 and 1962 and making frustrating runs at the PGA, which mysteriously escaped him, although he finished second three times. He later went on to win 10 PGA Senior Tour events.

Arnie was given his first set of clubs by his father, Milfred "Deac" Palmer, when he was four, and began caddying and working in the caddie shop of the nine-hole Latrobe course when he was 11. He shot a 71 and won a tournament when he was in the seventh grade. He attended Wake Forest University, spent three years in the Coast Guard and began playing golf regularly while working as a manufacturer's agent in Cleveland.

He won the National Amateur in 1954, and shortly afterward, while playing in an amateur tournament in Pennsylvania, met Winnie Walzer, to whom he proposed a week later. The two planned to spend their honeymoon in England while Arnie played with the U.S. Walker Cup team. Instead, Arnie and Winnie decided to hit the pro tour. With $600 borrowed from Palmer's dad, the two set out in a second-hand house trailer.

After the PGA's six-month probationary period, Palmer began collecting prize money almost immediately. He won his first tournament in 1955, two in 1956, four in 1957, virtually doubling his prize money each year. He was the leading money winner in 1958 with $42,608 after capturing his first Masters.

He became the game's first millionaire.

His greatest year was 1960, when he won the Masters, rallied with a stunning 65 to capture his only U.S. Open at Denver, then went to ancient St. Andrews, where he had the British Open virtually clinched before a rainstorm hit, allowing Australian Kel Nagle to edge ahead by a stroke. In January of 1997, Palmer underwent prostate cancer surgery, but made a full recovery and continued to play on the PGA Senior Tour.

Palmer was golf's first conglomerate. He set up his own company, which manufactured golf clubs, balls, shirts, slacks, shoes and gloves. He headed 11 clothing companies with branches in Australia, Japan and Europe. He was the largest stockholder in a chain of putting courses. He owned a printing company, insurance agency, investment firm and several golf courses.

In 1999, the American Society of Golf Architects presented him with the Donald Ross Award for his contributions to golf course design. Palmer's company has designed more than 200 courses around the world.

217

WALTER PAYTON DURING HIS FINAL REGULAR-SEASON HOME GAME FOR
THE CHICAGO BEARS IN 1987. (AP/WIDE WORLD PHOTOS)

WALTER PAYTON

A STANDOUT, DURABLE RECORD BREAKER

Walter Payton is certainly one for the books.

In his college days at Jackson State, when he ran, kicked field goals and extra points and passed, Payton broke into the NCAA record books with 66 touchdowns and 464 career points.

As a professional with the Chicago Bears from 1975-87, he continued to break records by the yard. In 1984, his 10th year in the National Football League, Payton surpassed Jim Brown's all-time rushing record of 12,312 yards finishing his career with 16,726. And in 1986, he became the first player in NFL history to amass 20,000 all-purpose yards.

En route to those magnificent statistical achievements, Payton generally became recognized as the game's quintessential halfback: He could run or receive with equal ability, and even throw the ball when the situation demanded.

Considering Payton's style as a punishing runner, and the pounding he took from opposing players, his longevity alone was remarkable.

"It's amazing," said former Bears' running great Gale Sayers, whose career was cut short by a knee injury. "It's as if the man upstairs said, 'Walter, I'm going to make you a football player. And for as long as you want to play, you can play.'"

Payton's durability was almost as much of a story as his statistical accomplishments. In his 13-year Hall of Fame career, he missed only one game, and that was in his rookie season, 1975.

"He follows the old gladiator code," Brown said.

Before the 1983 season, Payton had surgery on both knees, yet toughed it out for the entire year. Despite damaged knees, he rushed for 1,421 yards.

"He ran stiff-legged all year," Bears' coach Mike Ditka recalled, "and he ran for more than 1,400 yards. The doctors wondered how he did it on those knees."

Whether plunging through a hole in the line, cutting outside or squirming forward with tacklers draped all over him, Payton may well have been the hardest back to bring down in the NFL.

"I don't know if there's a way to stop him," said former Packers star Bart Starr. "I haven't seen anyone in the league do a good job of it. You just try to contain him. You don't reach and grab and arm-tackle him."

Payton also holds the NFL record for most rushing yards in a game, 275, against the Minnesota Vikings on December 29, 1977, and at one point won five straight National

WALTER PAYTON LOOKS FOR AN OPENING AGAINST THE NEW ORLEANS SAINTS IN 1984. (AP/WIDE WORLD PHOTOS)

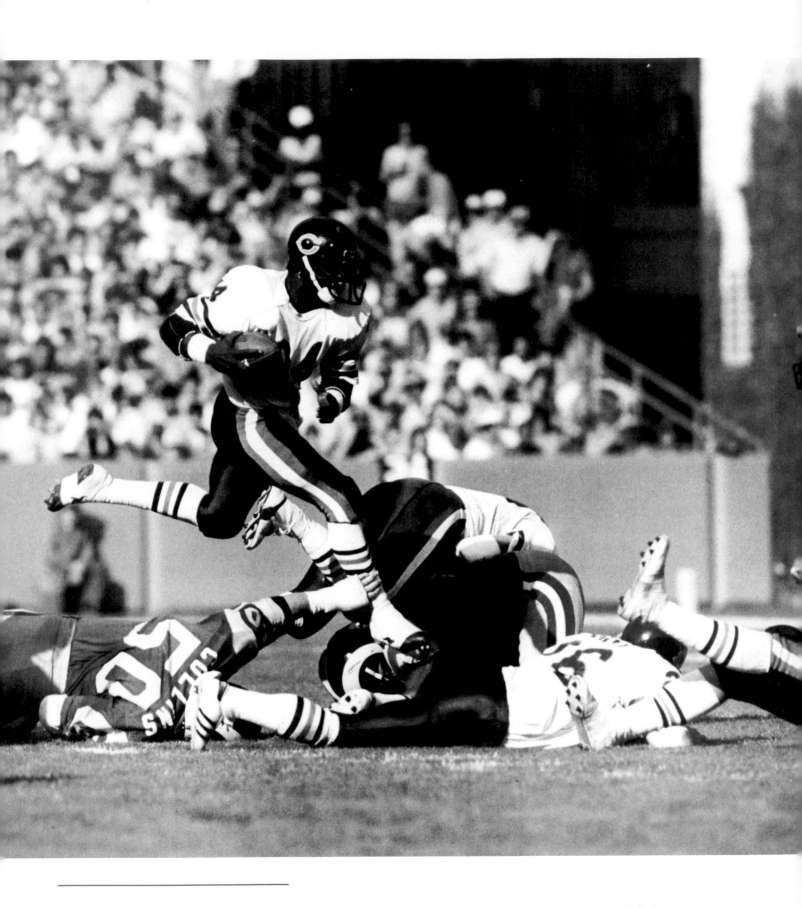

WALTER PAYTON LEAPS OVER THE LOS ANGELES RAMS IN THIS 1984
REGULAR-SEASON GAME. (AP/WIDE WORLD PHOTOS)

WALTER PAYTON CARRIES THE BALL UPFIELD AT SOLDIER
FIELD DURING HIS SUPER BOWL-WINNING SEASON IN
1985. (AP/WIDE WORLD PHOTOS)

Conference rushing titles, including the 1977 season when he gained 1,852 yards. At that point, Payton was the best running back in football, and he later was voted to the NFL's 75th Anniversary All-Time Team in 1994.

A self-effacing player who continually gave credit to the offensive line for his exploits, Payton not only was a good runner, but a good blocker. In short, Payton played bigger and stronger than he looks. He is actually 5-foot-10 1/2 and about 200 pounds.

On the field, Payton inflicted as much punishment as he received from tacklers.

"If you want to play a long time," Payton said, "you have to protect yourself. You can't always keep accepting the blows."

Having watched Payton reintroduce the wicked straight-arm to a new generation of safeties and cornerbacks, one teammate observed. "It's like a recoilless rifle. There are a number of defensive backs in the league with fewer neck vertebrae because of it."

Payton first attracted the attention of the pros with his accomplishments at Jackson State, where he earned the nickname "Sweetness," for his sweet moves on the football field.

Looking for a centerpiece in their efforts to rebuild, the Bears picked Payton in the first round of the 1975 draft, the fourth player chosen overall.

Ten years later, he led them to their first, and only, Super Bowl title.

Carrying him along, as much as anything, was a boyish enthusiasm for the game that he never lost. After tackles, Payton hopped up and rushed back to the huddle. During timeouts, he led the stadium in cheers.

"He's always snapping towels and lighting cherry bombs," Bob Avellini, a former Bears' quarterback once said. "In a meeting when everybody's half asleep, he'll give out an inhuman scream just for the heck of it."

Someone suggested that Payton was football's answer to Pete Rose and he liked the analogy.

"I'd like to be remembered like that, somebody who stands for hard work and total effort," Payton said.

After football, Payton dabbled in numerous business ventures and auto racing. He owns a pub and his own hall of fame museum and is a minority owner of a power equipment firm and an IndyCar team.

He's sat on the Bears' board of directors since 1997.

In February of 1999, Payton was being treated for a rare liver disease and needed a transplant.

PELE MOVES THE BALL UP THE FIELD DURING THE 1977 NORTH AMERICAN
SOCCER LEAGUE CHAMPIONSHIP GAME AS HIS NEW YORK COSMOS DEFEATED
SEATTLE 2-1 TO WIN THE CHAMPIONSHIP. (AP/WIDE WORLD PHOTOS)

PELE

THE WORLD'S MOST FAMOUS ATHLETE

To the world he was simply "Pele." Single names always have been sufficient to connote greatness. Caesar. Michelangelo. Garbo. In his field, there was none greater than Edson Arantes do Nascimento, the poor kid from a remote Brazilian village who became the most celebrated figure in the world's most popular sport—the sport known as football or "futbol," but called soccer in America.

If a universal poll were taken to determine the greatest athlete of the century, the honor almost certainly would fall on the slender shoulders of the leaping, dashing, ball-kicking wizard known as Pele, "The Black Pearl."

Relatively slight at 5 feet, 8 inches and 160 pounds, he was a veritable Houdini on the field—gliding along the green pitch, feinting, dribbling, legs moving like a marionette, as if controlled by invisible strings, and smashing the ball into the net with bow-and-arrow accuracy.

He was lionized by fans and world leaders.

It's said that when he visited Biafra, a civil war there was suspended for two days. In Spain, they cancelled bullfights rather than compete with Pele's appearance on television.

Pele learned to love soccer from watching his father, who played on a town team in their native Brazil. He quit school when he was 10 and got his big soccer break at 15 when a friend of his dad gave him the chance to play with the city team in Santos.

He was hired on a trial basis for $75 a month, a steal of a deal. A year later, he was starting and starring.

He led Santos to league championships in his first six seasons and averaged a goal a game over his 1,000-plus-game career with the team.

He helped Brazil win World Cup championships in 1958, 1962 and 1970.

Pele scored his 1,000th goal on November 19, 1969, in Rio de Janeiro's National Stadium, an event given precedence in many newspapers over the lunar landing of Apollo 12.

Pele made what was hailed as his final international appearance in 1971. But four years later, he signed a $4.7 million contract with Warner Communications to play three years and do promotional work for the New York Cosmos of the North American Soccer League.

"You can tell the world," Pele said, "soccer has finally come to America."

PELE DRIBBLES THE BALL DURING AN EXHIBITION GAME IN LOS ANGELES IN 1976. (AP/WIDE WORLD PHOTOS)

PELE

WILLIE PEP IN AN
UNDATED PUBLIC-
ITY PHOTO.
(AP/WIDE WORLD
PHOTOS)

WILLIE PEP

"THE GREATEST BOXER I EVER SAW"

Willie Pep, perhaps the most brilliant featherweight champion in ring history, could beat anybody in the world his weight, with two exceptions: a tall, bony jaw-bender named Sandy Saddler and, sadly, a guy named Willie Pep.

Pep fought Saddler four times for the 126-pound crown and lost three of them, each by a knockout. He outpointed Sandy once in a fight that rattled the rafters at the old Madison Square Garden and is still listed high in the annals of boxing for its 15 rounds of legal mayhem. That fight, on February 11, 1949, was probably Pep's peak as a boxer.

Willie was called his own worst enemy and worked at it. He made a lot of money but spent even more. His financial mistakes forced him to keep fighting long after he should have quit the ring. At the time of his last pro bout, a losing six-rounder to somebody named Calvin Woodland in 1966, Pep was 43.

Before he met Saddler, Pep lost only one bout in a string of 136. He began his career with 62 victories, lost an over-the-weight fight to Sammy Angott, a two-time lightweight champ, and then ran off 73 straight wins.

Born Guglielmo Papoleo in September 1942, in Middletown, Connecticut, he gravitated to the ring at an early age and was a star amateur in the late 1930s. Willie turned pro in 1940, changing his name to the Americanized version.

Angelo Dundee, who later trained Muhammad Ali, called Pep the greatest boxer he ever saw. Not trained. Saw. Pep, who won the featherweight title at age 20, summed up his talents this way: "I was strictly a boxer but, boy, could I box. When I got hit, I was sometimes hurt. But I won a lot more fights than I lost. And I fought a lot of times, once or twice a month, for a number of years."

He first took on Sadler in 1946 and lost his title on a four-round knockout. He won it back the next year but took a beating in the process and was never the same fighter. He lost to Saddler on an eight-round K.O. in 1950 and a nine-round K.O. in 1951.

He fought an unnerving 241 bouts.

"I guess everybody would like to know what happened to all the big money I made," he said, looking back on his career. "So would I. I have so much scar tissue I look as though I'm wearing blinders. But boxing was my business. And I think I was pretty good at it."

WILLIE PEP CONNECTS WITH A JAB IN A FEATHERWEIGHT BOUT WITH CHALKY WRIGHT. (AP/WIDE WORLD PHOTOS)

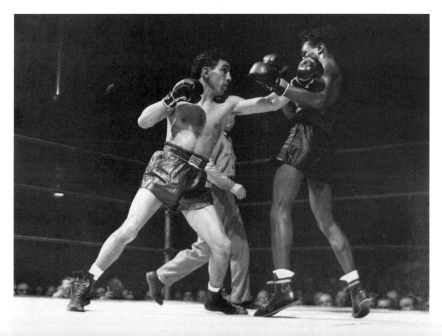

RICHARD PETTY GETS THE CHECKERED FLAG AS THE WINNER OF THE 1971 DAYTONA 500, HIS 120TH CAREER VICTORY. (AP/WIDE WORLD PHOTOS)

RICHARD PETTY

STOCK CAR RACING'S BEST

One can usually tell what part of the racetrack Richard Petty is in. Just look for the swarm that constantly surrounds him.

The "King" of NASCAR stock car racing for more than a quarter of a century holds court most of the time when he is at his place of business.

He isn't hard to spot. He usually is wearing a feathered cowboy hat, sunglasses and snakeskin cowboy boots, and smoking a long, thin cigar.

If he isn't signing autographs and talking to fans, Petty is telling stories to the media or talking with other racing people about the sport he has loved since he began helping his father, Lee, in the formative days of NASCAR.

The rest of the time, the tall, slim racing veteran helps work on the stock car he once drove and now owns.

Lee Petty was a NASCAR champion and winner of 54 races, but his eldest son has far surpassed not only him, but everyone else in the sport.

The native of Level Cross, North Carolina, won seven championships, seven Daytona 500s and, most amazing, a total of 200 races, almost double the amount accumulated by the runner-up—David Pearson. Only Dale Earnhardt has as many Winston Cup titles as "the King."

"I've had some good luck during my career," Richard said. "I had the good fortune to grow up with the sport and have my daddy to watch and learn from. Then I raced with some of the greats and they taught me a lot. And maybe I taught them a few things, too."

Petty, who was crew chief for his father for several years—one of the youngest ever—finally got behind the wheel of a NASCAR stock car in 1959. But he didn't win for the first time until 1960.

"After I drove a few races, I began to wonder if I wouldn't be better off taking care of Daddy's cars," Petty said. "I found out real quick how much I didn't know about driving a race car, even after watching Daddy for so long. But I found out quickly that I enjoyed it. And I learned from just about everybody."

He learned well enough that in 1960, at 22, he won his first three races. It could have been four.

RICHARD PETTY GIVES HIS PIT CREW A RIDE DOWN PIT ROAD AFTER PETTY WON THE FIRECRACKER 400 AT THE DAYTONA SPEEDWAY IN 1977. (AP/WIDE WORLD PHOTOS)

RICHARD PETTY FLASHES THE A-OKAY SIGN IN 1985 BFORE THE DAYTONA 500, A RACE HE WON SEVEN TIMES. (AP/WIDE WORLD PHOTOS)

RICHARD PETTY, RIGHT, LOOKS INTO AN EMPTY ENGINE WELL OF A
NEW RACE CAR WITH HIS FATHER LEE, CENTER, AND BROTHER
MAURICE, LEFT, IN THIS 1964 PHOTO.(AP/WIDE WORLD PHOTOS)

Early that season, still winless and admittedly beginning to wonder if he ever would win, Petty got his car "hooked
up" at the old Lakewood Speedway in Atlanta, one of the many dirt tracks of that era that no longer exist.

"I was just flying that day," he recalled. "All of a sudden, I was running out front. Funny thing, with all the traffic and
the dust, it didn't seem a lot different than being behind, but I knew the difference and I liked it.

"When I got the checkered (flag), I didn't know what to think. It was a great feeling. Then, just when they were
going to hand me the trophy, somebody came up and said, 'There's a protest.' Turned out that Daddy, who was second,
protested that I cut across the grass in one turn, which everybody did.

"They (NASCAR) decided for him, and Daddy got the win and the trophy. People usually tell that story to show
how competitive our family is. But, there was a lot better reason.

"I was disappointed, but Daddy explained it to me later. NASCAR wanted to get some of the guys to buy new cars
and not keep running the same old ones year after year. They paid more for winning in a new car. Daddy was in a new car
and I was driving our old one, so by him winning, we got more money for first place, and I still got second-place money.

"Besides, Daddy said I'd probably win some more races later."

By 1967, Lee was retired, and Richard, with brother Maurice as his crew chief and first cousin Dale Inman as the
team manager, was the dominant figure in the new and growing sport.

Petty won 27 races that year, a single-season record that is unlikely ever to be challenged, much less broken. In fact,
he finished in the top ten 39 times in 48 starts that season.

He won 21 in 1971, and in 1973, after the schedule had been shortened to about 30 races a year, he set the modern
standard of 13 victories in 30 starts.

"It's always been hard to win," Petty said. "But now, there's so much good equipment and so many good teams that
it's tough to dominate like we did in '67."

His landmark 200th victory came on July 4, 1984, in the Firecracker 400 at Daytona Beach, Florida. Among the
more than 100,000 spectators was President Ronald Reagan.

For Petty, who had just turned 46, it was a gratifying and fulfilling moment.

"Each time you win a race, you start thinking about the next one—if you'll get it, when you'll get it. The 200th,
though, was so special that I thought about it and enjoyed it for a while."

It turned out to be his last trip to Victory Lane. With $7,755,409 in career earnings, Petty retired in 1992 to watch his son
Kyle race and to concentrate on his owner duties.

DESPITE A HAND IN HIS FACE, JERRY RICE STILL MADE THIS CATCH IN 1998. (AP/WIDE WORLD PHOTOS)

JERRY RICE MAKES A CATCH BEFORE MAKING HIS COMEBACK FROM INJURY IN 1997. (AP/WIDE WORLD PHOTOS)

JERRY RICE

EXTRAORDINARY RECEIVER

Jerry Rice is the greatest wide receiver ever to play the game and arguably the greatest player in the history of the NFL.

In 14 NFL seasons he shattered almost every receiving record there is including records for touchdowns (164 entering the 1999 season), receiving yards (17,612), receptions (1139) and 100-yard games (64).

As a collegian, he set 18 NCAA Division II records during his four year career at Mississippi Valley State. He had more than 100 receptions in both his junior and senior seasons and exceeded 1,000 yards receiving during three consecutive years. In 1984, his senior year, he recorded 1,845 yards and scored 28 TDs as a senior in 1984.

The San Francisco 49ers maneuvered their way into position to take Rice as the 16th pick overall in the 1985 NFL Draft. He was perfect for Bill Walsh's West Coast offense. Rice could both go deep and take a short pass and make it into big play. Rice had an explosiveness that, combined with superb moves, got him wide open.

"Jerry is so much stronger and has so much more stamina than anyone else who has played at that position," said Walsh.

"They'll be tough records to ever duplicate because the game has changed so much and there are so many substitutions. It is tough for a single player to do as much as he used to."

Steve Young described Rice's accomplishments as both overwhelming and workmanlike. "The thing is, if he weren't so talented, you'd all be calling him a blue-collar guy because he works so hard at it," Young said.

"We all know what a great football player he is," ex-coach George Seifert said of Rice. "He's a great athlete, but he has all these intangibles; his work ethic and how he thrives on the competition, how much he wants to play. So it's fun to see somebody that works so hard have the success. A lot of times, guys work hard and they don't ever, because of circumstance, quite get there. Here's a man that's worked very hard and to see him succeed … is something very meaningful."

He also dominated in the Super Bowl. He was MVP in the 1989 Super Bowl, when he had 11 catches for 215 yards and a touchdown in the 49ers' 20-16 victory over Cincinnati. In 1990, he had seven catches for 148 yards and three TDs in a 55-10 victory over Denver.

Knee injuries hampered Rice during the 1997 and '98 seasons, but he returned healthy in 1999.

Young said Rice has set such high standards that it's hard to live up to them while he's playing hurt.

"What do I tell him?" San Francisco receivers coach Larry Kirksey once said.

"All I tell him is, just make sure you show up."

JERRY RICE BRINGS IN A PASS IN FRONT OF DEION SANDERS DURING THE 1993 REGULAR SEASON. (AP/WIDE WORLD PHOTOS)

MAURICE RICHARD IN ACTION IN 1954. (AP/WIDE WORLD PHOTOS)

MAURICE RICHARD

AND THE ROCKET'S RED GLARE

One of the many axioms in hockey for nearly 30 years was that there was no place on the ice for the unorthodox. Except, perhaps, in the net.

To place a left-handed shooter on right wing was as preposterous an idea in the 1940s as it was for a goaltender to wear a mask, until "The Rocket" launched himself into the Montreal Canadiens' lineup and toward the Hall of Fame.

Maurice Richard earned that nickname early in his career. He was "The Rocket" for many reasons—his skating speed, his ability to explode from a standing start; his strength and relentlessness. When Richard moved in on a target, usually the puck and then the enemy goal, there was no stopping him.

"'The Rocket' was the perfect description for Maurice," said Toe Blake, a teammate of Richard's and later his coach with the Canadiens. "When he would take off, nothing got in his way that could stop him."

"What I remember most about Rocket was his eyes," recalled goalie Glenn Hall. "When he came flying toward you with the puck on his stick, his eyes were all lit up, flashing and gleaming like a pinball machine. It was terrifying."

Just the thought of taking on Richard had to be terrifying for opponents. His intensity was matched by an explosive temper that often got him into trouble. He always fought back and sometimes was the instigator, although Richard usually felt he was the victim.

That fiery temperament spurred Richard to previously unattained heights. While players such as Bobby Hull, Phil Esposito, Mike Bossy and Wayne Gretzky made 50-goal seasons commonplace, Richard was the first player to reach the half-century figure. When he did it in 1944-45, it was in a 50-game season compared to 80 nowadays.

Richard scored 544 goals in his 18-year career. He did so without the benefit of a curved stick blade or a ripping slapshot. He did it playing the off wing.

And he did it in the pressurized atmosphere of Montreal, where hockey is a religion.

"We were supposed to win all of the time," he said. "When we did not win, it was a tragedy to many fans. They did not recognize how hard we tried, that we were beaten by better teams or that we maybe had injuries. All they knew was win, win, win."

Led by Richard, the Canadiens did win. Eight times, Richard was on a Cup winner, including his final five seasons, 1956 through 1960.

He also led the NHL in goals five times. His best season was 1954-55 when he scored 50 and 50.

"There were games when I felt everything I shot would go in," he said. "On some nights, if I touched the puck, I knew I would score."

As a meaure of his achievements, he made the Hall of Fame only nine months after his retirement. The usual waiting period is three years.

MAURICE RICHARD UNVEILS THE NEW NHL SCORING TROPHY NAMED IN HIS HONOR IN 1999. (AP/WIDE WORLD PHOTOS)

CINCINNATI'S BIG "O" LAYS IT IN. (AP/WIDE WORLD PHOTOS)

OSCAR ROBERTSON

"HE COULD BEAT YOU BY HIMSELF"

In today's basketball parlance, achieving a "triple-double" has become the epitome of all-around prowess.

Only a handful of players each season are able to accomplish the feat of reaching double figures in points, rebounds and assists in one game. Earvin "Magic" Johnson of the Los Angeles Lakers had a total of 72 "triple-doubles" in his first seven years in the NBA, an average of 10 a season, to easily become the best at putting together an outstanding all-around game.

But if "triple-double" figures had been kept during the 1960s, there was no doubt that Oscar Robertson would be the league's all-time leader.

Robertson, a legend as a high school player in Indianapolis and a college star at Cincinnati, arrived in the NBA in 1960 and became one of its greatest guards.

He was named to the all-time All-NBA team in a poll of sports editors of the nation's 100 largest newspapers, receiving more votes than any player except Wilt Chamberlain. In 1996, he was voted one of the NBA's 50 Greatest Players of All Time, a no-brainer.

In Robertson's first four seasons with the NBA's Cincinnati Royals, he averaged 30.2 points, 10.7 rebounds and 10.4 assists—"triple-double" figures—in 309 games.

The 6-foot-4 Robertson, known as "The Big O," went on to average 25 points, 9.5 assists and 7.5 rebounds during his 14-year NBA career, which included 12 All-Star appearances (he was the all-time leading scorer in All-Star games). He also was the NBA's Most Valuable Player in 1964 and led the league in assists six times.

"There is nothing he can't do," former Boston Celtics coach and general manager Red Auerbach said of Robertson. "No one comes close to him or has the ability to break open a game like Oscar. He's so great he scares me. He can beat you all by himself and usually does."

Robertson was his harshest critic.

"All passes aren't good passes just because the ball reaches the teammate you intend it for," he said. "Playmaking is getting the ball to the man so he is in a position to take his best shot."

For all his impressive statistics, an NBA championship eluded Robertson for 10 years with the Royals. Then he was traded to the Milwaukee Bucks in 1970 and joined with Kareem Abdul-Jabbar, then known as Lew Alcindor, to win an NBA title in 1971.

Robertson also was active in the fledgling NBA players union, serving as its president for one term. During his presidency,

OSCAR ROBERTSON LOOKS TO THE BASKET DURING HIS DAYS WITH THE CINCINNATI ROYALS IN 1961. (AP/WIDE WORLD PHOTOS)

Oscar Robertson wears a protective mask to protect a cut lip and still scores on the Philadelphia 76ers in this 1967 game. (AP/Wide World Photos)

OSCAR ROBERTSON SET ANOTHER COLLEGIATE RECORD WITH THIS FIELD GOAL, HIS **957**TH, AGAINST WICHITA IN 1960. (AP/WIDE WORLD PHOTOS)

he filed a suit in 1970 challenging the reserve clause that tied players to their teams. The suit led to the Robertson settlement in 1976 that refined college draft rules and brought about free agency.

As NBA salaries escalated during the 1990s, Robertson was amazed at the effect his suit had on the sport.

"I have to admit, the situation's gotten out of hand," Robertson said. "Why should an owner pay a player $1 million when he's only worth $100,000? Then the fans are misled. They get down on a player because they expect him to play like a million dollars, and he's not worth it."

But Robertson said he didn't begrudge today's athletes their large salaries.

"Athletes make big money, but so do movie stars and the presidents of auto companies," he said. "Don't direct your animosity at athletes; look at society as a whole. The salary structure has risen in pro basketball because the owners are impatient, and they're willing to pay whatever it costs to win."

Robertson, who made $33,333 in his rookie season, said players during his day were taken advantage of by NBA owners. "There were a lot of things the owners did that weren't considered All-American," he said. "A lot of guys were blackballed. If owners didn't like the way you dressed, the car you drove—anything—they could keep you from playing. Believe me, it happened."

He said that "owners had things their way for a long time, but now the players want their share of the money. The owners say 'Be patient,' but the players aren't settling for that anymore."

For a time, Robertson often was mentioned when coaching vacancies came up, but his sometimes rebellious nature probably turned off NBA owners.

"If I'm going to coach, I would want to run the whole show," Robertson said. "I'd want to control draft choices, trades, all of that. It only seems fair, since good players make the coach.

"If it's a situation I could live with and the money was right, I'd be interested. If I got the right offer, I would coach. But New York, for example, would be tough. In New York, I wouldn't have the time I'd need to build a winner.

"Owners want a winner. When they don't get it, they tend to blame the coach."

JACKIE ROBINSON BEORE SPRING TRAINING IN 1956. IT WOULD BE ROBINSON'S
TENTH AND FINAL YEAR WITH THE DODGERS. (AP/WIDE WORLD PHOTOS)

JACKIE ROBINSON

BREAKER OF THE COLOR LINE

During the 1972 World Series between the Cincinnati Reds and Oakland A's, Jackie Robinson, scheduled to throw out the first ball, was approached by a youngster as he waited in the catacombs of Cincinnati's Riverfront Stadium.

"Will you please give me your autograph?," the boy asked timidly, offering a clean baseball.

The sturdily built black man, with gray flecks creeping from his thick, close-cropped dark hair, took the ball, stared at it a few moments and replied apologetically: "Son, I don't know—I can hardly see the ball," He laboriously scrawled his name and limped away.

Two weeks later—stricken with diabetes, a heart condition and failing sight—one of the true all-time giants of baseball was dead at the age of 53.

Dead yet imperishable, he left an imprint on the game and on society that will prevail long after many greater deeds performed on the diamond are forgotten. He played a major part in restoring a nation's conscience. He broke the color line.

Jackie Robinson's plaque in the Hall of Fame in Cooperstown, New York, unveiled in 1962, told of no majestic feats to compare with the multiple home runs of Babe Ruth and Hank Aaron, the .406 batting average of Ted Williams or the 100-plus base thefts of Maury Wills or Lou Brock. He made his contributions on the field—a fine athlete, tough, competitive, productive—but he will be most remembered for the character he showed under extreme duress.

Jackie's Hall of Fame inscription is terse, cold and reveals only a small fraction of the man and his life. It reads:

"Jack Roosevelt Robinson; Brooklyn, N.L. 1947 to 1956. Leading NL batter in 1949. Holds fielding mark for second basemen playing in 150 or more games with .992. Led in stolen bases in 1947 and 1949. Most Valuable Player in 1949. Lifetime batting average .311. Joint record holder for most double plays by second baseman, 137, in 1951. Led second basemen in double plays 1949 50-51-52."

There wasn't much room to tell how this black man, born in the Jim Crow South, suffered through the indignities of racial bias; continued to stand up to abuse from players and fans after being thrust into the role of the first black man in modern times to play baseball in the major leagues; lost a son first to drugs and then to a terrible automobile accident and finally battled debilitating ailments until his untimely death on October 24, 1972.

Robinson was remembered during a 1997 ceremony in New York when Major League Baseball announced that no player on any team would wear number 42 again.

President Clinton and Robinson's widow were on hand for the announcement, which came on the 50th anniversary of Robinson's major league debut.

JACKIE ROBINSON SAFELY STEALS HOME UNDER THE TAG OF NEW YORK YANKEES CATCHER YOGI BERRA IN GAME 1 OF THE 1955 WORLD SERIES. (AP/ WIDE WORLD PHOTOS)

SUGAR RAY ROBINSON, RIGHT, SHAKES HANDS WITH HENRY ARMSTRONG
BEFORE THEIR WELTERWEIGHT BOUT. (AP/WIDE WORLD PHOTOS)

SUGAR RAY ROBINSON

"POUND FOR POUND THE GREATEST"

Legend has it that back in the late 1930s, a sportswriter, impressed after watching a scrawny, 19-year-old black kid polish off an opponent in a small fight arena in upstate New York, turned to the youth's handler at ringside and remarked:

"That's a sweet boy you have there."

"Yeah," replied Manager George Gainford, "sweet as sugar."

The sportswriter pounced on the phrase for his morning newspaper column and thus was born one of the most familiar and electrifying names in the annals of boxing.

Sugar Ray Robinson went on to become one of the most celebrated figures in the game, a classic boxer-puncher who rode a roller coaster to championships in two weight divisions—and almost a third—and to two fortunes squandered by high living.

From 1940 through 1965, he established a remarkable record of 202 professional fights, winning 175. He reigned as welterweight titleholder for four years, was five times winner and loser of the middleweight crown and barely missed making boxing history by losing a hard-fought light heavyweight title bout to Joey Maxim in 1952.

In his first 12 years, while at his peak, he lost to only two foes—Jake LaMotta, whom he beat on five other occasions, and Randy Turpin, whom he knocked out in a return meeting.

In an age when heavyweights were the glamor figures and dominated public attention, Sugar Ray was acclaimed "pound for pound, the greatest fighter who ever lived."

The phrase became one of the sport's most enduring clichés but, as the years passed, no one emerged seriously to dispute it.

A onetime street dancer, Robinson combined artistry and speed with bone-rattling power. Old-timers compared him with George Dixon, Joe Gans and Benny Leonard. Latter-day critics said Sugar Ray was the inspiration

---

SUGAR RAY ROBINSON LANDS A GLANCING BLOW TO THE BACK OF JAKE LAMOTTA'S HEAD DURING THEIR MIDDLEWEIGHT TITLE BOUT IN 1951. (AP/WIDE WORLD PHOTOS)

SUGAR RAY ROBINSON WAVES FOR THE CAMERAS DURING THE WEIGH-IN FOR HIS 1956 MIDDLEWEIGHT TITLE BOUT AGAINST CARL "BOBO" OLSON IN LOS ANGELES.   (AP/WIDE WORLD PHOTOS)

SUGAR RAY ROBINSON, CENTER, ENJOYS A ROUND OF GOLF WITH SAM SNEAD, LEFT, AND ED SULLIVAN IN NEW YORK IN 1957. (AP/WIDE WORLD PHOTOS)

of Muhammad Ali's "Float like a butterfly, sting like a bee" routine.

A superb ring tactician, Robinson used Leonard had a technique of rocking into range, unleashing a salvo of blows and then rocking back again. He had a flicking rat-tat-tat left that set his opponent up for a crunching left hook or right cross. Contemporaries marveled at his vast repertoire of moves.

After being floored in a welterweight title bout, Tommy Bell said, "He came at me with two punches, a right and a left. I don't know which hit me. I didn't feel hurt, but when I started to move, my legs wouldn't go with me and I fell over on my head."

Although a fierce gladiator who constantly pressed in for the kill when he had a foe in trouble, Sugar Ray professed in later years that he never really had a love for ring combat. He got his greatest kicks out of the high jinx that accompanied the role of ring idol.

Quite possibly, this lust for high living was a reaction to his grim and spartan background.

Robinson was born Walker Smith on May 3, 1920, in Detroit's tough, so-called "Black Bottom" district, but found himself in New York's Harlem at an early age after his mother was deserted by his father. He acknowledged that he ran with a street gang, danced for nickels and pennies on the sidewalks of New York's Times Square and shot craps all night with other gang members in the back alleys.

Befriended by a priest, he began working out in a neighborhood gym, where he caught the eye of Gainford. It was Gainford who pulled a stray card out of his pocket when "Smitty," as Ray was then called, showed up for an amateur fight without credentials. The name was that of another obscure fighter, Ray Robinson. The name stuck.

Robinson was brought along carefully by Gainford. He even fought an aging Henry Armstrong, carrying the old, legendary fighter for 10 rounds. He won his first pro title—the 147-pound championship in 1946, beating Tommy Bell. He defended the title only four times before moving into the middleweight division, where he produced his greatest fights.

Meanwhile, he was burning the candle at both ends. Frequently he would stay up until 4 a.m. at the Cotton Club, swinging with friends. He drove a bright red Cadillac. They said his closets housed 1,000 suits. He toured Europe with a dozen or more courtiers including a harem of interracial beauties, a valet, hairdresser and even a court jester. A family could have lived a year on his champagne bills.

Although his purses never compared with the exorbitant guarantees of the 1970s and 1980s, Sugar Ray never lacked for cash flow. He owned a string of apartment buildings on New York's Seventh Avenue and operated several variety shops. He was a landlord who needed a bevy of secretaries to handle his interests.

He actually had two careers. The first, starting in 1940, ended June 25, 1952, when he was overcome by heat prostration in the 13th round of a light heavyweight title challenge against Maxim.

Broke, having dissipated more than $4 million, his marriage dissolved, he announced his retirement the following December and began a career as a tap dancer, booked into nightclubs for $15,000 a week. When this venture dulled, he essayed a ring comeback in 1954, regaining some of his old magic and recapturing the middleweight title from Bobo Olson. He earned good purses in bouts with Gene Fullmer, Carmen Basilio and Paul Pender, losing regaining and then losing again the middleweight title. He earned more than $1.5 million, which subsequently evaporated.

Then, by his own admission, he saw the light. He remarried, settled in Los Angeles, reactivated the Ray Robinson Foundation and threw all his energies into working with kids and church.

He died April 12, 1989, at the age of 68.

WILMA RUDOLPH BRINGS HOME THE BATON AND THE GOLD MEDAL IN THE
4 x 100-METER RELAY AT THE 1960 SUMMER OLYMPICS IN ROME.
(AP/WIDE WORLD PHOTOS)

WILMA RUDOLPH

A SYMPHONY OF SPEED AND GRACE

They made a movie of Wilma Rudolph's life, and if one were not cognizant of the true story, one would believe it was padded with the fiction and tear-jerking stuff for which Hollywood is known. In Wilma's case, no such puffery was necessary. It was her life as she lived it and the most imaginative script writer would find it difficult to exaggerate.

It was a story that had all the ingredients of high drama—a black girl, daughter of a struggling handyman, born in the South, the 20th of 22 children, stricken with paralyzing illnesses at the age of four, apparently doomed to be a cripple, yet one who fought back to become the greatest American woman runner ever to compete in the Olympic Games.

After being stricken with scarlet fever and double pneumonia when she was 4, she went on to become a fine high school athlete, qualify for the 1956 Melbourne Olympics at age 15, returned four years later in Rome to sweep to three gold medals—the 100 and 200 meters and 400-meter relay—and seal her niche in the Olympic Hall of Fame.

Rudolph taught high school, modeled, worked as a Hollywood publicist, served as an analyst on the faculty of a university, lectured, campaigned as a fund-raiser and did television commercials.

She became very active in the Women's Sports Foundation, lobbied for Title IX (the law requiring equal treatment for women in college sports), and became the driving force in the establishment of the $1.5 million Track and Field Hall of Fame in Charleston, S.C.

Her madcap schedule intensified after the divorce from her husband in the mid-1970s, with her four children growing into adulthood. She served as a consultant on the movie of her life, "Wilma," produced by Bud Greenspan, did a cross-country tour for a bakery sponsoring the 20th Century Fox filming of the 1980 Olympics and maintained a busy travel schedule promoting causes for underprivileged children.

Even after her racing days were done, Rudolph was a favorite the world over as promoter of the Wilma Rudolph Foundation for underprivileged kids. She died in November 1994 at age 54.

THIS PHOTO FINISH OF THE 100-METER SPRINT AT THE 1960 SUMMER OLYMPICS SHOWS WILMA RUDOLPH WINNING THE GOLD MEDAL. (AP/WIDE WORLD PHOTOS)

RIVALS BILL RUSSELL AND WILT CHAMBERLAIN ARE BOTH ON THE RIM AS THE BALL FALLS INTO THE HOOP AFTER RUSSELL'S SHOT DURING THE 1969 NBA FINALS. RUSSELL'S CELTICS WOULD GO ON TO WIN THEIR 11TH TITLE WITH NO. 6 ON THE TEAM. (AP/ WIDE WORLD PHOTOS)

BILL RUSSELL

"BEST DEFENSIVE PLAYER OF ALL TIME"

When Boston picked Bill Russell, a two-time college All-America and Olympic gold medalist, in the first round of the National Basketball Association draft in 1956, many of the game's most astute critics, including Philadelphia owner Eddie Gottlieb, said wily coach Red Auerbach of the Celtics had pulled a boner.

"Russell wasn't a scorer in college," warned Gottlieb. "People say he can't shoot and can't score. What good is he?"

Auerbach apparently saw in his gangling, 6-foot-10 rookie what his peers had failed to observe—intangibles that were to be reflected and vastly instrumental in the Celtics' phenomenal success over the next two decades.

Sitting in his office, preparing to present a $24,000 contract, Auerbach reminded Russell of the negative appraisals. "Everyone says you can't shoot well enough to play with the pros," he said. "Does that bother you?"

Russell, who told of the incident years afterward, replied, "Yeah, I'm a little concerned about it."

"Okay, I'll make a deal with you," Auerbach said. "I promise as long as you play here, whenever we discuss contracts, we will never talk about statistics."

According to both men, they never did. In 1980—with the feats of Wilt Chamberlain, Kareem Abdul-Jabbar, Julius Erving, Elgin Baylor and other stars fresh in mind—the nation's basketball writers voted Russell "Greatest Player in the History of the NBA."

Russell couldn't stuff the ball through the hoop with the ease of seven-footers such as Chamberlain and Jabbar. He couldn't fly through the air as did Erving or exhibit the ballhandling of a slick Bob Cousy. What he could do—and did better than anyone else—was to keep the opposition from doing all those things he couldn't do. He was the great equalizer, generally regarded as the "best defensive player of all time."

He blocked shots. He exercised ball control. He turned defense into an exact science and revolutionized the game. John Havlicek, a Celtics' teammate, said he had seen Russell block a shot, gain control of the ball, feed it to one of his forwards and then follow the fast break to the other end of the floor, ready to grab a rebound.

Against Philadelphia in 1957, Russell had 32 rebounds in a half, an NBA record. He was the NBA all-time playoff leader in rebounds. He also set the league record for rebounds in the championship series—40 against St. Louis in 1960, repeated against Los Angeles in 1962.

BILL RUSSELL LEAPS FOR A REBOUND AGAINST THE LOS ANGELES LAKERS DURING THE FIFTH GAME OF THE 1968 NBA FINALS. (AP/WIDE WORLD PHOTOS)

RUSSELL PLAYING FOR THE UNIVERSITY OF SAN FRANCISCO WHERE HE WON TWO NCAA CHAMPIONSHIPS. (AP/WIDE WORLD PHOTOS)

BILL RUSSELL CELEBRATES THE CELTICS' 1968 NBA
CHAMPIONSHIP WITH CELTICS GENERAL MANAGER RED
AUERBACH, CENTER, AND JOHN HAVLICEK, RIGHT. (AP/WIDE
WORLD PHOTOS)

His defensive genius was credited with leading the Celtics to 11 NBA championships in the 13 years he played, eight in a row and the latter two times in 1968 and 1969 as player-coach. He was the NBA's Most Valuable Player five times and played in 11 All-Star games. Chosen in 1966, he had the distinction of being the first black coach in the NBA. He was elected to the Basketball Hall of Fame in 1974 and named one of the NBA's 50 Greatest Players of All Time in 1996.

Born February 12, 1934, in Monroe, Louisiana, William Felton Russell moved with his family to Oakland, California, when he was nine. He attended McClymonds High School, where as a 6-foot-2, 128-pound sophomore, he was so awkward, coaches paid no attention to him. Eventually, he added seven inches and 100 pounds to his muscular frame and improved enough to get a scholarship at the University of San Francisco, a small Jesuit school.

Russell and a teammate, K.C. Jones, who followed him to the Celtics, led San Francisco to No. 1 in the college rankings in 1955-56 and were stars in the United States' gold medal victory in the 1956 Olympics.

It had been a struggle, and Bill was the first to acknowledge it. "Basketball didn't come easy to me," he said. "Defense is not an innate talent or luck. You have to work years to perfect it. I should epitomize the American dream, for I came from long odds."

A striking figure, 6 feet, 10 inches tall and 220 pounds, the goateed Russell was almost immediately tossed into a personal conflict with the awesome 7-foot-1, 275-pound Wilt Chamberlain when the latter entered the NBA in 1959. It was offense vs. defense, differing styles, a clash of strong personalities, a natural rivalry that delighted fans.

Sparks were bound to fly—and they did.

Basketball writers drew comparisons. Contemporaries passed judgment, one of them, Jerry West, saying, "I think Wilt is a better all-around player but, for one game, I'd rather have Russell."

Chamberlain managed to outscore Russell in their personal confrontations, but it was usually Russell's team that came out on top. In the 10 years Russell and Chamberlain stalked each other, the Celtics won the NBA championship nine times and held an 84-57 edge over Wilt's Philadelphia, San Francisco and Los Angeles teams.

This was frustrating for the hulking Wilt the Stilt, who rationalized: "I outscored him (Russell) in head-to-head meetings 440-212, outrebounded him 333-161 and even blocked more of his shots than he did of mine."

Russell countered: "Only the first year against Wilt was a challenge. Then it became clear that he was great—but I was better."

Retiring after the 1969 season, Russell signed a lucrative contract with the telephone company, lectured on college campuses, did TV commentary and commercials and, in 1973, returned briefly as coach and GM of Seattle's NBA team. He became coach of the Sacramento Kings in 1987 but was replaced before the end of the season and moved into a vice president's role with the team.

"I have achieved the absolute in my fields," he said.

Babe Ruth wears his Yankee uniform for the final time on June 13, 1948, as he acknowledges the cheers of fans at Yankee Stadium on the 25th anniversary of the opening of Yankee Stadium, "The House That Ruth Built." (AP/Wide World Photos)

BABE RUTH

SAVIOR OF BASEBALL

In an era of flamboyant prose and graphic nicknames for sports heroes, they called him "Bambino," "The Sultan of Swat," "The King of Clout," "The Savior of Baseball," a superfluous exercise, since one word would have been enough.

Simply the "Babe."

He was hardly the textbook figure for an athletic idol. He was 6 feet, 2 inches tall and weighed variously between 215 and 250 pounds, with most of the avoirdupois concentrated in a mammoth belly that hung like bouncing jelly over his belt line.

He had a round, boyish face with a bulbous nose, and when he took up a bat, which looked like a toothpick in his beefy hands, and sent the ball on a lazy arc into the stands, he toured the bases with mincing, girlish steps on matchstick-thin legs.

Off the diamond, he was a big, overgrown kid, a glutton who gorged himself on beer and hot dogs, who flouted club rules and indulged heavily in the good life of wine, women and song.

Truly a king with earthly, human tastes.

Few will deny that Babe Ruth remains the most magical name in American sports—a name that is still spoken with reverence in such foreign countries as Japan and Britain, while names of other great performers are forgotten.

Baseball men will tell you he was the greatest all-around player of all time—a brilliant pitcher before becoming a home run-hitting outfielder, a man without a technical flaw.

More than that, the Babe was credited with saving baseball at a time the game had lost public confidence because of the 1919 "Black Sox Scandal," in which some members of the Chicago White Sox were suspended for allegedly throwing the World Series against the Cincinnati Reds.

A young star named George Herman Ruth was just emerging as a slugger with the Boston Red Sox. A winning left-handed pitcher, the beefy kid had just been turned into an outfielder that year and hit an all-time record of 29 home runs. Sold to the New York Yankees in 1920, the Babe, profiting from the introduction of a livelier ball, electrified the nation by hitting 54 home runs. The scandal was soon forgotten, and baseball was launched into an unprecedented era of prosperity and home run fever.

Turnstiles hummed and cash registers jingled as fans rushed to the ball parks to see the potbellied slugger slam baseballs out of the park, and he obliged: 714 career home runs, a record 2,217 runs batted in and a lifetime batting average of .342.

The Babe's home run marks—including the 60 he hit for a season high in 1927—

BABE RUTH SURROUNDED BY HIS FAVORITE FANS, CHILDREN. (AP/WIDE WORLD PHOTOS)

Babe Ruth watches one of his 714 career home runs on its way out
of Yankee Stadium during his 60-home run season in 1927.
(AP/Wide World Photos)

BABE RUTH BROKE INTO THE BIG LEAGUES AS A PITCHER WITH THE BOSTON RED SOX. HIS HITTING ABILITY FORCED THE RED SOX TO MOVE HIM TO THE OUTFIELD. (AP/WIDE WORLD PHOTOS)

became so sacred that many baseball fans were extremely upset when the Yankees' Roger Maris came along to hit 61 in 1961 and the Braves' Hank Aaron soared past the Babe's career total, hitting his 715th on April 8, 1974, in Atlanta.

In fact, the Babe's record of 60 home runs in one season was so sacrosanct that baseball was constrained to attach an asterisk to Maris' feat in 1961, specifying that it was attained over a longer (162 instead of 154) game schedule. The sports' hierarchy didn't see fit to treat subsequent records—and they were many—with the same disdain.

It emphasized Ruth's shadow over the entire game.

George Herman Ruth was born in 1895 on the Baltimore waterfront to parents who died when he was very young. An unwanted waif, he wound up in St. Mary's Industrial School, where a Catholic priest got him interested in baseball. The kid started out as a left-handed catcher but shifted to the pitcher's role. It was at St. Mary's that he caught the eye of Jack Dunn, owner of the minor league Baltimore Orioles, who signed him for $600 in 1914.

Historians say this also was the origin of the Babe's nickname. The youngster, 19 and timid, clung so closely to the boss's heels that players would say, "There goes Jack and his new babe."

Ruth was so impressive on the mound that he graduated to the Boston Red Sox just before the end of the year. He won two of his three decisions, and beginning in 1915, he reeled off winning seasons of 18, 23 and 24 games. He beat the Brooklyn Dodgers in the 1916 World Series. He faced the great Walter Johnson eight times and won six, three of them by 1-0 scores. Once, he struck out the Detroit Tigers' Bobby Veach, Sam Crawford and Ty Cobb with the bases loaded.

Overall, he had a career pitching record of 94 victories and 46 defeats, a 2.28 earned run average, a 3-0 record and an ERA of 0.87 in the World Series with a record of 29 2/3 consecutive scoreless innings that endured for 40 years.

Ed Barrow, manager of the Red Sox and later general manager of the Yankees, called Ruth "as good as any left-handed pitcher I ever saw," yet it was he who decided that the Babe would be more valuable with a bat in his hand playing every day and converted him into an outfielder.

In 1920, the Red Sox, in financial difficulty, sold the Babe to the New York Yankees for $125,000 and a $350,000 mortgage on Boston's Fenway Park—a price that seemed exorbitant at the time but proved to be a steal. The Babe responded with his 54 home runs. It changed the face of the game.

Previously, it had been a game of pitching and finesse, managers strategically squeezing out one and two runs at a time. Ruth turned it into a power exercise that produced runs in clusters.

A new dynasty was born. The Yankees moved out of the shadow of the New York Giants in the Polo Grounds in 1923 and into Yankee Stadium, their own concrete palace in the Bronx. The "Bronx Bombers" became a national fetish.

Ruth led or tied for the American League home run crown in 10 of his 14 years with the Yankees. He hit better than .300 in six World Series, twice belted three home runs in a single Series game and set a Series batting mark of .625 in 1928.

His most famous blow was struck in the 1932 World Series against the Chicago Cubs, when he took his stance at the plate, pointed to a center-field spot and then hit a home run in the bleacher section to which he had gestured. The incident became a source of debate among those on hand.

Chagrined that he never was given a chance to manage the Yankees, Ruth asked for his release in 1935, joining the Boston Braves. He batted only .181 but hit six home runs, three in one game. He died August 16, 1948 of lung cancer.

PETE SAMPRAS WITH HANDS RAISED IN VICTORY AFTER WINNING THE 1995 U.S. OPEN. (AP/WIDE WORLD PHOTOS)

PETE SAMPRAS SERVES IN THE 1997 WIMBLEDON MEN'S FINAL. (AP/WIDE WORLD PHOTOS)

PETE SAMPRAS

"HE WALKED ON WATER"

Pete Sampras left skid marks and blood stains on Centre Court.

He flew above the net for overheads, dived horizontally for volleys, and to hear an awestruck Andre Agassi tell it, "He walked on water" at Wimbledon.

Even Sampras couldn't quite believe the way he came up with some shots in a 6-3, 6-4, 7-5 victory that brought him his sixth Wimbledon championship in seven years and tied him with Roy Emerson for the men's record of 12 Grand Slam titles.

"I couldn't have played any better," Sampras said. "In the beginning, in the middle of the second set, I was on fire. In all aspects of my game, from my serving to my groundstrokes, I was playing in a zone."

If ever a shot deserved to be saved on film in the Tennis Hall of Fame, it's the one Sampras produced early in the second set.

Agassi had sprinted to his left and come up with a running backhand crosscourt that would have passed virtually anyone else at the net where Sampras stood. It was one of those brutally hard shots that make such a noise, and come off the racket at such an angle, that fans start roaring before it even lands.

But suddenly there was Sampras, diving flat out, flicking a backhand drop volley that fell ever so gently on the other side of the net for a winner. He belly-whopped hard to the tattered turf, skidded a yard and tore up the huge scab he had on his right forearm from other dives the past two weeks.

Agassi stood on the baseline and stared in amazement. Sampras inspected his open wound, wiped himself off, and served two straight aces at nearly 130 mph to take a 3-1 lead.

"He played some impeccable tennis at the most important times," Agassi said.

As if that wasn't convincing enough, Sampras tried to do it again as he served for the match at 6-5 in the third set.

This time Agassi ripped a forehand crosscourt, a shot that came off his racket once more with a thud. Sampras was beaten, but he didn't know it, or refused to believe it. He hurled his body through the air again, parallel to the court, and just missed the ball as he skidded on the grass and tore up his arm a little more.

Sampras' response to that miss? He wiped off the blood and struck his 16th and 17th aces to end the match, the first at 127 mph, the next at 110 mph on a gutsy second serve at 40-30.

PETE SAMPRAS, RIGHT, CELEBRATES THE UNITED STATES' VICTORY IN DAVIS CUP COMPETITION WITH TEAMMATE ANDRE AGASSI, LEFT, AND TEAM CAPTAIN TOM GULLIKSON, CENTER, AFTER DEFEATING RUSSIA IN 1995. (AP/WIDE WORLD PHOTOS)

SAMPRAS KISSES THE TROPHY AFTER WINNING THE 1998 WIMBLEDON MEN'S SINGLES FOR THE FIFTH TIME. (AP/WIDE WORLD PHOTOS)

PETE SAMPRAS REACHES OUT FOR A RETURN IN 1999. (AP/WIDE WORLD PHOTOS)

PETE SAMPRAS DIVES FOR A SHOT IN THE 1999 MEN'S SINGLES FINAL AT WIMBLEDON. SAMPRAS DEFEATED ANDRE AGASSI, 6-3, 6-4, 7-5, FOR HIS 12TH GRAND SLAM SINGLES TITLE, TYING THE RECORD HELD BY ROY EMERSON. (AP/WIDE WORLD PHOTOS)

"It's so hard to explain the feeling that I felt serving for the match," Sampras said. "All of a sudden the match is on your racket, and you start breathing heavier. You start thinking, 'Wow, this is it, this is going to go either way. I could go from winning the title to playing a tiebreaker in the third set.'

"I just kind of went for it, and I hit a great second serve. That's the one shot you need to have to win here. It was a great shot. I surprised myself. I went up the middle, and the next thing I knew I was holding the cup."

Sampras took control of the match with a rush of five straight games, from 3-3 in the first set to 2-0 in the second. It was, simply, Sampras at his best.

"That's how Pete plays," Agassi said. "You've got to weather his storm. And when you weather his storm, that's when he's vulnerable. But his storm was too strong today. I couldn't do it."

What amazed Agassi even more than the sight of Sampras flying through the air, was the way he dared to hit those second-serve aces at 110 to 120 mph. On this day, Sampras wasn't playing safe.

"He's taking chances out there," Agassi said. "People think he's walking on water until he starts missing a few of those. But he didn't. So he walked on water today."

Sampras moved beyond Bjorn Borg to become the winningest man at Wimbledon in the open era. He moved out of a tie with Borg and his longtime idol, Rod Laver, who each had 11 Grand Slam titles.

The $728,000 he collected for winning increased his career prize money to more than $37 million. He is the first player in the history of ATP Rankings (since 1973) to finish No. 1 for six consecutive years. He surpassed Ivan Lendl in 1999 in total week ranked No. 1. Through September of 1999, Sampras held the top ranking 276 weeks and had 60 singles titles.

At 28 and planning to play into his early 30s, Sampras should have many chances to pass Emerson, who collected his major titles in the less competitive era just before open tennis started in 1968.

That prospect, and his place in history, were more than Sampras could think about in the moments after winning.

"I'm still spinning a little bit," he said. "It's going to take a couple of weeks to have it all sink in. It's a little overwhelming to have won what I've won. To be honest, I don't know how I do it, I really don't."

Despite losing, Agassi will take over the No. 1 spot from Sampras, but it was a hollow consolation. What meant more to Agassi was that he knows he's playing well enough to take a measure of revenge at the U.S. Open next month.

Agassi had sought to become the first player since Borg in 1980 to win the French Open and Wimbledon in succession. He's completed a career Grand Slam, something Sampras is missing because of his failures on the French clay.

But asked whether Sampras is the greatest player ever, Agassi didn't hesitate:

"Yes," he said. "He's accomplished more than anybody else has, in my opinion. No question about it. The guy's dominated the grass, and he's finished the year No. 1 six years in a row. His achievements speak for themselves."

BARRY SANDERS CARRIES THE BALL FOR A TOUCHDOWN AGAINST THE PHILADELPHIA EAGLES IN 1996. (AP/WIDE WORLD PHOTOS)

BARRY SANDERS BREAKS THROUGH THE ARIZONA CARDINALS' DEFENSE DURING THE 1995 SEASON. (AP/WIDE WORLD PHOTOS)

BARRY SANDERS

BARRY, BARRY GOOD

Barry Sanders was the best running back of his era and one of the most electrifying players ever to play in the NFL. He could make a loss of two yards exciting enough to appear in highlight films.

Sanders' eye-popping moves dazed and dazzled NFL defenders and frustrated defensive coordinators for 10 years. He regularly led the league in yards for losses—his style was zigzag, not straight ahead, and when he zigged for a hole that wasn't there, he'd get trapped—yards behind the line of scrimmage.

But a play or two later, he'd break for 30 or more, sometimes bending his body at a 45-degree angle from the ground, then bouncing up to dart through a small hole. At 5-foot-8, 200 pounds, he had the flexibility of a gymnast, the ability to twist and turn in ways an Emmitt Smith or a Terrell Davis, the best of his contemporaries, wouldn't even attempt.

In Sanders' 10 years, his team was 78-82 in regular-season play and 1-5 in the five years they made the playoffs. In the Wayne Fontes era, which covered Sanders' first eight seasons, the Lions were constantly changing coordinators and systems—from the run-and-shoot, to a one-back system with no blocker, to a more conventional pro set.

He'd gain his 1,500 or 1,700 or 1,800 yards regardless and got 2,058 in Bobby Ross' first year, 1997, carrying Detroit to the playoffs in a brilliant final regular-season game. Naturally, they lost their first postseason game, 20-10 in Tampa. In 1997, Sanders had an NFL-record 14 consecutive 100-yard games.

Sanders, 31, had 15,269 career rushing yards and gained 1,000 or more yards in each of his 10 seasons. He is the only player to record five 1,500-yard rushing seasons and won the rushing title four times.

After the Lions finished 5-11 last season, Sanders apparently had enough. He'd had an "off" year, 1,491 yards, and there were no Super Bowl rings in sight.

Sanders retired on the eve of the 1999 Detroit Lions' training camp, a shocking decision that prevented him from becoming the NFL's career rushing leader this season. He left only 1,458 yards shy of breaking Walter Payton's NFL career rushing record of 16,726 yards.

He won the 1988 Heisman Trophy in his final season, his junior year, at Oklahoma State, where he set 13 NCAA records. That year he rushed for a record 2,628 yards, scored 37 touchdowns and averaged 238.9 yards a game.

He was selected in the first round of the NFL draft by the Lions as the third overall selection.

BARRY SANDERS IS CARRIED OFF THE FIELD BY HIS DETROIT LIONS TEAMMATES AFTER RUSHING FOR 184 YARDS IN A COME-FROM-BEHIND VICTORY IN THE 1997 REGULAR SEASON. (AP/WIDE WORLD PHOTOS)

WILLIE SHOEMAKER, AGE 44 IN THIS PHOTO, WAS CLOSING IN ON THE 7,000-VICTORY MARK. (AP/WIDE WORLD PHOTOS)

WILLIE SHOEMAKER

AGELESS SULTAN OF THE SADDLE

Fifty-four years after his 2 1/2-pound frail body was placed in a shoebox and shoved into an oven to keep it alive, Willie Shoemaker nursed a 17-1 shot, a colt named Ferdinand, to victory in the 1986 Kentucky Derby.

It was one of sport's most memorable achievements. It would have been a historic feat, no matter who was in the saddle, but, coming as it did from the gifted hands of the world's greatest jockey at such an advanced athletic age, the feat took on miracle proportions. The sports world was awed and delighted.

The victory put a crown of gold on a 41-year career that saw the pint-sized Texan ride more horses, win more races, capture more stake purses and earn more prize money than any jockey who ever lived. Before retiring in 1990, Shoemaker rode 8,833 winners, 1,009 of them in stakes races and 250 with purses of $100,000 or more. He also won 10 national money titles and over $123 million in purses.

Shoemaker considered Eddie Arcaro his toughest rival and envied his two sweeps of horse racing's Triple Crown events the Kentucky Derby, Preakness and Belmont Stakes with Whirlaway and Citation, the only prize to escape him. "He was terrific," Shoemaker said of Arcaro. "I think he beat me more than I beat him." They had some great duels.

Shoemaker needed no excuses for his own record in Triple Crown events. He won the Kentucky Derby four times, with Swaps, Tomy Lee, Lucky Debonair and Ferdinand; two Preakness Stakes, with Candy Spots and Damascus; and five Belmont Stakes, with Gallant Man, Sword Dancer, Jaipur, Damascus and Avatar.

Then there was his notorious blunder in the 1957 Derby when, seemingly cruising to victory aboard Gallant Man, he mistook the sixteenth pole for the finish line, stood up in the stirrups and allowed Iron Liege to win by a nose.

"An error like that would have destroyed most men," Arcaro said. "Only a guy like Willie could have survived it. He's a tough son-of-a-gun."

That toughness was tested from the day of his birth and throughout a career that saw him labeled at first "too small to be a jockey," suffer two life-threatening accidents during the late 1960s, undergo marital problems, and temporarily lose some of his competitive drive after being lured into the fast lane of California celebrity life.

Then, on April 8, 1991, a little more than a year after retiring to become a trainer, Shoemaker was involved in a one-car accident that left him paralyzed frm the neck down.

Shoemaker retired as a trainer in 1997 following Santa Anita's Oak Tree meet.

WILLIE SHOEMAKER, ABOARD SWAPS AFTER WINNING THE AMERICAN DERBY IN 1955. (AP/WIDE WORLD PHOTOS)

MARGARET SMITH COURT DURING HER FINALS MATCH AND EVENTUAL VICTORY IN THE 1970 WIMBLEDON WOMEN'S SINGLES. (AP/WIDE WORLD PHOTOS)

MARGARET SMITH COURT

QUEEN OF GRAND SLAM TENNIS

They called her "Maggie." She was a scrawny, skinny-legged lass of 11, living in the country town of Albury, Australia, when she first heard mention of the term "Grand Slam" in tennis. Margaret Smith had been playing the game for two years and was showing great promise as a junior in a land where tennis was more than a sport—it was a religion. Every day the train would arrive with newspapers from Sydney, and Maggie would scan the sports pages zealously for reports of the Australian National Championships then in progress.

She was particularly interested in American star Maureen "Little Mo" Connolly. The court experts had tabbed "Little Mo" the world's best prospect for sweeping all the major titles—the Australian, Wimbledon, U.S. and French championships—for a Grand Slam no woman had ever achieved.

The country girl was thrilled when Little Mo won and went on to fulfill her destiny in 1953. She never dreamed that 17 years later she would duplicate the feat and establish herself as one of the game's immortals.

"Whenever you talk of great women tennis players, you have to start with Margaret," said Marty Riessen, who shared many mixed doubles titles with the Australian. "She should go down as the finest woman player of all time."

Seven years almost to the day after Maggie had thrilled to Maureen Connolly's successful invasion of her country, she found herself in center court receiving the trophy as the youngest woman—at 17—to win the Australian championship, a distinction that now belongs to Martina Hingis, who did it at age 16 in 1997. It was merely the beginning of a long reign that saw her not only capture the Grand Slam but amass a cache of worldwide crowns, unmatched by any other player, before or after.

Margaret Smith, later playing under her married name of Court, won 26 Grand Slam tournament singles titles alone and 62 overall. Her closest challenger on the all-time list is Martina Navratilova with 56.

Margaret won the Australian singles championship a record 11 times between 1960 and 1973. She captured the American crown seven times, the French five and Wimbledon on three occasions.

She retired in 1966, made a comeback in 1968, won the Australian and French in 1969 and swept all four Grand Slam crowns in 1970.

After becoming pregnant in 1971, she left competition again, only to return in 1973 and lead all women's players in winnings.

She went out on top, retiring for good after the 1973 season.

MARGARET SMITH COURT REACHES FOR A RETURN IN THE 1968 U.S. OPEN. (AP/WIDE WORLD PHOTOS)

SAM SNEAD TAKES A PRACTICE SWING AT A TOURNAMENT IN 1937.
(AP/WIDE WORLD PHOTOS)

SAM SNEAD

THE SLAMMING MOUNTAINEER

It is one of the regrettable ironies of sports that golf annals will always record Sam Snead as the remarkable talent who never won the United States Open Championship.

This rugged, long-hitting Virginia hillbilly enthralled galleries for half a century with a swing as smooth as molasses pouring over a stack of flapjacks and as explosive as a cannon shot. He won more than 100 tournaments throughout the world, 84 on the PGA tour. He won more tour events than Arnold Palmer and Jack Nicklaus.

He played in the era of such giants as Ben Hogan, Byron Nelson, Lloyd Mangrum and Jimmy Demaret, beating them more often than he lost. Fellow pros rated him as the finest striker of the ball who ever lived.

Yet it was his fate to carry the negative tag: He couldn't win the U.S. Open.

An amazing athlete, he seemed to defy the aging process. Long after many of his contemporaries, including Hogan and Nelson, had retired, Sam continued to tee it up with the Palmers and Nicklauses and even the so-called young lions. They all would stop, watch and admire when he prepared to swing. He became one of the game's irrefutable legends.

He shot his age many times. When the day's round was complete, even after he had moved past age 70, Snead would entertain fellow players in the locker room by doing a complete flip from a standing start or kicking the top of a door frame. His body was so limber, it seemed to lack bones.

If Snead felt that fate dealt him a bad hand in his pursuit of the U. S. Open—he had a chance to win a half-dozen of them only to be thwarted by some bizarre incident—he never allowed his frustration to surface.

"It gives you an eerie feeling sometimes," he acknowledged in the sunset of his career. "I've won tournaments I had no business winning, and I've had tournaments snatched right out of my hands when by all rights they should have been mine. It's almost as if your name is written on a tournament before it starts."

Snead couldn't complain much. He won three Masters, between 1949 and 1954, and was runner-up twice. He won three PGA titles in tough match-play competition and was a finalist on two other occasions. He won the British Open in 1946 in his first try.

He was the tour's leading money winner in 1938, 1949 and 1950 and the Vardon Trophy winner (lowest scoring average) in 1938, 1949, 1950 and 1955. Seven times he was a member of the U.S. Ryder Cup team, compiling a 9-2 record.

"Slammin' Sammy" won six PGA Seniors, five World Seniors and, with Don January, the Legends title in 1982.

Snead played in his last Masters in 1983, but still rturns to Augusta National each year, where he's an honorary starter.

SAM SNEAD MAKES AN IRON SHOT FROM THE EDGE OF A SAND TRAP IN THE 1949 PGA CHAMPIONSHIP IN RICHMOND, VIRGINIA. (AP/WIDE WORLD PHOTOS)

Mark Spitz waves to the crowd after his sixth gold medal in the 100-meter freestyle at the 1972 Summer Olympics in Munich. (AP/Wide World Photos)

MARK SPITZ

CONQUERER OF THE WATER WORLD

He was tall, slim, dark with a dashing mustache—and he could swim like a fish. For one minuscule moment in time—seven days in the late summer of 1972 in the Olympic pool at Munich, Germany—he proved himself the greatest swimmer of all time. Then, like a chameleon, he was supposed to shed his old skin and take on a new image to become Johnny Weissmuller, Errol Flynn and Clark Gable all wrapped into one neat, marketable package.

Mark Spitz fulfilled his destiny when he swept to seven swimming gold medals, including three for relays, all in world-record time. It was perhaps the most astounding individual feat ever in the Olympic Games. Yet, having conquered the water world, he found himself ill equipped to measure up to the expectations of his fans and commercial advisers.

Despite all his medals—with their attendant glory—and his physical assets, he turned into a major disappointment. All the multimillion-dollar efforts to make him a public idol collapsed almost immediately. His fame faded.

"I was a porpoise out of water," the handsome Californian said poignantly afterward. "All my life I had done little except concentrate on my swimming. I was determined to be the best in the world. I never learned how to relate to my friends and the public."

Spitz, cocky and often arrogant, was always at loggerheads with his teammates. Some found him immature—a characteristic that he openly acknowledged. A close friend said he was a hypochondriac, a complainer, and a worrier.

Spitz had the misfortune to compete in what is possibly the most snobbish, clannish and insensitive sport in the Olympic Games. A historian once commented that the only way you could tell swimmers apart was to throw them in the water and see which stroke they swam. Spitz concentrated on the freestyle and butterfly.

Born February 10, 1950, of well-to-do parents in Modesto, California, he grew up in the shadow of Don Schollander, the blond and popular Yale man who won four gold medals in Tokyo in 1964 and a gold and silver in Mexico City in 1968.

In the tradition of the sport—that swimmers reach their peaks as teenagers and are over the hill before they can vote—Spitz and Schollander, the latter four years older, were of two different eras although their paths crossed in Mexico City.

Spitz was 18, just arriving on the launching pad for his meteoric career. Schollander was an "old man" of 22, still basking in the limelight of his four golds in the previous Games,

MARK SPITZ SURGES AHEAD TO WIN HIS HEAT IN THE 200-METER BUTTERFLY AT THE 1972 SUMMER OLYMPICS. HE TOOK THE GOLD IN THE EVENT. (AP/WIDE WORLD PHOTOS)

MARK SPITZ SHOWS THE FIVE GOLD MEDALS HE WON IN THE 1972 OLYMPICS IN MUNICH. HE WAS THE FIRST MAN TO WIN FIVE GOLD MEDALS IN A SINGLE OLYMPICS. (AP/WIDE WORLD PHOTOS)

MARK SPITZ,
CENTER, DURING THE
MEDAL CEREMONY
FOLLOWING HIS GOLD
MEDAL
PERFORMANCE IN
THE 200-METER
BUTTERFLY IN THE
1972 OLYMPICS.
(AP/WIDE WORLD
PHOTOS)

and the highly respected dean of the U.S. team.

Spitz had been a national champion in high school and had been lured by a scholarship to Indiana University, an institution renowned for its water program. He quickly alienated his Olympic teammates by brashly predicting that he expected to win six gold medals at Mexico City. The result was that he soon found himself "frozen out" by veteran members of the squad.

Spitz's life was made miserable for the six weeks the team spent in a training camp in Colorado Springs, Colorado, prior to the Games. Mark was moved out of the main dormitory into a small room of his own. The older members stuck together, and when they elected to speak to Spitz, who is Jewish, it was often to make fun of him. They aimed anti-Semitic remarks at him and scoffed at his grandiose goals.

A teammate, Gary Hall, acknowledged that there was a group scheme to shake Spitz's confidence. "He was really susceptible. You could psych him out," Hall said. Other team members admitted sheepishly later that Mark had been given a bad deal.

Instead of winning six gold medals, Spitz captured a disappointing two, both in the freestyle relays. He finished third in the 100-meter freestyle and second in the 100-meter butterfly, failing to qualify for the medley relay. Schollander had to settle for second in the 200-meter freestyle and a share of a single gold in the 800 freestyle relay.

Mexico City proved a disheartening experience for Spitz, who later confessed that he thought he might never compete in another Olympics.

"I told myself," he said, "that even if I never go to another Olympics, I could still say 30 years from now, 'Well, I got two golds, a silver and a bronze. I didn't win any individual events, but I held 35 world records. That isn't all that bad.'"

Dreams don't die that easily.

Three years after Mexico City, Spitz, having established himself as the world's best swimmer, swept to five gold medals in the Pan American Games. Then he set his sights on Munich, 1972.

They were the "Horror Olympics," scene of the Arab massacre of the Israeli athletes, disqualification of U.S. sprinters for failing to report on time; a pratfall by America's top miler, Jim Ryun and the first defeat ever for the U.S. basketball team. But there was no denying Spitz his cascade of gold.

A more mature man now, admired by his teammates and hailed by the fans, he reeled off victories night after night, setting one world record after another. He captured the 100- and 200-meter freestyle and butterfly events and helped the Americans win two freestyle and one medley relay.

A few hours after Mark had won his seventh gold, the terrorists moved in, leaving a carnage of death. Because he was Jewish, Spitz was quickly whisked out of the country.

He returned to the United States a genuine hero, his earlier problems forgotten. He signed with one of Hollywood's biggest talent agencies for a reported $6 million. He was groomed for the movies, TV and commercial shots. The ventures all flopped. Critics were brutal, declaring that he was a drab personality with no sex appeal.

"I wasn't an actor, and I wasn't an entertainer," he said. "I knew I could make money in other ways. I am not bitter. I reached my goal and went out gracefully."

INGEMAR STENMARK IS HELD ALOFT BY HIS FELLOW MEDAL WINNERS AFTER HE WON THE GOLD MEDAL IN THE GIANT SLALOM IN THE 1980 WINTER OLYMPICS IN LAKE PLACID. (AP/WIDE WORLD PHOTOS)

INGEMAR STENMARK

KING OF THE MOUNTAIN

Ingemar Stenmark, the master technician who racked up more World Cup victories than any other skier, hung up his bindings in 1989.

It was an anticlimatic end to a brilliant career for the Swedish star, because he missed a gate just seconds after he started the first run of a World Cup slalom race in central Japan.

"It's a sunny day, a good day to end," he said. "I'm tired and want to stop.

"You have to stop sometime, and now's a good time."

It's not the forgettable finale his fans remember but the 86 world cup victories he posted—all in the slalom and the giant slalom. As records go, that will be tough to top.

"Eighty-six wins—and in only two events … is an incredible accomplishment," Stenmark's coach, Herman Nogler, said.

Stenmark won over a world of fans during his spectacular 16 years on the slopes. His three world championship titles and two Olympic gold medals made him a legend.

A month after his last run, 10,000 Stenmark supporters braved bone-chilling conditions to wish him a fond farewell in Salem, Sweden.

The event was billed as "Ingemar's Races," and it featured two of skiing's all-time greats. Italian Gustav Thoeni, a five-time World Cup Champ, wouldn't have missed it for the world. To him and others, Stenmark was a hero.

"I don't speak English very well, but there is not much to say whatever the language," Thoeni said. "He is the best."

INGEMAR STENMARK ON HIS WAY TO THE GOLD MEDAL IN THE GIANT SLALOM AT THE 1980 WINTER OLYMPICS. (AP/WIDE WORLD PHOTOS)

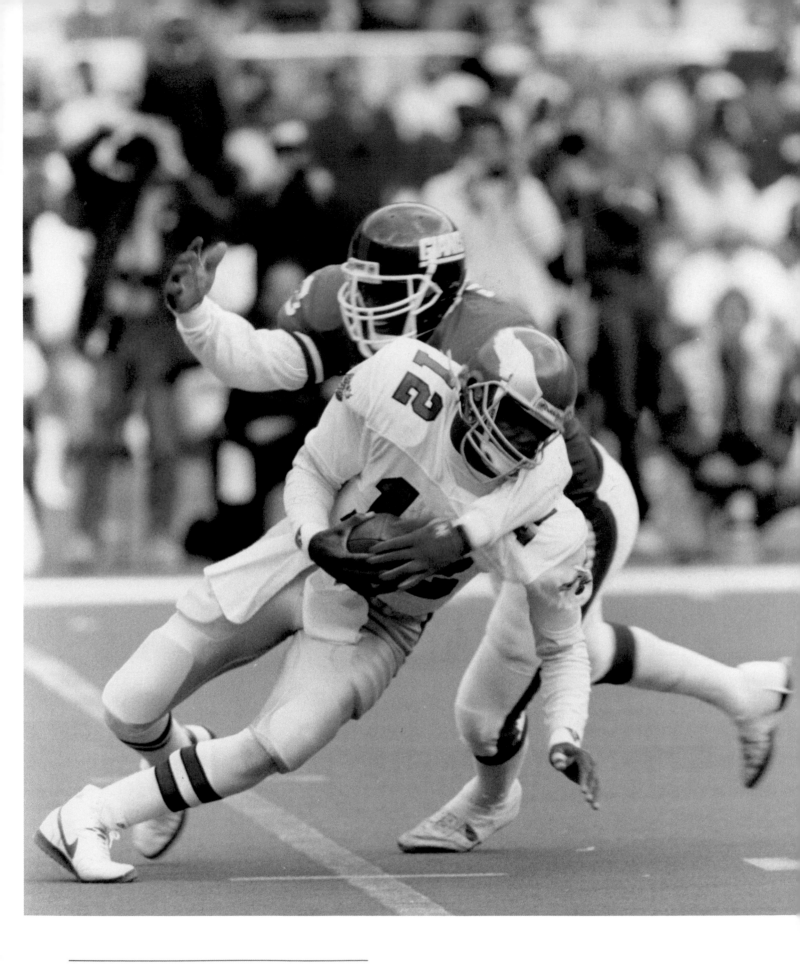

LAWRENCE TAYLOR SACKS THE PHILADELPHIA EAGLES' QUARTERBACK IN A 1989 REGULAR-SEASON GAME. (AP/WORLD WIDE PHOTOS)

LAWRENCE TAYLOR

LAWRENCE THE GIANT

Lawrence Taylor once described himself as a wild man in a wild game.

Many former teammates, opponents and football analysts simply call Taylor the greatest linebacker ever.

"He is the Michael Jordan of football," former New York Giants teammate and defensive end George Martin said. "There is just that dominance."

People describe the 1999 Hall of Fame inductee as intense, passionate, determined, ferocious, powerful, fast, a raw talent. And, of course, there's the dark side.

Taylor was all of that off the field, too. He has had well-publicized problems with substance abuse, money, temper, taxes and marriage both during his career and since his retirement after the 1993 season.

During a 13-year career with the Giants that was highlighted by two Super Bowl championships and 10 straight Pro Bowl berths, Taylor forced offenses to change.

When a quarterback got to the line of scrimmage, he had to know where No. 56 was on the field.

Pass plays that were supposed to be a simple as 1-2-3 were foiled when Taylor got to the quarterback on two with a hit usually preceded by a karate chop across the arms.

Running away from Taylor was just as problematic. He would run from sideline to sideline and stop backs for 2-yard gains.

"He could have played in any decade and been outstanding in any decade," former Giants general manager George Young said. "The distinction that sets him apart is his ability to maintain his intensity over the longest period of time in a game and a career."

Fox Sports analyst John Madden calls him "the best defensive player in the last 20 years."

And Taylor has the numbers to back it up.

He finished his career with 132 1/2 sacks, which didn't count 9 1/2 as a rookie because sacks weren't an official stat until 1982.

The former University of North Carolina standout hated to lose, and he found ways to put his team over the top, be it the late interception against Detroit one Thanksgiving or the forced turnover or the big tackle.

"There are a lot of people who can make tackles, but I always seemed to look for the big play," Taylor said. "The big play got noticed, the big play was the one that changed the game.

"I have always wanted to be the one who made those plays."

LAWRENCE TAYLOR IN ACTION DURING HIS FIRST SUPER BOWL SEASON IN 1986. (AP/WIDE WORLD PHOTOS)

Jim Thorpe did just about everything for the Carlisle Indians School Football team, including kicking off. (AP/Wide World Photos)

JIM THORPE

THE GREATEST OF THEM ALL

By the sheer enormity and breadth of his exploits and the assessment of sports historians whose job it is to gauge them, Jim Thorpe must be acclaimed indisputably the greatest athlete of all time.

He should have received a dozen calls from the president and been honored with a reception at the White House. He should have been in more than one Hall of Fame. A statue of him should stand on the city square and he should be memorialized in bronze. Children should read about him in school.

But this remarkable athlete, master of many sports, was destined to receive the back of the hand from a cruel and insensitive society. His Sac and Fox Indian ancestors were uprooted from their native lands in Iowa by greedy white neighbors. With the aid of blue-coated U.S. troops, they were driven into Kansas and finally herded to an arid, godforsaken territory in Oklahoma.

It was in this grim, hopeless atmosphere that Jim Thorpe was born on May 28, 1888 one of 19 children, son of a farmer and Indian mother. The father, part Irish, had five wives. The mother, part-French, weighed 200 pounds.

Rare athletic skills saved the youngster from this bleak existence. He got a scholarship to the Carlisle Indian School in Pennsylvania, became an All-America football star, excelled in numerous other sports and made the Olympics.

In the 1912 Olympics in Stockholm, Sweden, Thorpe won gold medals in both the decathlon, a gruelling variety of 10 different specialties, and the pentathlon, five events—regarded as the premier tests of versatility and endurance in the entire Games.

Six months afterward, a sportswriter disclosed that Thorpe had received money for playing professional baseball in a small league in North Carolina during summer vacations while at school ($2 a game plus expenses). The austere and hypocritical International Olympic Committee stripped Thorpe of his medals and had his records erased from the Olympic book.

Thorpe went on to play both professional football and major league baseball, but the shadow of his Olympic experience never left him. For years, friends and advocates of justice sought to have the medals restored and Thorpe's record cleansed, but without success.

The International Olympic Committee, later headed by the United States' Avery Brundage, refused to yield.

THORPE PRACTICES HIS KICKING BEFORE A 1912 FOOTBALL GAME FOR CARLISLE INDIAN SCHOOL. (AP/WIDE WORLD PHOTOS)

Jim Thorpe, left, leads two young blockers for Red Grange, right, in this 1947 photo taken at a football school where Thorpe and Grange worked as coaches. (AP/Wide World Photos)

JIM THORPE IS
GREETED BY A
GROUP OF
FELLOW
NATIVE
AMERICANS IN
THIS 1926
PHOTO.
(AP/WIDE
WORLD
PHOTOS)

Thorpe's plea was that he was just an innocent Indian kid who was unaware of any wrongdoing. His supporters used the argument that Thorpe's offense was minuscule compared with other flagrant violations of the Olympic amateur code.

"Ignorance of the law is no excuse," cracked Brundage, who was Thorpe's decathlon and pentathlon rival in the Stockholm Games and who some said bore a deep jealousy of the man who beat him.

Thirty-odd years after his death, Thorpe's medals finally were restored, thanks to a Swedish researcher who discovered an escape hatch in the Olympic charter that specified that protests of professionalism had to be made within 30 days after the Games. It brought small solace to Thorpe's family and friends. The Olympic hierarchy, however, never restored his records.

After the Olympics, Thorpe had the distinction of playing both major league baseball and pro football at the same time. He earned what could be considered respectable salaries at the time—he had natural drawing power at the gate—but was careless with his money. By the time the 1930s Depression occurred, he was virtually broke, married for a second time with four children to support.

He tried his hand at a variety of jobs—painting and acting, winding up making $4 a day wielding a pick and shovel. When a newspaper photographer caught him doing this menial work, the nation was shocked. Charles Curtis, vice-president of the United States at the time, invited him to sit in the presidential box at the 1932 Olympics in Los Angeles. The crowd gave him a huge ovation.

Thorpe served in the merchant marine during World War II and virtually dropped from sight until his death in 1953 at age 65. There was one last splash of glory. In 1951, a poll of sportswriters by The Associated Press named him both "Greatest All-Around Athlete" and "Greatest Football Player" of the first half century.

He was indeed the athletic marvel of the age.

Thorpe wasn't a big man, by modern standards. He was 5 feet, 11 inches tall and weighed 185 pounds, with narrow shoulders and hips but thick thighs and legs, and arms like railroad ties. He ran with such an easy gait that he was accused of being lazy. He called it relaxation.

At Carlisle, playing under the legendary coach, Glenn S. "Pop" Warner, he was a brutal runner, averaging close to 10 yards a carry and 16 points a game in a conservative, low-scoring era. The Carlisle Indians were national champions.

Thorpe was the spearhead of the Carlisle team that crushed Army, a power of the time, 27-6, provoking an Army end named Dwight Eisenhower to say, "We could have won if it hadn't been for Thorpe. He's the best I've ever seen."

From Carlisle, the rugged Indian went to the Canton (Ohio) Bulldogs of the American Pro Football Association, forerunner of the National Football League, where his ball carrying and dropkicking brought three national crowns.

He played with the New York Giants baseball team, under crusty John McGraw, for six years, 1913-1919, and briefly for Cincinnati, as an outfielder. He finished his career with three years in the minors, hitting over .300. Thorpe was adept at tennis and could shoot in the 70s in golf with practice. His bowling average was over 200. He also excelled in handball, billiards, rowing and gymnastics.

Proving his versatility had no limits, he even won a ballroom dancing contest with a Carlisle coed in 1912.

The International Olympic Committee restored Thorpe's amateur standing in 1982 and returned the medals to his family at a ceremony during the 1984 Olympic Games in Los Angeles.

BILL TILDEN IN ACTION DURING A 1933 TOURNAMENT.
(AP/WIDE WORLD PHOTOS)

BILL TILDEN

"BIG BILL" PROVIDED THRILLS

William T. Tilden II was a society blueblood from Philadelphia's swank Main Line who fancied himself a Shakespearean actor and author, yet found his stage to be the lush grass tennis courts of Germantown, Wimbledon and Forest Hills.

Years after advancing age and chronic injuries forced his retirement in 1933 at age 40, tennis buffs acclaimed him the greatest of all time.

"A rare genius," said Berkeley Bell, a contemporary.

"No one ever studied the game as he did. No one ever produced a repertoire of spin, speed and variety to compare. An astounding man," added Vincent Richards, his onetime doubles partner.

They were assessments that found no dispute among the court experts of succeeding generations. In 1969, an international panel of tennis writers voted Tilden the "Greatest Player of All-Time." Earlier, an Associated Press half-century poll placed him alongside Babe Ruth, Jack Dempsey, Bob Jones and Red Grange as the greatest in his particular sport.

They called him "Big Bill," a designation to differentiate him from his sternest rival, "Little Bill" Johnston, a frail, 5-foot-8, 120-pound retriever who wore a size 4 1/2 shoe.

Tilden was a magnetic figure on or off the court. Six feet, two inches tall with broad, sloping shoulders, a receding hairline and lantern jaw, he moved with a long stride and flowing grace. When he walked onto the Center Court at Wimbledon with his long white flannels, V-neck cable stitch sweater and half a dozen wooden Top Flight racquets cradled in his arm, one could imagine that occupants of the Royal Box should stand and bow to him instead of the reverse ritual.

"Big Bill" gave every indication that it was indeed he who was tennis royalty, and let no one forget it.

In 1921, "Big Bill" became the first American male to win the men's singles title at Wimbledon and he added two more. He put together a string of six U.S. crowns and added a seventh in 1929. He won seven National Clay Court titles and went 17-5 in Davis Cup action.

"The greatest—there can never be another like him," fellow American player J. Gilbert Hall once said.

He was a showman off the court, too, later appearing in several Shakespearean plays on stage as well as "Dracula." He wrote several tennis books— some fiction, none successful.

"Big Bill" retired in 1933 and died 20 years later, a bachelor, a broken man still seeking to reclaim some of his old glory on the tennis court or the stage.

BILL TILDEN GETS IN A WORKOUT IN 1930. (AP/WIDE WORLD PHOTOS)

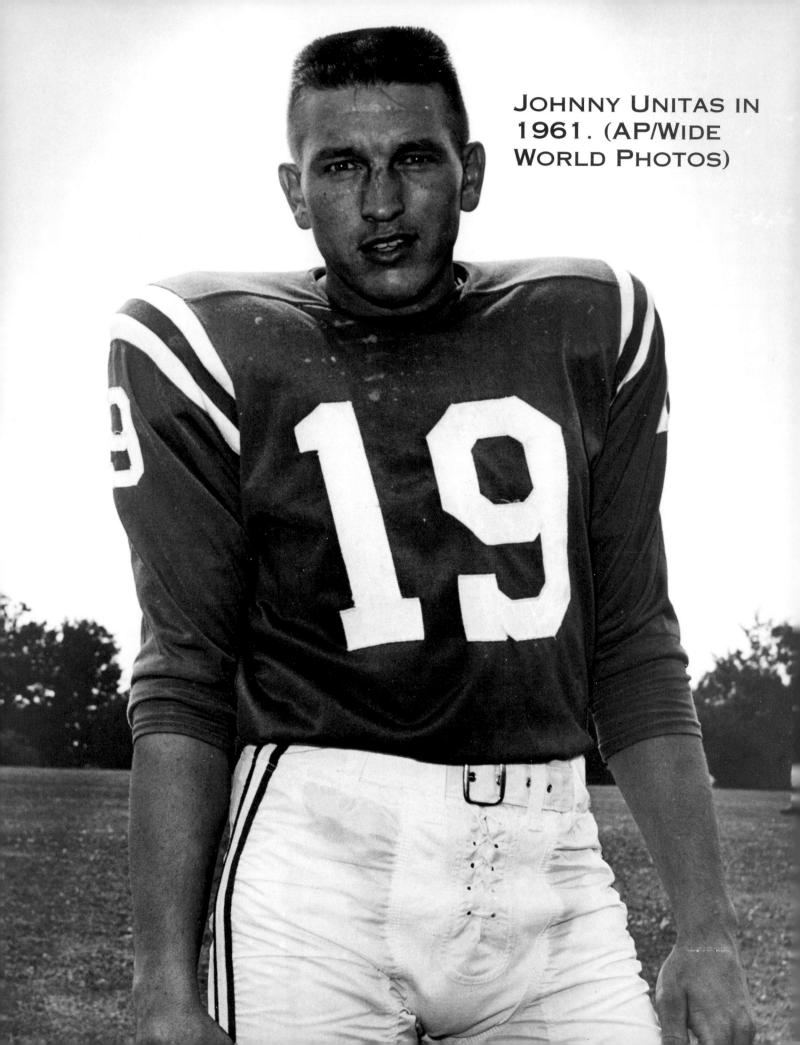

JOHNNY UNITAS IN 1961. (AP/WIDE WORLD PHOTOS)

JOHNNY UNITAS

"LIKE BEING IN A HUDDLE WITH GOD"

The National Football League is a multimillion-dollar operation, rich in scouts, ecstatic press-agentry and sophisticated terminology. But the case of Johnny Unitas makes one suspect that the NFL was not all that accomplished in the mid-1950s.

Nobody wanted Unitas in 1955. However, he eventually became one of the greatest players in the game's history. In 1957, he was named the league's most valuable player—the first of three occasions he was to receive this honor. In 1958 he led his team—the Baltimore Colts—to the league championship, a dramatic 23-17 overtime victory against the New York Giants that has been called "the greatest game ever played."

He also guided the Colts to the 1959 title, a 31-16 triumph over the Giants, and took Baltimore into the 1964 championship game, before losing to the Cleveland Browns 27-0.

In commemoration of the NFL's 50th anniversary, Unitas was voted the greatest quarterback in its history. He also was chosen the Pro Football Athlete of the Decade for the 1960s in a poll of the nation's sports media.

In his 18-year NFL career—17 years with the Colts, one year with the San Diego Chargers—Unitas completed 2,830 passes for 40,239 yards and 290 touchdowns, including at least one scoring pass in a record 47 consecutive games.

And in 1979, Unitas was inducted into the Pro Football Hall of Fame at Canton, Ohio.

In an emotion-packed ceremony on the steps of the domed shrine, the calm and dignified Unitas told a crowd of several thousand: "A man never gets to this station in life without being helped, aided, shoved, pushed and prodded to do better. I want to be honest with you; the players I played with and the coaches I had . . . they are directly responsible for my being here. I want you all to remember that. I always will."

It was a typical speech for a man who never was flamboyant, never overly enthusiastic, never boastful...who just did his job thoroughly and quietly.

About the only criticism Unitas ever received was a charge that as his fame increased, he became conceited. But Unitas said, "There is a difference between conceit and confidence. A quarterback has to have confidence. Conceit is bragging about yourself. Confidence means you believe you can get the job done. I always believed I could."

And most often, he did.

JOHNNY UNITAS GETS OFF A PASS OVER GREEN BAY PACKERS DEFENSIVE TACKLE HENRY JORDAN DURING THE 1964 SEASON. (AP/WIDE WORLD PHOTOS)

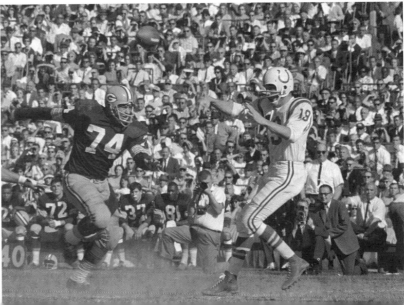

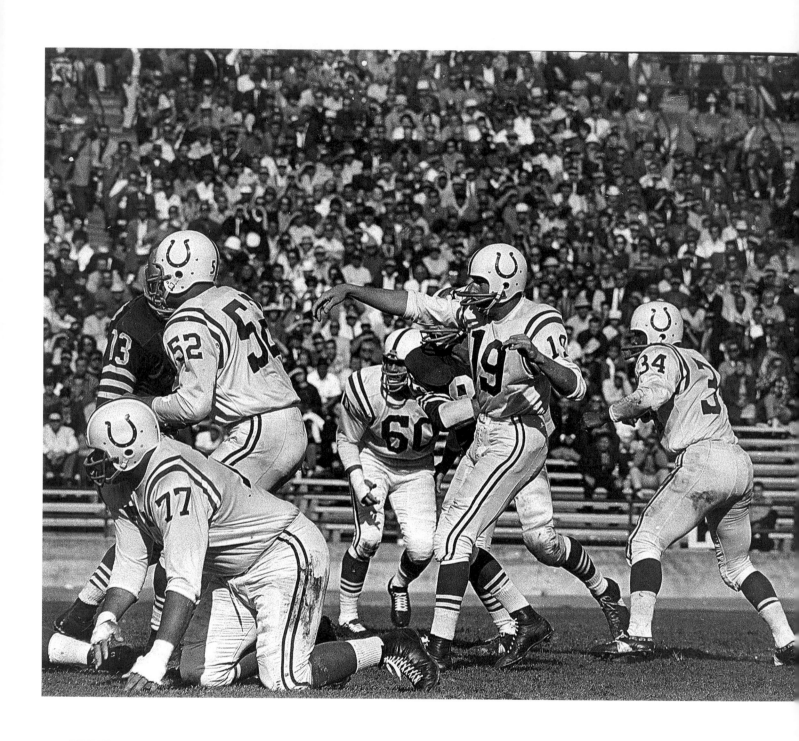

JOHNNY UNITAS CONNECTS AGAIN. THIS TIME IT WAS AGAINST THE SAN FRANCISCO 49ERS DURING THE 1962 SEASON, (AP/WIDE WORLD PHOTOS)

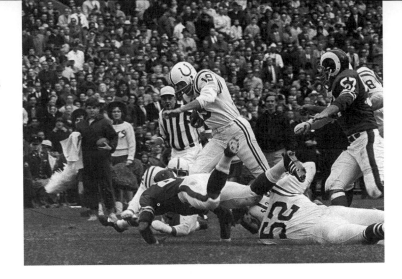

JOHNNY UNITAS RUNS
FOR A TOUCHDOWN
AFTER FAKING A
HANDOFF IN THIS
1965 PHOTO.
(AP/WIDE WORLD
PHOTOS)

Sid Luckman, also ranked among pro football's great quarterbacks, said, "Johnny Unitas is the greatest quarterback ever to play the game, better than I was, better than Sammy Baugh, better than anyone."

Raymond Berry, Unitas' teammate on the Colts and later coach of the New England Patriots, said, "What can I tell you about John Unitas? Well, I can tell you about his uncanny instinct for calling the right play at the right time, his icy composure under fire, his fierce competitiveness and his utter disregard for his own personal safety."

"I'm sure no one predicted such greatness for John Unitas in 1955," Berry added.

In 1955, after the Steelers had selected Unitas in the ninth round of the NFL draft out of the University of Louisville, they cut him late in training camp. Before leaving, Unitas sent a telegram to Paul Brown asking for a tryout with Cleveland. Brown told him the team's quarterbacking positions were filled, but to contact him the following year.

If it were not for Brown's encouraging reply, Unitas' football career might have ended then. He still seriously considered going into teaching. He had graduated from Louisville with a B.S. in physical education and economics.

Meanwhile, a former Louisville teammate, Freddie Zangaro, suggested that Unitas join him on a semi-pro club, the Bloomington Rams. Unitas was hesitant. He was married, with one child and another on the way.

"I didn't want to get busted up to where I wouldn't be able to work," he said, "but I finally decided to give it one year so that I'd be in shape if Paul Brown brought me to camp."

With the Rams, Unitas played on fields in Pittsburgh that were strewn with rocks and shattered glass. And he earned $6 a game!

If nothing else, the experience toughened him up for the NFL, which came calling in 1956. But instead of the Browns who sought his services, it was the Colts.

There are two stories of how Baltimore came to pick up Unitas. In one, General Manager Don Kellett insisted that in going over old waiver lists, he came across Unitas' name. "We had scouted him . . . and . . . had him down as a late draft choice if he was still eligible," Kellett said.

The other story, according to Coach Weeb Ewbank, is that "Unitas was signed after we received a letter from a fan—addressed to the club, not to me—telling us there was a player in Bloomington deserving a chance."

"I always accused Johnny of writing it," Ewbank said.

At any rate, Kellett offered Unitas a contract for $7,000. In his workouts with the Colts, Unitas was impressive, and Ewbank kept him as a backup to George Shaw.

But in the fourth game of the season, Shaw suffered a broken left leg, and Unitas was rushed into action. He did not make a very auspicious debut. His first pass was intercepted by Chicago's J.C. Caroline and returned for a touchdown. On the next play from scrimmage, Unitas collided with fullback Alan Ameche on a handoff and fumbled. The Bears recovered and scored again. Again the Colts received, again Unitas botched a handoff and again the Bears scored. The final score was Chicago 58, Baltimore 27—after Unitas had inherited a 20-14 lead.

Ewbank was not discouraged about Unitas' dismal showing. The following week, Unitas was ready, and he guided the Colts to a 28-21 victory over Green Bay. He also led them to three more victories that season, and finished with the highest completion average ever recorded by a rookie, 55.6 percent. He had become Baltimore's starting quarterback—and held the job for 16 more years.

During that stretch, he had the utmost respect of his teammates.

When Unitas gathered the offensive unit around him to call a play, tight end John Mackey said, "It's like being in a huddle with God."

JOHNNY WEISSMULLER IN HIS MOVIE ROLE AS TARZAN. (AP/WIDE WORLD PHOTOS)

JOHNNY WEISSMULLER

TARZAN OF THE SWIM LANES

When Mark Spitz electrified the 1972 Olympic Games in Munich, Germany, by sweeping to an unimaginable seven gold medals in swimming, there was one man who was relatively unimpressed. Living out his days more renowned as the movies' "Tarzan," 68-year-old Johnny Weissmuller said, "I was better than Spitz. I never lost a race."

Whether or not he was correct on his first premise, which shall forever be a matter of conjecture, he found no dissenters of the latter, which probably was stated more in honest conviction than in idle boast.

Johnny Weissmuller was king of the water in sport's Golden Age of the 1920s, which bred such athletic giants as Babe Ruth, Jim Thorpe, Jack Dempsey, Bill Tilden and Babe Didrikson, all of whom were voted the greatest of their crafts over the first half century in a 1950 poll of the nation's sportswriters and broadcasters by The Associated Press.

This strapping, handsome son of struggling Viennese immigrants dominated his sport as none ever did before and none has done since, although changing times, scientific research, diet and new techniques have enabled 15-year-old girls to record faster times in events in which he excelled.

Weissmuller was unbeatable for more than a decade in every distance from 50 yards to half a mile. He won a total of five gold medals in two Olympics, captured 52 national titles and shattered 67 world records in his incredible career. He touched first in every race he ever swam.

Weissmuller competed under primitive conditions compared with later conditions in the sport. When he raced, there were no starting blocks, flip turns or lane ropes. He didn't have the benefit of all the intricate coaching ideas developed in ensuing generations. Yet he was far ahead of all his rivals.

Weissmuller was born June 2, 1904, in Windber, Pennsylvania, in the heart of the coal country. His father worked in the mines. Johnny was a tyke of eight when the family pulled up stakes and moved to Chicago, where the elder Weissmuller, a moody and often abusive man, got a job as a saloon keeper and died shortly afterward.

The Weissmullers' modest second-floor, frame apartment was near Fullerton Beach on Lake Michigan, and that's where Johnny and a younger brother, Peter, spent their idle hours splashing around in the surf that lashed the shoreline boulders. "It was dangerous but to a couple of kids like us, very adventurous," Johnny was to recall later. "Swimming just came natural to us."

With his mother struggling to make ends meet, Johnny quit school and took odd jobs to help the family survive. He worked as an errand boy for a while, and later got a job as a bellhop at the Chicago Plaza hotel.

"Your guts get mad when you try to fight poverty and its constant and

JOHNNY WEISSMULLER SHATTERED 67 WORLD RECORDS IN HIS INCREDIBLE CAREER. (AP/WIDE WORLD PHOTOS)

Johnny Weissmuller in competitoin in Japan in 1928. Shortly following
this race, Weissmuller turned professional. (AP/Wide World Photos)

JOHNNY WEISSMULLER WITH
FELLOW OLYMPIC GOLD
MEDALIST ELIZABETH
ROBINSON AT A RECEPTION IN
NEW YORK CITY FOR OLYMPIC
CHAMPIONS. (AP/WIDE WORLD
PHOTOS)

inevitable companion—ignorance," he said. "I made up my mind to fight my way out of it any way I could."

When Johnny was 16, he was persuaded by a friend to try out for the swimming team at the Illinois Athletic Club. There the youngster, tall and skinny, fell under the influence of a coach, a bulbous, 350-pound man named Bill Bachrach, naturally called "Big Bill." Johnny, wearing a swimming cap to control a head of hair that fell below the nape of his neck, was impressive in a junior meet and, because he showed a lot of natural ability, captured the undivided attention of "Big Bill."

"Stick with me, son," said Bachrach, "and I'll make you a champion." After Weissmuller won a junior 100-yard freestyle in the 1921 Central AAU Championships, Big Bill began hustling well-heeled members of the club by betting them the scrawny kid could swim certain distances in faster time than the world record. With timekeepers and stopwatches on hand, Johnny kept padding Big Bill's wallet.

Later in 1921, Weissmuller, at age 17, won the 50-yard freestyle in the National AAU Championships in 23.2 seconds, a fifth of a second off the world mark, and shortly afterward broke the world 150-yard record in 1 minute, 27.4 seconds at Brighton Beach, New York. Still just a kid, he married the first of his five wives, a beach girl named Lorelei.

Johnny had hit big time. With Bachrach as tutor, he made a trip to Hawaii for an exhibition and then set his sights on the 1924 Olympics in Paris. He qualified by beating the marks of Hawaii's Duke Kahanamoku, a two-time Olympic champion.

Having beaten the Duke's time, Weissmuller now had to beat the Hawaiian in person in their first confrontation in the 100-meter finals—not just one Kahanamoku, but two, since the Duke's younger brother, Sam, also was in the race.

Off winging, Johnny won the 100 meters in 59 seconds flat. He also took the gold in the 400-meter freestyle in 5:04.2 and shared the victory in the 800-meter relay. Four years later, he won Olympic gold medals in the 100-meter freestyle and the 800-meter relay in Amsterdam.

Johnny toured Europe and returned to find himself much in demand in American cities. It was while in Hollywood that he met the swashbuckling Douglas Fairbanks Sr., who looked over the swimmer's sleek, muscled 6-foot-3, 195-pound figure and suggested him for a movie part which he had turned down.

The movie was *Tarzan of the Apes*, based on the Edgar Rice Burroughs novel. Johnny beat out more than 100 candidates for the title role in which he co-starred with demure Maureen O'Sullivan as Jane and a chimpanzee named Cheetah.

With his long hair and lithe, muscled physique scantily clad in loin cloth, Weissmuller became an American staple for generations, his long-running series of Tarzan movies repeated later in TV reruns. Meanwhile, he had a succession of wives, including actress Lupe Velez, but children by only his fifth, Maria, who bore him three heirs. He retired to Fort Lauderdale, Florida, site of the International Swimming Hall of Fame, and died January 21, 1984, at the age of 79.

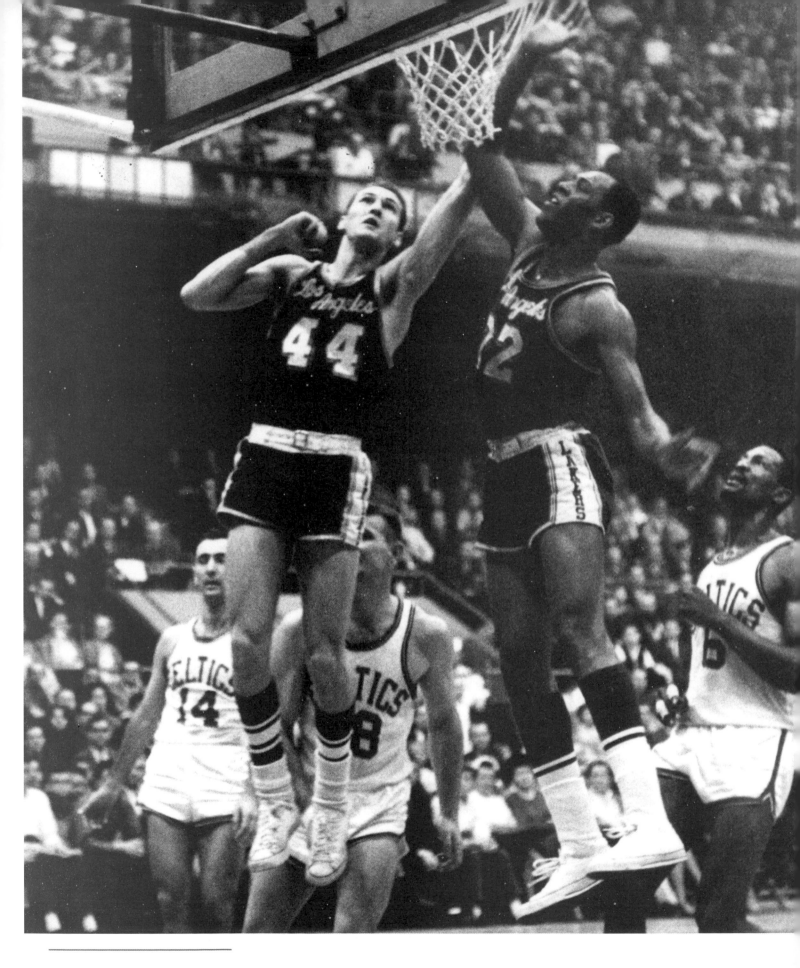

JERRY WEST, LEFT, AND ELGIN BAYLOR LEAP TOGETHER TO TAP IN A BASKET AGAINST THE BOSTON CELTICS. (AP/WIDE WORLD PHOTOS)

JERRY WEST

THE LAKERS' "MR. CLUTCH"

There are two ways to sum up the brilliance of Jerry West. With a record book—or simply with a nickname.

The record book shows that West was a two-time college All-America at West Virginia University, captain of the 1960 U.S. Olympic gold medal-winning team, a 10-time first-team NBA All-Star with the Los Angeles Lakers, a Basketball Hall of Famer and one of the NBA's 50 Greatest Players of All Time.

West's career playoff average is No. 2 all-time, behind only Michael Jordan's 33.4. He also was named to four NBA All-Defensive teams in the first five years the award was given.

West's nickname, "Mr. Clutch," best describes his play under pressure.

"Jerry West is by far the greatest clutch player who ever played," said longtime Lakers' broadcaster Chick Hearn. "He made basket after basket to win games."

"He was undoubtedly the greatest shooter when the game was on the line," said Lakers' president Bill Sharman who coached the Lakers to the 1972 NBA championship. "Throughout his career, he must have won 40 to 50 games with the last basket."

Ironically, West's most famous shot may have come in a game that the Lakers didn't win.

The Lakers and New York Knicks were tied in the final seconds of regulation play in Game 3 of the 1970 NBA finals, when Bill Bradley sank a jumper to give the Knicks an apparent victory.

West took the inbounds pass and let fly from the top of the foul circle in his backcourt . . . a shot of more than 60 feet. The ball went through the net.

If West had made that shot today, he would have had another game-winner. But in the pre three point field goal era, all his shot did was tie the score. The Knicks went on to win in overtime and eventually captured their first NBA crown.

Despite his heroics, West wasn't fond of the "Mr. Clutch" label.

"I really don't like that name," he said late in his career. "I've had some bad games, too, and when I do, when I miss the winning shot or something, people can use it to make fun of me."

West's on-court success has followed him into his post-playing career. He coached the Lakers to three straight playoff berths in the late 1970, took over as general manager in 1982 and has been working in the front office ever since.

"His concern was No. 1 for basketball, No. 2 for the team and No. 3 for Jerry West," longtime Lakers broadcaster Chick Hearn said. "That's about the highest accolade you can give a player."

JERRY WEST IN GAME ACTION DURING THE 1971-72 SEASON WHEN THE LAKERS WON 69 REGULAR-SEASON GAMES, A VICTORY TOTAL THAT WOULD NOT BE EXCEEDED FOR OVER 20 YEARS. (AP/WIDE WORLD PHOTOS)

KATHY WHITWORTH WATCHES HER TEE SHOT DURING A TOURNAMENT IN 1963.
(AP/WIDE WORLD PHOTOS)

KATHY WHITWORTH, GOLF

ALWAYS A WINNER

Kathy Whitworth is the winningest golfer, male or female, in U.S. Tour history. The seven-time LPGA Player of the Year posted 88 professional tournaments victories.

She captured the New Mexico State Amateur two consecutive years (1957, 1958) before turning professional in December 1958. She dominated women's professional golf from 1965 to 1973. She is also seven-time winner of the Vare Trophy for the lowest scoring average.

Whitworth has been the leading money winner eight times (1965-1968 and 1970-1973). With her third-place finish at the 1981 U.S. Women's Open, Whitworth became the first LPGA player to record $1 million in career winnings.

In 1984 she won her 85th victory, breaking the record held by American Sam Snead for career titles. Her last official victory and the 88th of her career was recorded at the 1985 United Virginia Bank Classic.

Six of her victories came in a major: the 1967, 1971, and 1975 LPGA Championships; the 1966 Western Open and the 1965 and 1966 Titleholders Championships. The only major to elude Whitworth is the U.S. Open where she finished second once and third two times.

Whitworth was known as a long-ball hitter, with 11 holes-in-one to her credit, but her putting was outstanding.

In 1974, the LPGA Tournament Division membership voted to drop the requirement that a player must be retired to be eligible for the Hall of Fame. She was inducted in 1975 with 72 wins. She was Associated Press Athlete of the Year in 1965 and 1967.

Paired with Mickey Wright, they made golf history as the first women's team to compete in the PGA sanctioned Legends of Golf.

Whitworth was named the golfer of the decade for 1968-77 by *Golf* magazine as part of the sport's centennial celebration in 1988.

KATHY WHITWORTH BLASTS OUT OF A SAND TRAP IN THE 1967 LPGA MIDWEST OPEN. (AP/WIDE WORLD PHOTOS)

BOSTON'S "SPLENDID
SPLINTER.
(AP/WIDE WORLD
PHOTOS)

TED WILLIAMS

LAST OF THE .400 HITTERS

They said his eyesight was so keen, he could read the autograph of the American League president on the ball as it sped to the plate. When he served in the military, they said he had the vision of one in 100,000. He almost never swung at a ball an inch out of the strike zone, and umpires came to respect his judgment.

If Ted Williams was not the greatest hitter in baseball, he was acknowledged to be the purest—a tall, stringbean of a man with a classic upright, left-handed stance, a long and flowing swing and wrists like bear traps that could uncoil in a lightning instant and propel the ball to distant targets as accurately as a William Tell bow.

Legend is that, once in batting practice, he wagered he could hit the painted footage figure on an outfield wall. He bounced the ball off the "0."

Playing half his games in Boston's Fenway Park, with its nearby left-field wall providing favoritism for right-handed hitters, the so-called Splendid Splinter was the only batter in modern times to break the .400 mark. His .406 in 1941 was the first to reach that elusive plateau in the American League since Harry Heilmann in 1923 and the first in the majors since Bill Terry of the New York Giants in 1930.

Despite two tenures of military duty, which took five full seasons out of his career, Williams poled 521 home runs and compiled a lifetime batting average of .344. He led the league six times in batting average and runs scored, four times in home runs and four times in runs batted in.

At 39 years of age, Williams became the oldest player in major league history to win a batting crown, winning his fifth in 1957. He won it again at 40 in 1958.

He had a lifetime slugging average of .634, second only to Babe Ruth. In this statistic, based on times at bat and total bases, he set a club record with .735 in 1941 and an astronomical .901 in 1953 while playing only 37 games after returning from the service. He hit 13 home runs and batted .407 in that abbreviated stretch.

He also ranked second to Ruth in bases on balls. He had 2,018 walks. Twice he was walked 162 times in a single season, including a streak of 19 straight games in 1941. Pitchers rarely attempted to brush him back or knock him down.

Five times he hit 35 or more home runs in a year. Three times he hit three homers in a single game. He had 17 grand-slam and seven pinch-hit home runs, blunting some critics' charges that he couldn't hit in the clutch.

Battling such criticism became the negative and galling aspect to his brilliant 19-year career with the Boston Red Sox, covering four decades. Williams was both a sports idol and an antihero in a

TED WILLIAMS WITH NEW YORK YANKEES SLUGGER JOE DIMAGGIO BEFORE A 1942 REGULAR-SEASON GAME.(AP/WIDE WORLD PHOTOS)

A SERIES OF HIGH-SPEED PHOTOS OF THE SWING OF TED WILLIAMS. IN 1957, AT THE AGE OF 39, HE WON THE AMERICAN LEAGUE BATTING TITLE WITH AN AVERAGE OF .388. HE WON IT AGAIN IN 1958 WITH AN AVERAGE OF .328. (AP/WIDE WORLD PHOTOS)

TED WILLIAMS THROWS
OUT THE FIRST PITCH OF
THE 1999 ALL-STAR GAME
WITH HELP FROM TONY
GWYNN. (AP/WIDE WORLD
PHOTOS)

city notorious for its demanding fans and caustic, competitive press.

"I've got the best pair of rabbit ears in all of baseball," the great slugger acknowledged later. "Those fans in the left-field stands were vicious. I admit I blew my top."

High-strung and sensitive, he developed early an adversarial relationship with a small and ugly segment of the fans and much of the news media.

He sulked and refused to talk to newsmen who he felt never gave him a fair shake. In his rookie year he became so angry at being booed for a miscue that he decided never again to tip his cap—a cherished baseball ritual—when the fans gave him an ovation. It was a vow that he never broke—even after the stands exploded in wild acclaim in 1960 when he closed out his career with his 521st, and longest, home run.

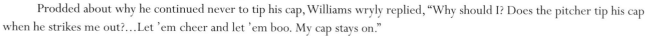

Prodded about why he continued never to tip his cap, Williams wryly replied, "Why should I? Does the pitcher tip his cap when he strikes me out?…Let 'em cheer and let 'em boo. My cap stays on."

In 1950, razzed by the fans for a couple of errors, temperamental Ted responded with a profane gesture, for which he was fined $5,000. "I was out of line," he said later. "When those buzzards poured out the abuse, I blew my cork."

Baseball's complex clouter was born August 30, 1918, in San Diego, California, and given the proud handle of Theodore Samuel Williams by his mother, a Salvation Army worker who later was deserted by his unstable father.

Ted's religious mother kept him under tight restraint. She refused to let him play on a local team run by a liquor store owner. But he played American Legion, high school and semipro baseball, where he showed outstanding promise as both a pitcher and a hitter. He batted .586 and .403 in high school, attracting scouts. He joined San Diego in the Pacific Coast League as a pitcher at age 17, earning $150 a month.

It was there that Eddie Collins saw the lean and hungry-looking youngster—then 6-3 and 143 pounds—and recommended him to millionaire Tom Yawkey, owner of the Boston Red Sox, who signed the kid with reluctance in 1938.

At Boston's spring camp, "The Kid," as Ted became known, was brash and cocky, antagonizing teammates. So Manager Joe Cronin assigned him to the club's Minneapolis Triple-A farm team for both seasoning and humbling. The latter didn't take.

Williams still had a chip on his shoulder when he joined the Red Sox in 1939, but there was no way to keep The Kid's big bat out of the lineup. In his rookie year, Ted batted .327, hit 31 homers and knocked in a league-leading 145 runs.

He grew bigger and stronger, finally reaching 200 pounds, and continued to dominate pitchers. Yet, he never mellowed. He spat at hostile customers and shunned the press.

When Lou Boudreau of the Cleveland Indians devised the "Boudreau Shift," packing fielders on the right side of the field, Williams ignored the challenge and refused to finesse the ball to the left. "I'm paid to hit," he said.

Despite a three-year hitch in World War II as a Marine fighter pilot and a recall for the Korean War, he never lost the symphony and power of his swing. He retired at the end of the 1960 season at age 42, managed the defunct Washington Senators briefly and finally settled down to his other two loves—Florida fishing and his Jimmy Fund for crippled children.

At age 80, Williams threw out the first pitch at the 1999 All-Star Game at Fenway Park. "I can only describe it as great," Williams said.

HELEN WILLS MOODY WARMS UP BEFORE A MATCH IN 1932.
(AP/WIDE WORLD PHOTOS)

HELEN WILLS MOODY

LITTLE MISS POKER FACE

Helen Wills Moody could have been a great author, a great painter or a great designer. She could have been royalty—a real-life queen sitting upon an ivory throne. In a way, she was all of these—brilliant, complex, stately, enigmatic—and no one would ever question her claim to royalty.

She was truly a queen. Her crown was a green-lined eyeshade, her robe a middy blouse and pleated skirt, her scepter a tightly strung wooden tennis racket. Her realm reached from the lush grass courts of Wimbledon and Forest Hills, New York, to the asphalt surfaces of California and the red clay of Roland Garros in Paris.

She was Queen Helen. During her prime, no one raised a voice to dispute it.

This serene, introspective daughter of a California country doctor dominated the courts from 1923, when she won the first of her seven United States ladies' singles championships until 1938, when she crushed her keenest rival, Helen Jacobs, 6-4, 6-0, for the last of her eight Wimbledon crowns.

With that, she said goodbye to competitive tennis, leaving the sports world to ponder whether it was fire or ice that lurked behind that mystic facade that never showed a flick of emotion on the court, never glared at an errant linesman and never changed expression, regardless of the course of the match, good or bad.

In a mad age when sports heroes were given colorful nicknames, Helen was dubbed "Little Miss Poker Face."

William Lyon Phelps, a well-known writer of the period, insisted that Helen's lack of expression during a match did not connote grimness or tension but meant she was "calm, placid, showed only equanimity."

W.O. McGeehan of the *New York Herald Tribune* wrote: "She plays her game with silent, deadly earnestness. That is the way to win games but it does not please galleries."

Helen Wills was born in October 1905, in Berkeley, California. Her father, who drove a buggy to visit patients in the country, was a fair player. On Helen's 14th birthday, he bought her a junior racket and enrolled her in a junior program under teacher William "Pop" Fuller.

Less than a year after taking up the game, Helen was good enough to be sent to the U.S. Junior Championships at Forest Hills where, at age 15, she won the title for girls 18 years and under.

At 17, she crushed the great Molla Mallory 6-2, 6-1 at Forest Hills and launched a reign that included seven national singles titles—one less than Mallory's total—over nine years.

Her 18 Grand Slam singles titles rank third all-time.

After tennis, she settled in Carmel, California, to pursue her loves of writing and painting. She wrote five mystery novels before dying at age 92 in January of 1998.

HELEN WILLS MOODY IN A 1938 PHOTO. (AP/WIDE WORLD PHOTOS)

EMIL ZATOPEK IN
ACTION IN THE
10,000 METERS IN
1948. (AP/WIDE
WORLD PHOTOS)

EMIL ZATOPEK

THE INDEFATIGABLE CZECH

"Za-to-pek! Za-to-pek!"

Like the clackety-clack of the wheels of a rumbling train under a tall head of steam, the chant reverberated through Helsinki's spacious Olympic Stadium and seemed to reach into the heavens and fall like thunder on the ears of the world.

It might well have been the theme song of the 1952 Games, the second of the great international sports festivals following the 12-year hiatus caused by World War II. It was also the first in history to produce the head-to-head confrontation on the athletic field of the two surviving powers—the United States and the Communist giant of the Soviet Union and its satellites.

Emil "The Indefatigable" Zatopek ran under the red colors of Czechoslovakia, a part of the Iron Curtain bloc. But politics and ideologies were forgotten, as this balding, reed-thin Czech army officer churned to long-distance running feats that never before had been achieved and, according to most track-and-field authorities, probably will never be duplicated.

Zatopek swept to victory in three of the most demanding tests in sports—the 5,000 meters, the 10,000 meters and the marathon, the latter a footrace covering 26 miles and 385 yards. Finland's fabulous Paavo Nurmi had won the 1,500 and 5,000 meters in 1924 and the 10,000 meters in 1920 and 1928, but to capture all three in a single meet would have defied his own comprehension.

Emil Zatopek was a scrawny man with a seemingly frail frame at 5 feet, 8 inches tall and 145 pounds. As he ran, it appeared he might collapse at any minute, falling prostrate on the track, gasping for breath.

His style was far from classic. As his pounding spikes chewed up the yards, his head bobbed from side to side, his arms flailed the air and his face became contorted, as if he were suffering the severest pain.

Red Smith, the famous columnist who covered the Helsinki Games, wrote that Zatopek ran "like a man with a noose about his neck…on the verge of strangulation…his hatchet face crimson, his tongue lolled out."

No matter. The crowd loved it. And as the inexhaustible Czech moved from event to event, his popularity grew. He became the Games' cult hero and fans by the thousands jammed the stadium to appreciate his awkward brilliance and cheer him on.

Zatopek, son of a laborer and second youngest of eight children, left home at 16 and got a job in a shoe factory. In Communist countries, clubs and factories engage heavily in sports competitions. Emil first ran for the shoe factory. He showed enough speed and dedication to be chosen for special

EMIL ZATOPEK GETS A KISS FROM HIS WIFE, DANA, AFTER WINNING THE MARATHON IN THE 1952 SUMMER OLYMPICS. (AP/WIDE WORLD PHOTOS)

EMIL ZATOPEK REGAINS THE LEAD IN THE 5,000-METER EVENT AT THE 1952 SUMMER OLYMPICS IN HENSINKI. (AP/WIDE WORLD PHOTOS)

EMIL ZATOPEK WON THIS RACE, THE 5,000-METER RUN, THE 10,000 AND MARATHON AT THE 1952 OLYMPIC GAMES. (AP/WIDE WORLD PHOTOS)

training. He decided to concentrate on distance running.

He ran at night, wearing heavy boots and carrying a flashlight. He initiated his own routine, which confounded his coaches. He said he got the idea from the great Nurmi.

"I heard that Paavo Nurmi, in one hour, was able to run four times 400 meters in excellent time," he explained later. "I thought, What if I make six times 400 meters, more then Nurmi, and what if I run a short distance, 100 meters, at full speed and then not sit but jog, and do that over and over again."

Trainers scoffed at his regimen, but Zatopek continued it. To practice for the 10,000, he would run five times 200 meters, 20 times 400 meters and five times 200 meters. He never sat. He jogged between routines.

Soon he was the best long-distance runner in Czechoslovakia. He did what most good Communist athletes do—he joined the army. In the 1948 Olympics in London, the first in 12 years, he won the 10,000 meters going away but finished second in the 5,000, rallying from 30 yards back to lose by two-tenths of a second. He skipped the marathon. In 1949, he broke Viljo Heino's world record in the 10,000 with a clocking of 29 minutes and 28 seconds.

At Helsinki in 1952, Zatopek won the 10,000 meters easily. The Finns took to him naturally. Nurmi had left in them a deep-seated devotion to long distance running. Zatopek said he worried about the 5,000 meters not only because of the stronger field, but also because the shorter race left him confused on strategy. Should he set the pace or lay back and unleash a kick at the end?

Zatopek relied on instinct and confidence in his staying powers. With 200 meters to go, he trailed Chris Chataway of Britain, Alain Mimoun of France and Herbert Schade of Germany, but with the roar of "Za-to-pek" ringing in his ears, he spurted to win by four meters.

He called it the most rewarding day of his career. He not only had two gold medals, but his wife, Dana, added another for the family cabinet by winning the javelin. In addition, it convinced Zatopek he should also try for the marathon, a race he had never won, and a shot at the "impossible triple slam" of distance running.

Helsinki was beside itself. The big stadium was jammed with chanting fans. Zatopek didn't disappoint. Running a strategic race, he burst into the arena amid a deafening roar, his face grimacing, head bobbing and arms flying. He set an Olympic record.

Zatopek became a national hero. He was a colonel in the army. He received all the government gratuities lavished on sports heroes—home, car, the works. The honeymoon was short lived.

A liberal and supreme patriot, he openly criticized the USSR's stranglehold on his homeland.

He argued that, to survive, Communism must give its adherents "air to breathe."

He was stripped of his rank. He was reduced to menial jobs such as cleaning toilets. He and Dana lived for a while in a trailer before moving to a modest home in the country. But no one could destroy the legend of the indefatigable Czech.